Career,
Work, and
Mental
Health

Rosalie, my wife and best friend for more than 57 years of never a dull moment, and an abundance of inspiration and love. All accomplishments in this relationship have been the result of a joint venture in this exciting journey.

Robert Partain, my appreciation for and enjoyment of our neighborly talks, encouragement, and sincere interest in this book. Dr. Partain should also be recognized for his skills as a neurosurgeon and for the countless lives he has restored and saved.

Career, Work, and Mental Health

Integrating Career and Personal Counseling

Vernon Zunker
Texas State University

Los Angeles • London • New Delhi • Singapore

For information:

SAGE Publications, Inc.
2455 Teller Road
Thousand Oaks,
   California 91320
E-mail: order@sagepub.com

SAGE Publications India Pvt. Ltd.
B 1/I 1 Mohan Cooperative
   Industrial Area
Mathura Road, New Delhi 110 044
India

SAGE Publications Ltd.
1 Oliver's Yard
55 City Road
London EC1Y 1SP
United Kingdom

SAGE Publications Asia-Pacific Pte. Ltd.
33 Pekin Street #02-01
Far East Square
Singapore 048763

Printed in the United States of America

Library of Congress Cataloging-in-Publication Data

Zunker, Vernon G., 1927–
Career, work, and mental health: Integrating career and personal counseling / Vernon Zunker.
     p. cm.
Includes bibliographical references and index.
ISBN 978-1-4129-6423-4 (cloth)
ISBN 978-1-4129-6424-1 (pbk.)
    1. Vocational guidance—Psychological aspects. 2. Work—Psychological aspects. 3. Mental health. 4. Counseling psychology. 5. Psychology, Industrial. I. Title. II. Title: Integrating career and personal counseling. III. Title: Career and personal counseling.

HF5381.Z865 2008
658.3'14—dc22   2008006241

This book is printed on acid-free paper.

08   09   10   11   12   11   10   9   8   7   6   5   4   3   2   1

Acquisitions Editor:	Kassie Graves
Editorial Assistant:	Veronica K. Novak
Production Editor:	Diane S. Foster
Copy Editor:	Kathy Anne Savadel
Typesetter:	C&M Digitals (P) Ltd.
Proofreader:	Theresa Kay
Cover Designer:	Gail Buschman
Marketing Manager:	Carmel Schrire

Brief Contents

Detailed Contents_____

Preface _____

A few years ago, I was director of a counseling center at a large state university. The career center was housed within the counseling center. During my 18 years as director, I observed that some students who came for career counseling were actually testing the waters while waiting for a chance to see a counselor about a troubling personal problem. Likewise, some students who were there for personal concerns also participated in career counseling. Over the years, my colleagues and I found that integrating our services had some definite advantages. It also became clear that there was a definite interest in a broad-based approach to selecting a career that went beyond the typical measure of interest and ability. We came to the conclusion that students wanted to explore a broad range of topics that included personal concerns and lifestyle dimensions. Evaluations from students who completed counseling programs, for example, rated discussions on the interrelationship of life roles as most informative.

It should not surprise anyone that those early experiences in a counseling center and teaching experiences in graduate school have inspired me to address the issues you will read about in this book. What I have attempted to compile are valid examples of the connectedness between career and personal concerns. Such mental health issues as depression and other mood disorders, for example, serve to develop the case for spillover effect from one life role to another. Substance abuse, personality disorders, and somatoform concerns are other examples that are used to illustrate the interrelationship between personal and career concerns. Faulty beliefs and negative cognitions are highlighted as to their pervasive nature. The focus of this book is on how personal and career concerns can affect all life roles and how career, work, and mental health are intertwined.

This book is not a theoretical one. It is offered as a text that provides a solid scientific basis for evaluating influences that contribute to the development of behavior and follows this with solutions that are effective and practical. It will offer you step-by-step procedures for delivering intervention strategies that have proven to be effective. Where we go from here in the development of future helping programs that address personal and career concerns as being intertwined perhaps will be the subject of someone else's book, and I wish him or her the best of luck!

Overview of the Book

The theme of this book is that career choice and development comprise a process that is intertwined and connected with mental health issues. A whole-person approach to counseling is considered to be an effective way to address concerns that are interrelated. An integrative approach developed by Barlow and Durand (2005) provides a solid foundation upon which one can evaluate the unique individuality of each client. The whole-person perspective touted in this book is a means of evaluating a broad spectrum of individual needs and how they are interrelated. Interventions are suggested as solutions for clients who experience interrelated concerns. This book is divided into two parts. Part I is entitled "Career Counseling Perspectives," and Part II is entitled "Mental Health Issues and Solutions." A brief overview of Chapters 1 through 12 follows.

The first chapter contains an introduction to an integrative approach that is used throughout this text as a means to uncover three dimensions of influences on behavior. Some comparisons of career and personal counseling are made; however, career counseling has been viewed as a separate domain. In a whole-person approach to counseling the interrelationships of concerns take precedence. Basic issues introduced in Chapter 1 include how multidimensional influences shape behavior, the pervasive nature of psychological disorders, the pervasive nature of work stress, the case for the client's unique cognitive schemas, recognizing and uncovering constraints of career choice, and cultural diversity and acculturation.

The second chapter is entitled "Career Development Theories: An Overview." Nine career development theories are introduced in this chapter. The overview of each theory includes basic assumptions, key concepts, and implications for career counseling. The nine theories are grouped according to the following categories: trait oriented, social learning and cognitive, developmental, and person-in-environment. At the end of each group of theories, each group's contribution to the practice of career development is summarized.

Chapter 3, entitled "Career Counseling Practices," is devoted to the practical application of the theories discussed in Chapter 2. A learning theory of career counseling model is presented as an example of current counseling practices that are very inclusive. The stages of this model suggest a progressive agenda that begins with establishing a working consensus relationship. A discussion of the intake interview includes an outline that is straightforward but very inclusive. Other sections of the chapter include using assessment in career counseling, effective interventions, and an example case of a whole-person approach to career and personal concerns.

Chapter 4, "Constraints Affecting Career Choice and Development," is the first of two chapters that focus on constraints of career choice. This chapter is primarily devoted to constraints that are associated with social class, socialization, and socioeconomic status. A review of an updated version of social class in America is presented in which class status is primarily determined by the income level of one's family and status of the breadwinner's occupational position. One's ability and financial resources to obtain an education have been found to be strong determinants of social mobility (moving to a higher level in the class structure). Aspirations for social mobility with accompanying career constraints may be influenced by environmental factors that promote the position that one's future is a matter of fate or luck and, most important, has nothing to do with self-determination.

Chapter 5, "Career Choice and Development and the Changing Nature of Work," is a continuation of career choice constraints but with quite a different twist. It begins with the position established in the preceding chapter that many social forces shape human development. A discussion of identity crisis and four identity status groups follows. One of the problems addressed is that an increasing number of young adults are delaying career commitment. Uncertain and unpredictable job markets are barriers faced by many young adults in the initial career choice process. Constraints in the career choice process may be the result of economic restructuring and external markets that have changed the nature of work and the workplace. The responsibility for the career development of employees in organizations has been diminished, and with it job security is no longer guaranteed. These factors and others may have intimidated prospective employees to the point that a career commitment is delayed. A list of career barriers is provided at the end of the chapter.

The rationale for the use of the biopsychosocial model is developed in Chapter 6, "Depression and Its Impact on Career Development." This interactive model is the basis of an integrative approach that is used to determine influences in the development of the mood disorder of depression. The interrelationship of concerns provides the helper with a perspective from which concerns are conceptualized. In the case of depression, interrelationships of concerns are addressed through technical eclecticism in four categories: (1) career, (2) affective, (3) cognitive–behavioral, and (4) culture.

Chapter 7, "Other Mental Health Issues and Career Concerns," focuses on several psychological disorders that can influence one's ability to function in society. Some anxiety, somatoform, and substance-related disorders are selected as examples to illustrate symptoms. The purpose of this chapter is to point out that psychological disorders can affect all life roles, including the work role; personal and career concerns share negative consequences. Being preoccupied with unfounded medical conditions, as in hypochondriasis, for example, can negatively influence social interactions and relationships and be responsible for performance impairment, absenteeism, job instability, and the loss of a work identity.

Chapter 8, "Cultural Diversity Dimensions," takes you beyond the usual and focuses on the understanding of human behavior from a cultural perspective. Culturally developed cognitive schemas are thought to be shaped by cultural context and, as such, may influence behavior that is based on culture specific beliefs, values, attitudes, and customs. Cognitive schemas create expectations that influence behavior; cognitive development is not the same universally. Helpers should focus on different worldviews in the helping process, including the meaning of family, cooperation versus competition, communication style, and locus of control. One must realize that there are distinct and vast differences as well as similar behavior patterns embedded in cultural contexts.

Chapter 9 is entitled "Personality Development and Disorders and Their Effect on Career." This chapter contains a brief review of four personality perspectives: (1) predispositions, which are inherited influences on personality development; (2) both genes and environment drive human development, which in turn contributes to the formation of human traits; (3) personal goals in life tasks are viewed as a unifying concept of understanding personality and career development; and (4) work experiences also contribute to personality and career development. Studies of gender and cultural factors are also reported. Ten personality disorders that are grouped into three categories, labeled *Cluster A*, *Cluster B*, and *Cluster C*, are described by standard symptoms. The severity of symptoms in each personality disorder and the length of time one has experienced abnormal behavior patterns are the major criteria for identifying a true personality disorder. Some symptoms of personality disorders that are related to personal and career concerns are highlighted.

Chapter 10, "Assessing Personality Development Through Personality Inventories," focuses on the use of personality inventories in the helping process. The Sixteen Personality Factor Questionnaire (Cattell, Cattell, & Cattell, 1993) and NEO Personality Inventory—Revised (Costa & McRae, (1992) and also known as the *Big Five Personality Inventory*, support the position that personality factors are thought to be personality traits derived from factor analysis. Studies involving these inventories suggest that personality appears to be related to vocational interests, career progression, job performance, and work behavior. In addition, the NEO Personality Inventory—Revised studies indicate that personality factors can be used across cultures.

Chapter 11, "Work Stress," is focused on the dynamic process of stress and stressors that can lead to physiological, psychological, and behavioral outcomes. In this chapter, we learn that work stress can be responsible for health problems of workers and for negative reactions to work, other employees, absenteeism, and poor work performance. Work role demands can interfere with family roles demands, and vice versa. Work–family conflicts are thought to be the result of spillover effect from stressors experienced in the workplace.

Chapter 12, "Interventions and Case Studies," is devoted to the topic of how and why to use cognitive–behavioral interventions. The major focus of cognitive–behavioral approaches is on client concerns and symptoms involving cognitive schemas that are thought to influence behavior. One of the basic assumptions is that behavior is learned and can be unlearned; negatively oriented schemas can be changed to self-enhancing thoughts. Readers will find that the following cognitive–behavioral approaches are practical as well as therapeutic: problem solving, assertiveness training and behavioral rehearsal, systematic desensitization, cognitive restructuring, role of cognitive schemas, Ellis's A-B-C theory of personality, self-enhancing thoughts, homework assignments, behavioral change by Meichenbaum, and stress inoculation training.

Three case studies provide examples of how personal and career concerns are interrelated.

Acknowledgments

I wish to thank the reviewers of this book for their suggestions, which were most relevant and helpful. Their insightful recommendations have made this book a better one! In alphabetical order of last name: Charlene Alexander, Ball State University; Darlene M. Hannigan, LaSalle University; Henry L. Harris, The University of North Carolina at Charlotte; Harvey Hoyo, National University; and Chadwick Royal, North Carolina Central University. My sincere appreciation and gratitude go to Kassie Graves for her immediate recognition of this book's potential to fill a void in current counselor training programs. I greatly appreciate the editing skills of Kathy Savadel and the production oversight of Diane Foster. I also want to recognize the faithful companionship of my canine friend Toddi, who made this task easier and enjoyable.

PART I

Career Counseling Perspectives

1

Introduction

This book is about integrating career and personal counseling. Its focus is on how helpers view clients from a "whole-person" perspective of concerns that clients bring to counseling. Helpers address not just career concerns or personal ones, but both, as well as how they interrelate. A holistic philosophy of counseling suggests that client concerns are inseparable and intertwined. Helpers do not limit their ability to understand that a client's belief systems and interests are interrelated. Helpers are alert to personal concerns that might interfere with a client's ability to adequately process information and make optimal decisions and/or a worker's ability to perform at work; helpers also address how reactions to work stressors can limit a client's ability to function in other life roles. The relationships between career and mental health concerns suggest that these concerns should be addressed by intervention strategies in an integrative counseling approach. Throughout this book, the following terms are used interchangeably: *counselor* and *helper*, and *counseling* and *helping*.

Some Perspectives of Personal and Career Development Counseling

In most contemporary books that address the counseling profession one can usually find an excellent introduction to this field. Theories of counseling and psychotherapy are the centerpiece for addressing personal concerns. Books devoted to personal counseling as well as career development generally present a number of counseling approaches that have been developed over time. What stands out is the diversity of approaches that have been developed in the counseling profession to address all clients' concerns. One can conclude that there are many reasons for different counseling approaches, including basic research that has enlightened our knowledge of human behavior as well as the increased diversity of concerns clients bring to counseling. One would suspect that even more theories of counseling will come forth in the future, theories that are designed to meet the needs of an ever-changing society. One life role that has maintained prominence, however, is the work role.

What is most significant in current counseling practices is the recognition of multiple influences that drive behavior. That in itself is not necessarily a new position, but a reciprocal interrelationship between influences has provided additional opportunities for establishing counseling goals. The three domains of biological, psychological, and social/cultural influences on behavior present new challenges to helpers. Viewed from this position, the helper's perspective of behavior is that it is indeed multidimensional. The three domains of influence are labeled as an *integrative approach* in the counseling process. The integrative approach to understanding behavior also provides the tools to evaluate causes of behavior from several dimensions that have been supported by extensive research (Barlow & Durand, 2005).

An integrative approach views the development of behavior as consisting of biological, psychological, and social/cultural influences; thus, multiple influences are the key to understanding behavior: It is not one dimensional. The integrative approach comprises a much broader concept of behavior that includes one's genetics, chemical imbalances, a wide range of psychological influences, and unique experiences from the total ecological environment. What is most interesting is the reciprocal relationship between influences—for example, counseling that includes psychological interventions can positively affect the functioning of the client's immune system. The integrative approach to understanding behavior also provides the tools to evaluate causes of behavior from several dimensions that have been supported by extensive research (Barlow & Durand, 2005). I illustrate the integrative approach in several of the chapters that follow.

Personal and career counseling have generally been viewed as separate entities in both training and practice. Theories of career development have primarily addressed the processes involved in making an optimal career choice. There are similarities between career and personal counseling in the way helpers address client concerns. The goals of career and personal counseling, however, are determined by sets of client needs. What I emphasize in this book are the interrelationships among needs. In practice, career counselors devote their skills to helping clients in the decision process, whereas in personal counseling a variety of personal concerns are addressed. Career choice and development traditionally have been viewed as distinct and separate from personal counseling. In the last several decades, however, the focus of career counseling has been extended to include personal concerns that interfere with the choice process. In addition, there has been a growing interest in addressing concerns of adults who have experienced outsourcing and workplace changes. Adults in career transition can present multiple concerns that helpers need to address by observing the interrelationship of concerns. Some concerns may be career specific, whereas other, more personal ones are interrelated to all life roles. Depression, for example, is indiscriminate in that it can affect all life roles. Faulty beliefs cannot be ignored in career development or in personal counseling. Symptoms of mental health problems clearly point out the need to address all concerns clients bring to counseling. What I am suggesting is that helpers need to focus on identifying and addressing the interrelationship of concerns as in a whole-person approach to counseling.

An overview of development of the counseling profession also provides a very instructive perspective. The concept of person-in-environment has become a major focus of helpers. Behavioral influences that are internalized through socialization have been of most interest to helpers who offer personal and career counseling. Over time, there has been a shift from an emphasis of intrapsychic explanations of behavior to the impact of self-in-situation (Gelso & Fretz, 2001). What is important here is the belief that there are both internal and external explanations of behavior that need to be incorporated in the helping process. Cognitive–behavioral techniques have grown in popularity as helpers deal with the here and now rather than uncovering past events and experiences that lead to awareness and insight.

What is not lost in these latest developments is the spillover effect of personal problems. Super (1984) made the relevant point that what happens in one life role can influence what happens in other life roles. Work–family conflict is a good example to illustrate this point. Work stress and subsequent problems in relationships at work can lead to conflicts in the home and with other relationships. The spillover affect studied by Zedeck (1992), which I discuss in a later chapter, underscores the assumption that personal and career/work problems are interrelated. In the case of spillover affect, career, work, and mental health have a connectedness that should be addressed. The same would be true for a client who is presenting paranoid symptoms. Helpers would address irrational and distorted thinking triggered by cognitive schemas that need to be unlearned and/or moderated. Helpers would direct a client's attention toward how faulty thinking can affect all life roles. The major message here and throughout this book is the position that career, work, and mental health are intertwined.

A holistic perspective of helping is particularly relevant for clients who present a combination of career concerns and symptoms of psychological disorders. For example, clients with a mood disorder, personality disorder, or both would likely experience serious functional problems in all life roles. Thus, mental health concerns of a personal nature present potential problems for clients in the initial career decision-making process and the processes that follow as well as in interpersonal interactions in the workplace and the ability to perform appropriately. On the other hand, workers who experience job loss likely will also present work–family conflicts and other relationship problems. Counseling progress for clients with both career and personal concerns may be limited unless helpers address the interrelationship of concerns: Clients appraise life situations in similar ways; that is, they can overgeneralize negative feelings to most life situations. This chapter includes an introduction to some basic issues that provide clarity to the role of the helper who assumes a whole-person approach to helping, not necessarily in order of importance: Multidimensional Influences Shape Behavior, Focusing on Multiple Life Roles, The Pervasive Nature of Psychological Disorders, The Pervasive Nature of Work Stress, The Case for Each Client's Cognitive Schemas, Recognizing and Uncovering Constraints of Career Choice, and Cultural Diversity and Acculturation.

Multidimensional Influences Shape Behavior

Perspectives of counseling from a whole-person point of view are grounded in an integrative interactive approach to causes of psychological problems from three dimensions: biological, psychological, and social/cultural. Influences that can lead to symptoms of psychological disorders are indeed multidimensional, suggesting that the uniqueness of each individual is the key to finding pathways to building tailored interventions. In the whole-person counseling approach helpers are to focus on all life roles; the spillover affect from one life role can negatively affect other life roles. This important principle suggests that psychological disorders can negatively affect the work role, although they do not always do so. In some cases, however, such as when a client has faulty beliefs, one may find major problems in career choice and development as well as with other life roles (Mitchell & Krumboltz, 1996).

The important point emphasized by this basic issue is that behavior is influenced by multidimensional forces, suggesting that helpers are to adopt a whole-person perspective for determining diagnostic procedures and tailored interventions. Thus, one is not to conceptualize influences that shape behavior as being one-dimensional; on the contrary, one looks for interactive reciprocating influences. From this perspective, helpers recognize the importance and relevance of the case for the individual and support the position that the uniqueness of each client provides direction to the process of establishing counseling goals.

Focusing on Multiple Life Roles

Life roles and developmental stages are major topics of interest in developmental psychology as well as career development theories. Super (1984) created a *life-career rainbow*, for instance, in which life roles designated as child, student, "leisurite," citizen, worker, and homemaker are assumed by individuals as they progress through life stages. Of interest to helpers are the following two suggestions: (1) Because people are involved in several roles simultaneously, success in one role facilitates success in another, and (2) life roles are not mutually exclusive; they affect each other in a wide variety of events, experiences, and circumstances. What is made clear here, however, is the relevance of the interrelationships of life roles in the counseling process. Helpers have long touted the benefits of a balanced lifestyle.

It is important for helpers to recognize that the value individuals give to life roles can vary during different life stages and ages as well as by gender and culture. Work, for instance, may be valued differently by people of different ages and across different cultures. As I discuss in Chapter 4, one also would likely find that the work role is valued differently within social classes. The important concept of life roles is addressed in most of the chapters in this book. Of particular interest is the spillover effect of one life role to another and the significance of addressing the interrelationship of all life roles.

_____ The Pervasive Nature of Psychological Disorders

Mental health professionals have worked tirelessly to reach a consensus for symptoms of mental illness that can be used in the diagnosis and treatment of psychological disorders. The *Diagnostic and Statistical Manual of Mental Health Disorders*, fourth edition, text revision (American Psychiatric Association, 2000), contains the current standard categories of disorders and symptoms.

Counseling psychologists, licensed professional counselors, and social workers, for example, have unified their counseling efforts to meet the concerns of the intact "normal" person as opposed to one who is profoundly disturbed (Gelso & Fretz, 2001). Nevertheless, there are indications that this trend has been changing over time, partly because helpers function in a variety of counseling centers that expose them to people who have been diagnosed with one or more psychological disorders (Corazzini, 1997).

The components of psychological disorders, according to Barlow and Durand (2005), are psychological dysfunction, distress or impairment, and atypical response. *Psychological dysfunction* is observed in individuals who are no longer "intact" but have a breakdown in behavioral functioning that involves cognitive and emotional factors. *Distress* reactions are often very severe: A person may be extremely upset to the point that he or she no longer meets daily obligations, and social functioning is also *impaired*.

As the name implies, *atypical responses* are behaviorals that appear to be odd or eccentric but in essence violate traditional norms. Be aware that some professionals do not use the term *psychological disorders* but prefer *mental disorders*, *mental illness*, or even *mental dysfunctions*. The preferred term in this book is *psychological disorders* because of the well-defined components provided by Barlow and Durand (2005). Also be aware that norms of behavior vary from culture to culture, and what may appear to be abnormal in one culture may be acceptable or expected behavior in another (see Chapter 8). In this book, examples of psychological disorders are discussed with an emphasis on how their symptoms impact all life roles. Helpers usually are involved with clients who have been diagnosed as having full-blown psychological disorders as well as with clients who have symptoms of certain disorders but do not meet all the criteria of a particular disorder. In both of these circumstances, helpers evaluate the relationships between what may be labeled as *personal problems* and an individual's ability to fulfill the requirements of a work role and maintain career development.

The Pervasive Nature of Work Stress

Stress reactions to daily life by adults and stress experienced in the workplace have become major topics of interest among the helping professions, including members of medical professions and management professionals in industrial organizations, among other groups. Stress reactions are common daily occurrences for many people, and most of them have developed unique coping methods that can diminish the negative consequences of stress. For some people, stressful life events and constant oppression have conditioned them to develop coping techniques that moderate effects of stressful events and situations. Others will need assistance in learning to effectively use coping strategies. The point is that reactions to stress are an individual matter that can be a very pervasive lifestyle issue; the effects of stress are not limited to any one life role but may negatively affect all of them. Chapter 11 is devoted to the discussion of work stress; also included are psychological symptoms that underscore the pervasive nature of stress.

The *diathesis–stress model* can assist helpers in developing a better understanding of the stress process. According to this model, some people inherit tendencies to express certain behaviors that are activated by stress. Each inherited tendency is considered to be a *diathesis*, or a condition that is necessary for the development of a psychological disorder. More specifically, a diathesis can be a genetic predisposition or vulnerability to illness, including mental illness. The precipitating force that triggers the vulnerability depends on the amount of stress an individual experiences and her or his coping ability. Further discussions on the subject of work stress will include its causes, consequences, and suggested interventions. A model of stress reactivity is also presented in Chapter 11.

The Case for Each Client's Cognitive Schemas

The growing interest in faulty beliefs is well documented in the career development literature as well as in published materials involving general counseling concerns and clinical psychology. This growing interest has been touted by cognitive–behavioral oriented helpers and major career development theorists (Mitchell & Krumboltz, 1996; Trull, 2005). The focus has been on the content of negative beliefs rather than how they were developed. Some researchers, however, have suggested that cognitive schemas developed through the socialization process trigger autonomic responses to events, situations, and even people (Castillo, 1997; Doyle, 1998). How a client interprets events, situations, and the actions of others can lead to a better understanding of his or her reactions to other personal interactions with others, including work associates. Thus, cognitive schemas have much to do with one's belief system. The rationale is that if one falsely believes that he or she cannot adequately perform in the workplace, then his or her ability is indeed diminished. On the other hand, if one is bolstered by feelings of self-efficacy and a sense of well-being, chances are that person's performance will be satisfactory. Clearly, interventions that encourage the learning of more positive self-thoughts and self-talk are essential ingredients for better mental health as well as for the ability to effectively evaluate future career prospects. Cognitive schemas are discussed in several chapters of this book, and the significance of cultural cognitive schemas is discussed in Chapter 8.

Recognizing and Uncovering Constraints of Career Choice

The American dream includes the belief that each person has the right to choose a career that will meet his or her financial needs and provide him or her with a work identity. Is this American dream achievable for everyone, including members of the poor and working class? Are those hard-working people who have achieved social mobility from working class to upper class the exception to the rule? The consensus is that most people remain in their social class of origin (Andersen & Taylor, 2006; Gilbert, 2003). The issues involved in constraints of career choice involve much more than a dream that did not come true. There appear to be both internal and external factors that contribute to what are known as *constraints* in the career choice process. Some people are of the opinion that getting a job is a matter of luck or fate. Those who have internalized these beliefs do not endorse the concept of self-determination; thus, they believe that their career prospects are very limited. Others who do endorse the idea that hard work and persistence will pay off with a job that offers numerous opportunities are usually not constrained when choosing a career. How these two different points of view evolve is a most relevant question.

Social/cultural influences that contribute to one's reluctance to make a choice include social class, environmental experiences that discourage feelings of self-efficacy, and the assumption that self-determination does not matter. Contextual interactions can greatly influence how each individual views his or her future lifestyle, including options for careers. It appears that class and race differences in perceptions of life and work are a reality. An additional reality is the changing nature of work and the disappearance of internal ladders in organizations that provided, among other things, job security and feelings of well-being. The rapidly changing workforce can be very intimidating to prospective employees. Some career barriers that are discussed in Chapters 4 and 5 include contextual experiences, external market forces, mental health issues, and negative cognitions.

Cultural Diversity and Acculturation

People are not to be stereotyped because of their cultural background; on the contrary, there is recognition that each person is biologically, socially, and psychologically unique. Helpers should uncover each client's unique qualities; this is especially true for members of culturally diverse populations. A major focus of helping is centered around the worldview of culturally different people. The rationale for this focus is that each cultural group has developed unique traditions, rituals, and ways of thinking; cultural norms, values, attitudes, and beliefs have been shaped by specific cultural contexts. Several dimensions of worldviews include the meaning of family, cooperation and competition, communication styles, and locus of control (Gelso & Fretz, 2001). In many non-Western societies the extended family traditionally asserts significant influence and control over individual opportunities of family members. A consensus of opinion about one's career choice, for instance, is highly sought after in families. Under these conditions, children are conditioned to think of their future in terms of how they can best meet the needs of their family rather than their individual aspirations. Feelings of connectedness formed in family relationships carry over to community relationships, where again, important decisions may be based on the approval of community as well as family. Under these circumstances, individual goals are thought to be selfish and inconsiderate of the group's welfare. Thus, the intention of some clients of other cultures may be misinterpreted. Other cultural considerations include styles of communication with another person that are influenced by perceived status differences. One may be reluctant to speak out for fear of being judged as outspoken or to talk about one's accomplishments for fear of being perceived as selfish. Some culturally diverse individuals believe that their future is determined by fate or the gods rather than through individual efforts. These examples and more are discussed in Chapter 8. Finally, one should be reminded that the context in which one is reared can have a tremendous influence on the development of life roles; contextual experiences influence the development of one's worldview.

The term *acculturation* refers to the adoption of beliefs, values, and practices of the host culture (Comas-Diaz & Grenier, 1998). Acculturation is considered to be important in discussions of cultural norms of behavior that may be different from those of the dominant culture. Behavior that is considered normal in one culture may not be judged that way in Western societies. For example, in chapter 8 I discuss some behaviors that may seem odd, eccentric, and quite strange but that in some remote places in the world could be judged as normal behavior that is associated with reactions to distress or loss of honor. Acculturation is a process in which people from other cultures who live in the United Stated for long periods of time adopt the norms of behavior of the host country. Therefore, traditional ways of behavior within the contexts of their culture of origin may have been significantly modified. A list of acculturation scales is provided in Appendix A.

Cross-culture studies continue to point out, however, that there are some universal norms of behavior and some behaviors that are considered to be culture specific in origin (Matsumoto & Juang, 2004). Acculturation, universal, and culture-specific behaviors can be important keys to a client's perception of the work role, relationships, and a way of life. An understanding and awareness of culture-specific beliefs, attitudes, and values is essential in the helping process, which is devoted to finding client uniqueness. It should not surprise anyone that the development of emotional problems is significantly influenced by an individual's perception of racial discrimination (Paniagua, 2005).

The whole-person approach to counseling introduced in this book is very inclusive and individually oriented. This broad-perspective approach suggests that the uniqueness of each client is supported to the point that helping is in essence a client-centered endeavor. The focus on client uniqueness suggests that helpers search for individuality from biological, psychological, and social/cultural perspectives, as in an integrative approach to personal and career counseling. Multidimensional influences on behavior present the opportunity to observe relationships between personal and career concerns. What is likely to be observed are both career-specific and personal-specific concerns that can be addressed separately while some concerns are addressed simultaneously. The whole-person perspective is, as the name implies, a position that encourages helpers to address concerns that can affect all life roles.

This book includes chapters that introduce psychological disorders with an emphasis on causes uncovered from biological, psychological, and social/cultural dimensions. The pervasive nature of psychological disorders must be recognized and addressed by valid interventions. Some suggestions for effective interventions are contained within several chapters. Chapter 12, however, is completely devoted to examples of interventions and case studies designed to address personal problems that can affect all life roles. The consequences of dysfunctional behavior are a major concern of helpers; therefore, the focus of helping is on solutions rather than on diagnostic labeling. On the other hand, symptoms of psychological disorders contained in the diagnostic process are most helpful in finding specific information that can be used in interventions. A clerk who has recently experienced episodes of depression, for instance, may not be diagnosed as having full-blown depression but can manage to cope with negative thoughts through cognitive restructuring and eventually return to work. In this case, cognitive restructuring can address symptoms of depression as well as the goal of moderating work role problems. In the next section, I provide an overview of the development of career counseling that will be used as a backdrop for the Part I of this book.

The Practice of Career Counseling: An Overview _____

The career counseling movement has a long and interesting history. Most researchers have focused on rise of the Industrial Revolution in the late 1800s. The beginnings of career counseling are traced back to the need of placement services in urban areas as a result of the Industrial Revolution. This was followed by a growth of guidance programs in public schools circa 1920–1940. The pace of the movement increased with the growing number of students attending colleges and universities beginning in the 1940s. The focus on the career development of employees by industrial organizations significantly expanded the role and scope of career counseling during the 1960s and beyond. Accompanying this spurt of growth, work itself was viewed as a very pervasive life role; the work role was considered to be a most important part of one's life story. Changes in the nature of work continued to move rapidly with the introduction of information technology and other technological advances. Organizations established outplacement services as workers were outsourced. In the 1990s, multicultural counseling called attention to the need of addressing diversity issues in all counseling programs, including the practice of career development. The call to address mental health issues in the career counseling process was also issued in the 1990s. Now, at the beginning of the 21st century, workers have voiced their complaints about how the changing nature of work does not offer them the opportunity of a lifetime job. Many have viewed the changing rules of working as a broken promise and a breach of contract that lessens their chance of achieving the American dream. The issues that adults must confront during the process of career transition represent a significant challenge to helpers in the practice of career development. Helpers can expect to find that the needs of adults in career transition have a connectedness with all life roles.

In the meantime, the practice of career development is also growing internationally. There are comprehensive school-to-work programs in England. Personal study programs for vocational training have been created in Finland. A very extensive job network has been developed in Australia. Denmark has developed one-stop centers that are referred to as *counseling houses*. Career education and guidance are mandatory in The Netherlands. Japan has a network of public employment security offices. Canada has developed a national career development policy that encourages more career counseling services. Finally, in Hong Kong, career services focus on career-related workshops (Herr, Cramer, & Niles, 2004).

What is most significant here are stages of changes that have evolved from ever-changing global networks of societies. The chronology of the career counseling movement in the United States does indeed reflect influences from social, political, economic, and other changes in the United States as well as in other nations around the world. We can expect to experience more stages of growth and significant changes in the career counseling movement as our nation continues to be transformed.

How This Book Is Organized

This book is divided into two parts. Part I is entitled "Career Counseling Perspectives." The major purpose of the five chapters contained in this part is to provide an overview of some selected career development theories followed by examples of current practices in career counseling. Two chapters are devoted to addressing current constraints on the career choice process. The rationale for this part of the book is that career development theories, current counseling practices, and an update on constraints of career choice provide the reader with background and reference sources as well as examples of the practice of career development. A philosophical, theoretical, and practical focus is introduced.

Part II, entitled "Mental Health Issues and Solutions," contains seven chapters that introduce you to a number of mental health concerns identified by symptoms and labels as well as how these concerns can affect one's ability to function in all life roles. A major focus, however, involves how the symptoms of psychological disorders can affect a client's ability to make career choices and/or maintain a work role. The interrelationship of concerns is the focus of interventions that address clients' needs from a whole-person perspective. One complete chapter is devoted to intervention strategies, and another is devoted to diversity issues. At the end of each chapter are supplementary learning exercises in the form of questions developed from the chapter content.

Summary

Integrating career and personal concerns is the major premise of this book. The relationship between career and mental health concerns are addressed through an integrative counseling approach. Personal and career counseling have traditionally been viewed as separate entities. The focus of this book is to address the interrelationships of client concerns.

Career counseling has a long history, beginning in the 1800s. There have been stages of growth in the career counseling movement that have addressed emerging needs of a changing society. The practice of career development is also growing internationally.

Supplementary Learning Exercises

1. Briefly describe a whole-person approach to counseling. Near the end of the semester, describe factors you would add to your earlier description.

2. Debate the pros and cons of career counseling as a separate entity.

3. Describe how you would use symptoms of a psychological disorder to choose intervention strategies. Give examples.

4. Which of the basic issues discussed in this chapter do you consider to be the most important? Rank order them and defend your rankings.

5. Describe the importance of acculturation when counseling clients from different cultural backgrounds.

2 Career Development Theories: An Overview

This chapter focuses on theoretical orientations of career development theories designed to foster career decision making. The intent is to introduce important perspectives of career development theories that have influenced career counseling practices. Although the relationship between theories and practice is not always clear, there is little doubt that theoretical underpinnings of career development theories have important links to the current practice of career development. Helpers who build an understanding of theoretical orientations for counseling practice enhance their ability to effectively address needs that clients bring to counseling. In a whole-person approach to career counseling helpers address both career and personal concerns. Consistency of methods and procedures when addressing multiple concerns requires a working knowledge of theoretical orientations of career development as well as theories of psychotherapy and personal counseling. Thus, this chapter is more philosophical in nature, but it is followed by an entire chapter devoted to the practical application of career counseling models that have evolved since the 1950s.

Career Development Theories

Career development theories have evolved from the need to match the skills of prospective workers with job requirements in the early 1900s. The focus was on techniques that could be used to match individual traits with requirements of occupations. The early theories were built within what was referred to as *vocational counseling*, the primary objective of which was to place individuals in work environments that gave them the best chance of being successful. Although that same goal exists today, many more variables are used to determine an optimal career choice. Around the 1950s, vocational counseling expanded its boundaries to include such factors as self-concept, self-knowledge, and other human developmental issues. *Career counseling* eventually became the preferred term in the 1970s, to emphasize the growing knowledge of human development and subsequently of career development issues as well. Ironically, some researchers have recently argued that career development should be more inclusive to focus on mental health concerns as well. Furthermore, changes in the workplace brought on by external markets in a global economy have made it more difficult for individuals who are in the process of choosing a career to satisfy their short- and long-term interests. The uncertainty of the future job market can be a significant barrier for some clients who are attempting to make an optimal career choice.

In the meantime, career development theories have received criticism from practitioners. The major concern has been that career development researchers have failed to provide more direct links between theory and the practice of career development. One counterargument has been that career development theories present different views of important relevant elements, and all have contributed to counseling practice. More information about career development theories has been detailed by D. Brown and Associates (2002); D. Brown, Brooks, and Associates (1996); Gelso and Fretz (2001); Sharf (2002); and Zunker (2006).

This chapter's overview of career development theories will include trait-oriented theories, social learning and cognitive theories, developmental theories, and person-in-environment theory.

This grouping of theories was recommended by Gelso and Fretz (2001) and used by myself (Zunker, 2006). Within each group, individual theories are highlighted, with a brief explanation of their basic approaches and assumptions. This information is followed by a summary of how each group of theories has contributed to the practice of career development.

Trait-Oriented Theories

Trait-oriented theories include trait-and-factor theory, person–environment correspondence (PEC) counseling, and John Holland's typology.

Trait-and-Factor Theory

Trait-and-factor theory was among the very early theories and provides a means of matching individual traits with requirements of occupations. It was heavily oriented toward placing clients in jobs through the matching of aptitudes and interests with specific work roles. The development of assessment instruments was closely associated with trait-and-factor theory. Among early vocational counseling theorists, Parsons (1909) maintained that vocational guidance is accomplished first by studying the individual, second by surveying occupations, and finally by matching the individual with the occupation. This process, which he called *trait-and-factor theory*, became the foundation of many vocational counseling programs, including the Veterans Administration, the YMCA, Jewish vocational services, and colleges and universities.

The development of assessment instruments and refinement of occupational information are closely associated with trait-and-factor theory. Currently, there are countless assessment devices designed to measure individual human traits. Computerized versions of some assessment instruments also provide interpretation profiles. Individual strengths and weaknesses are currently evaluated through a variety of assessment devices. Assessment data are also used to predict job satisfaction and success. In the early years of vocational counseling, however, decisions were primarily based on aptitudes and interests.

Sharf (2002) summarized the advantages and disadvantages of trait-and-factor theory. He suggested that it is a static theory instead of a developmental one and that it focuses on identifying individual traits and factors but does not account for how interests, values, aptitudes, achievement, and personalities grow and change. What this theory does not address is that clients can benefit from dialogue that is directed toward continually evolving personality traits and how changes affect career decision making. In general, trait-and-factor theory has been criticized as being too narrow in scope to be considered a major career development theory.

Some defenders of trait-and-factor theory have argued that it has never been fully understood. Advocates of this theory suggest that test results have always been one means of evaluating individual differences; thus, excessive use of testing results was not the intent of the trait-and-factor theory. Furthermore, the early approaches and assumptions of this theory remain a viable part of many current theories that include the use of assessment accompanied by many other factors in the career decision-making process. Contemporary practices, for example, stress the relationship between human factors and work environments (D. Brown et al., 1996).

In current practice, multiple individual traits are obtained from assessment data. A similarity model is used to help clients focus on exploring careers. One practice is to view assessment results as a measure that indicates how similar an individual's results are to people who are employed successfully in a particular occupational group. The rationale here is that the chances of being accepted and successful are higher if one has traits that are similar to those of successful people employed in certain occupational groups.

Person–Environment Correspondence Counseling

PEC is often referred to as a *work adjustment theory*; in fact, in the early 1990s PEC was referred to as *TWA* or the *theory of work adjustment*. Its focus has been on long-range issues that one encounters in the workplace as compared to many other theories' overwhelming focus on vocational choice. Work is perceived to involve one's personality and adjustment styles; thus, one should focus on human interactions to achieve and maintain a positive relationship with one's work environment. Individuals bring requirements to a work environment, and the work environment makes its requirements of the individual. The role of satisfaction one can derive from work roles is a key concept in making an optimal career choice. Satisfaction with the work role, according to PEC, is gained through work reinforcers found in different work environments. Thus, one is encouraged to find amenable work environments; career choice must include procedures to first help clients determine their work satisfaction needs and, second, to uncover work reinforcers (work activities that reinforce needs) in prospective workplaces. According to PEC, job satisfaction includes several factors, such as the possibility of satisfactory relationships with coworkers and supervisors, type of work, autonomy, responsibility, and opportunities for self-expression, among others.

Four key concepts of PEC are summarized as follows: (1) work personality and work environment should be amenable, (2) an individual's fit into a work environment is largely determined by individual needs, (3) important aspects of stability and tenure in a work setting are referred to as a *correspondence between individual needs and systems of reinforcement*, and (4) job placement is best accomplished through a match of worker traits and requirements in work environments (Dawis & Lofquist, 1984).

A very important element of PEC is the identification of personality traits, ability, and values. In addition, an individual's needs are derived from six values measured by the Minnesota Importance Questionnaire (Rounds, Henly, Dawis, Lofquist, & Weiss, 1981): (1) achievement, (2) comfort, (3) status, (4) altruism, (5) safety, and (6) autonomy. The measured value of comfort, for example, translates to the needs of activity, independence, variety, compensation, and security. Potential reinforcers of needs are determined by examining specific occupational requirements and work environments. Some of the major criteria used to determine reinforcers involve the characteristics, abilities, and values of individuals in certain work environments. The constantly changing nature of work in the 21st century and advances in technology, however, have made finding consistent and stable workplace reinforcers more difficult.

Work adjustment counseling is viewed differently at present, primarily because workers are now faced with constantly changing work environments. Work adjustment and job satisfaction concerns, however, remain key concepts for helpers today. In an ideal situation, individuals locate groups of occupations that hold the greatest potential for job satisfaction. In current practices the unique needs of clients also include gender, national origin, cultural and ethnic background, and sexual orientation. Five implications for career counseling have emerged from PEC: (1) job satisfaction should be evaluated by type of work, satisfaction with coworkers and supervisors, autonomy, responsibility, and opportunities for self-expression; (2) job satisfaction is only one measure of work adjustment—there are many variables that measure work adjustment or what is often referred to as one's *fit* between work environment and an individual worker; (3) job satisfaction is an important predictor of job tenure; (4) the position that individual needs and values are significant components of job satisfaction is an important contribution to the study of career development; and (5) the case for the unique needs of each individual as an important factor in career choice and development underscores the significance of individual uniqueness in the counseling process.

John Holland's Typology

John Holland believes that people are attracted to certain jobs because of their personalities and because of numerous variables and activities derived from early experiences; thus, career choice is an expression or an extension of personality into the world of work. Congruence of one's view of self with an occupational preference establishes what Holland refers to as *modal personal style*. Four basic assumptions underlie Holland's (1992) theory:

1. In our culture, most persons can be categorized as one of six types: realistic, investigative, artistic, social, enterprising, or conventional. (p. 2)

2. There are six kinds of environments: realistic, investigative, artistic, social, enterprising, or conventional. (p. 3)

3. People search for environments that will let them exercise their skills and abilities, express their attitudes and values, and take on agreeable problems and roles. (p. 4)

4. A person's behavior is determined by an interaction between his or her personality and the characteristics of his or her environment. (p. 4)

In Holland's system of typology, the code for six types that represent both individuals and environments is Realistic, Investigative, Artistic, Social, Enterprising, and Conventional (RIASEC). This coding system is used to represent the order of individual preferences that are measured by interest inventories. One person, for instance, may find his three top types to be SIC (i.e., Social, Investigative, and Conventional), and another person might find her three top types to be CRI. Work environments that match each combination of categories or measured types are available for clients to consider in the choice process. Holland has developed an impressive amount of supplementary material that can be used in the career choice process. A complete list of typical occupations, for example, is provided for each of the six types. Descriptions of Holland's six types are arranged according to personal style and occupational environments are presented in Table 2.1.

There are four key concepts in Holland's theory that are relevant to understanding his model of career development: (1) congruence, (2) consistency, (3) differentiation, and (4) identity. There is *congruence* when an

Table 2.1   Holland's Modal Personal Styles and Occupational Environments

Personal styles	Themes	Occupational environments
May lack social skills; prefers concrete vs. abstract work tasks; may seem frank, materialistic, and inflexible; usually has mechanical abilities	Realistic	Skilled trades, such as plumber, electrician, and machine operator; technician skills, such as airplane mechanic, photographer, draftsperson, and some service occupations
Very task-oriented; is interested in math and science; may be described as independent, analytical, and intellectual; may be reserved and defers leadership to others	Investigative	Scientific, such as chemist, physicist, and mathematician; technician, such as laboratory technician, computer programmer, and electronics worker
Prefers self-expression through the arts; may be described as imaginative, introspective, and independent; values aesthetics and creation of art forms	Artistic	Artistic, such as sculptor, artist, and designer; musical, such as music teacher, orchestra leader, and musician; literary, such as editor, writer, and critic
Prefers social interaction and has good communication skills; is concerned with social problems, and is community-service-oriented; has interest in educational activities	Social	Educational, such as teacher, educational administrator, and college professor; social welfare, such as social worker, sociologist, rehabilitation counselor, and professional nurse
Prefers leadership roles; may be described as domineering, ambitious, and persuasive; makes use of good verbal skills	Enterprising	Managerial, such as personnel, production, and sales manager; various sales positions, such as life insurance, real estate, and car salesperson
May be described as practical, well-controlled, sociable, and rather conservative; prefers structured tasks, such as systematizing and manipulation of data and word processing	Conventional	Office and clerical worker, such as timekeeper, file clerk, teller, accountant, keypunch operator, secretary, bookkeeper, receptionist, and credit manager

SOURCE: Adapted from Holland (1992).

individual's personality type is consistent across types. *Consistency* is used to illustrate the typology paradigm; for example, one is considered to be more consistent if his or her highest two or three scores on an interest inventory are more similar in nature than for individuals who have less consistent scores. To illustrate, an individual's highest two interests scores of RI are consistent in that Realistic and Investigative characteristics have much in common, compared with a score of CA, in which the two characteristics (Conventional and Artistic) are considered to be almost opposite types. The relevance of this principle is that the more consistent people are, the higher the odds are that they will find success and satisfaction. *Differentiation* also has much to do with personality types. Pure personality types, for example, will have less resemblance to other types in Holland's typology. Individuals who have poorly defined personalities are considered to be *undifferentiated* and as a result may be more indecisive in the career choice process. *Identity* is used to signify a person who has clear and precise goals, interests, and talents. People who have many occupational goals with no clearly defined occupational choice are labeled as having a low identity; thus, *identity* refers to the clarity of occupational goals and one's skills and aptitudes.

The above principles have been widely endorsed by users as being practical and straightforward. Holland's typology emphasizes both self-knowledge and knowledge of career information. Personality development is a primary consideration in Holland's career typology theory of vocational behavior. Chapters 9 and 10 are devoted to discussions of personality dimensions and traits.

Finally, Holland's theory is known for its practical usefulness, and it has become one of the most widely used for career decision making. Holland's typology has been studied in more than 500 research projects. Most of his propositions are clearly defined, and thus they lend themselves to empirical evaluation.

Trait-Oriented Theories in Perspective

As the name of this group of theories implies, they emphasize human traits such as aptitudes, interests, and personality in the career choice process. Standardized tests are prominently used in trait-oriented theories. Trait-oriented approaches focus on work requirements and environments, person–environment fit, and reinforcers that lead to job satisfaction. Most significant to the choice process is the recommendation that people choose *work environments* rather than attempting to focus on only one occupation. In the 21st century, workers may need to make multiple career choices because of the changing nature of work, which is expected to continue with the introduction of new technology and the potential growing influence of external markets in a global economy. Even though most helpers use assessment instruments in current career counseling practice, and the role of assessment results is considered to be important in the career choice process, assessment does not dominate the practice of career development.

Social Learning and Cognitive Theories _____

This group consists of Krumboltz's learning theory of career choice, career development from a cognitive information processing perspective, and social cognitive career theory.

Krumboltz's Learning Theory of Career Choice

Krumboltz's learning theory of career choice is an attempt to simplify the process of career selection and is primarily based on life events that are influential in determining career selection. According to this theory, the process of career development involves four factors: (1) genetic endowments and special abilities, (2) environmental conditions and events, (3) learning experiences, and (4) task approach skills. *Genetic endowments and special abilities* include inherited qualities that may set limits on the individual's career opportunities. The major implication here is to recognize that genetic endowments can influence the career decision-making process, but one should not view inherited qualities as determining one's destiny. Special abilities as determinants in the career choice process can best be illustrated by such special talents as artistic, musical, and inherited physical abilities that are needed to become an outstanding athlete. All of these are thought to have some genetic component.

Environmental conditions and events, Factor 2, are considered to be influences that are often beyond the control of the individual. The experiences from one's total ecological system are thought to influence skill development, activities pursued, and career preferences. A listing of 12 categories of environmental conditions that have significant influence on career development includes job opportunities, changes in social organizations, educational systems, labor laws, and neighborhood and community events and situations. Factor 3, learning experiences, includes both instrumental learning experiences and associative learning experiences. *Instrumental learning experiences* are those that individuals learn through reactions to consequences (positive and negative), through direct observable results of actions, and through the reactions of others. Actions (behaviors) are repeated when they are positively reinforced and decrease when they are not; for example, if an associate praises one's ability to perform on a work task, then that action is likely to be tried again or may even encourage one to attempt other, more difficult tasks. *Associative learning experiences* include negative and positive reactions to pairs of neutral situations; for example, statements such as "All politicians are dishonest" and "Bankers are all rich" can influence one's perceptions of these occupations. The fourth factor, task approach skills, includes the sets of skills the individual has developed, such as problem-solving skills, work habits, mental sets, emotional response, and cognitive responses. These are thought to be the results of an interaction of biological conditions (innate abilities), environmental conditions, and learning experiences. An important point to remember is that task approach skills can be modified by other experiences.

What we have here is a process of interaction of the above four factors—innate abilities, environmental conditions and events, instrumental and associative learning experiences, and task approach skills. From this process emerge self-observation generalizations concerning one's attitudes, work habits, values, interests, and developed skills. In learning theory of career choice, an individual's worldview generalizations significantly influence one's view of self, others, and the world; thus, one's beliefs can indeed influence how one views future life roles, including the work role. Important to the principles of this theory, however, is that self-generalizations can be modified.

Of major significance is the recommendation that individuals are to expand their skills and interests to meet changing requirements of future occupations; learning experiences can increase one's range of occupational possibilities. Preferences for occupations are influenced by three factors: (1) relevant work experiences that are viewed as positive especially if one succeeds at tasks required, (2) role models being observed are reinforced for their activities, and (3) when someone speaks positively about a career. Several observations for career counseling include the following:

1. Career decision making is a learned skill.

2. Persons who claim to have made a career choice may also need help. Career choice may have been made from inaccurate information and faulty alternatives.

3. Success is measured by a student's demonstrated skill in decision making; evaluation of decision-making skills is needed.

4. Clients come from a wide array of cultural, socioeconomic, and occupational groups.

5. Clients need not feel guilty if they are not sure of a career to enter.

6. No one occupation is seen as the best for any one individual. (Krumboltz, Mitchell, & Gelatt, 1975, pp. 11–13)

Career Development From a Cognitive Information-Processing Perspective

This theory highlights cognitive information-processing skills that are most important when using career information and problem-solving skills to make career decisions. The stages of processing information are used to evaluate an individual's skills. Client problems with processing information are aggressively addressed. Helpers use individual learning plans developed collaboratively with clients to assist in the career planning process, particularly the information processing phase. The individual is encouraged to use self-talk to debunk faulty cognitions; one goal is to increase self-awareness. Ten basic assumptions of this theory are as follows:

1. Career choice results from an interaction of cognitive and affective processes.

2. Making career choices is a problem-solving activity.

3. The capabilities of career problem-solvers depend on the availability of cognitive operations as well as knowledge.

4. Career problem-solving is a high–memory-load task.

5. Motivation (to become a better career problem solver).

6. Career development involves continual growth and change in knowledge structures.

7. Career identity depends on self-knowledge.

8. Career maturity depends on one's ability to solve career problems.

9. The ultimate goal of career counseling is achieved by facilitating the growth of information-processing skills.

10. The ultimate aim of career counseling is to enhance the client's capabilities as a career problem-solver and a decision maker. (Peterson, Sampson, & Reardon, 1991, pp. 7–9)

Most significant is a seven-step sequence of career delivery services. Step 1 includes the initial interview, in which helpers determine the client's typical method of making a decision. Of special interest are cognitive clarity and self-awareness. Faulty beliefs are aggressively addressed. Step 2 consists of preliminary assessment to determine readiness for decision making. Of major interest are indications of dysfunctional thinking. Step 3 includes a conceptualization of client problems and their potential causes. In Step 4, client and counselor collaborate to determine problem-solving and decision-making goals. Individual learning plans are developed and discussed in Step 5. In Step 6, the client works through the individual learning plan, and in Step 7 the client and counselor review what has or has not been accomplished and eventually consider future career planning.

The cognitive information-processing perspective stresses problem solving as the most efficient method of making an optimal career decision. Therefore, effective career information processing is highlighted in what is referred to as *CASVE*: Communication, Analysis, Synthesis, Valuing, and Execution. In *Communication*, an individual learns to identify needs. *Analysis* is used to determine interrelating problem components. *Synthesis* describes the process in which one creates likely alternatives when solving a problem or problems. In the fourth step, *Valuing*, the individual prioritizes alternatives. The final step in CASVE is *Execution*, in which one forms the end strategies in the problem-solving scheme. These are all strategies for developing effective interventions based on a careful analysis of each individual's needs. Career problem-solving is primarily seen as a cognitive process.

This theory is user friendly and is one of the few that offers a counseling model that incorporates theoretical concepts. The authors have also developed the Career Thoughts Inventory (Sampson, Peterson, Lenz, Reardon, & Saunders, 1996) and workbooks that address negative thoughts, decision-making problems, and external conflicts.

Social Cognitive Career Theory

The underlying assumptions of social cognitive career theory are drawn from general social cognitive theory, in which cognitive processes are thought of as being self-regulatory and blend with motivational processes into a lifelong phenomenon. This theory suggests a broad approach to variables that shape career behavior, almost all experiences, events, and situations that are thought to influence career behavior. The authors of this theory subscribe to Bandura's (1997) model of causality known as the triadic reciprocal interaction system that includes three variables: (1) physical and personal attributes, (2) external environmental factors, and (3) overt behavior. All three variables interact as causal influences on individual development. Thus, this approach to individual development is a person–behavior–situation interaction. Interests develop through activities, especially when individuals view themselves as competent. When negative outcomes are perceived by the individual, however, certain interests fail to develop. This theory also focuses on the social, cultural, and economic conditions that shape learning opportunities, as well as the opportunity of performing certain activities. The pathways to career choice according to this theory are as follows: self-efficacy and outcome expectations promote career-related interests, interests in turn influence goals, goal-related actions lead to performance experiences, the outcome determines future paths (determined by whether self-efficacy is strengthened or weakened), and one finally establishes a career decision or redirects goals (Lent, Brown, & Hackett, 2002).

Self-efficacy, which is discussed in several chapters of this book, is a key concept in social cognitive career theory. There is support that self-efficacy does indeed promote better performance (Gelso & Fretz, 2001). Helpers therefore might serve their clients well by offering suggestions or training programs designed to improve or modify self-efficacy precepts. Although there is much to be learned about self-efficacy, career status counseling strategies for improving self-efficacy have great potential for enhancing career development. More information on overcoming barriers to career choice is discussed in Chapters 4 and 5.

Social Learning and Cognitive Theories in Perspective

These theories promote the idea that social conditioning, social position, and life events significantly influence career choice. Key elements in the career choice process are problem-solving and decision-making skills. Individuals should process information effectively and think rationally. Learning programs are most important for increasing the range of career choices. Observational learning and self-efficacy are major elements that influence career choice. Skills learned in the initial career choice process may also be used for future career choices. These theories are embedded in social cognitive theory.

This group of theories greatly expands the variables that affect career choice and development over the life span. Individuals are influenced by many factors, including genetic endowment; contextual experiences, including social conditioning; social class; and learning experiences, including skills learned in managing tasks. The ability to process information is one of the major skills emphasized in this group of theories. Faulty cognitions are aggressively addressed through cognitive restructuring.

Developmental Theories of Career Choice

This group consists of two theories: (1) the life-span, life-space approach and (2) circumscription, compromise, and creation: a developmental theory of occupational aspirations.

Life-Span, Life-Space Approach

When one is discussing developmental approaches to career development, one usually begins with probably the most well- known and influential of all career development theorists, Donald Super. It is generally agreed that his innovative thinking, research, and publications have significantly influenced the career development movement since the 1940s. His death in 1994 did not end his influence on current practices of career development—on the contrary, his work will continue to be a driving force well into the future. In this overview of a very small part of what he contributed, highlights of some of his major works are presented. Numerous insightful discussions of Super's contributions to career development can be found in the Reference section of this book.

Super developed his theory of career development from multiple sources; therefore, he viewed his work as the development of segments of possible future theories. As early as the 1940s, Super voiced a strong belief that career counseling approaches were too narrow in scope and that career development should be viewed as an ongoing process that gradually unfolds over the life span. This observation was made at a time when the overwhelming emphasis in career counseling was on initial career choice. The message that most young people were receiving during this time was that initial career choice should be made as early in one's development as possible. Super stressed, however, that initial career decisions should be made only when one has reached *career maturity*, which includes planning skills, accepting responsibility, and awareness of various aspects of a preferred vocation. In addition, he claimed, counseling should be extended to include potential multiple adult concerns that evolve from the work role. These insightful perceptions of career development underscored the need to extend career counseling and helped broaden its scope. In essence, helpers are to address client concerns over the life span of development that is both continuous and discontinuous. For more than 50 years, Super was involved in research projects and publications that underscored the need to broaden the scope of approaches used in the practice of career development. My discussions of the life-span, life-space approach to career development will be limited to developmental stages and tasks, the life-stage model, career pattern studies, and the concepts of self-concept and career maturity.

One of the core elements of Super's developmental approach was developmental stages and tasks over the life span. His early conception of stages and tasks was modified in the 1990s to provide an updated framework for observing vocational behavior and attitudes. He uses the terms *cycling* and *recycling* through developmental tasks, because he viewed ages and transitions as very flexible and not necessarily occurring in a well-ordered sequence. Thus, individuals can recycle through one or more stages, often depending on individual situations and current conditions. Each stage includes tasks that begins with adolescence and end with late adulthood, thus the name *life-stage model*. The tasks for each stage are divided into four periods of life span: (1) adolescence (ages 14–25), (2) early adulthood (ages 25–45), (3) middle adulthood (ages 45–65), and (4) late adulthood (ages 65+). Five life stages—growth, exploratory, establishment, maintenance, and decline—are labeled. The tasks for each life stage are considered examples of development over the life span.

The *growth* stage is characterized by development of capacity, attitudes, interests, and needs associated with self-concepts in adolescence. In early adulthood one learns to relate to others, and by middle adulthood one learns to accept one's limitations. In late adulthood, one reduces working hours.

The *exploratory* phase is a tentative one in which choices are narrowed, but not finalized, in adolescence. From early adulthood to late adulthood, one learns about and finds work opportunities, discovers potential problems in middle adulthood, and in late adulthood eventually finds a good retirement community.

The *establishment phase* is characterized by trial and stabilization through work experiences, beginning in adolescence. One learns about work per se and finds opportunities in the workplace while developing new skills in middle adulthood. In late adulthood, one turns toward tasks that are more pleasurable and relaxing.

The *maintenance* phase is characterized first by verifying an occupational choice in adolescence. In early adulthood, one seeks to secure an occupational position. Middle adulthood is characterized by keeping up with the competition in the workplace. In late adulthood, one turns to keeping up with what is most enjoyable.

The *decline* phase is characterized by reducing sports participation in early adulthood. In the middle adult years, one turns attention to essential activities, and by late adulthood one begins to reduce work commitments (Super, 1990).

Another of Super's hallmarks is the use of *self-concept* in the career decision-making process. By projecting one's self-concept into potential occupational environments, individuals evaluate occupational choices. Underlying this proposition is the assumption that self-concept is developed over time through life experiences and situations and through interactions with others. Super's position is that one individual is not likely to match all requirements and dimensions of a given occupation, and some individuals may have characteristics that are appropriate for multiple occupations. Self-concept is not viewed as static in that life role experiences, including the work role, can lead to changes in one's self-concept. Important for helpers to remember is that, according to Super, work congruence is a matter of how each individual's self-concepts fit career requirements. Helpers are to be prepared to address client concerns over a lifetime of development.

The term *career maturity* evolved from Super's study of the vocational development of ninth-grade boys in Middletown, New York (Super & Overstreet, 1960). The career development of these boys was followed and evaluated well into their adulthood. Numerous findings were reported, including the observation that some ninth-graders were judged to be vocationally immature on the basis of their knowledge of an occupation, planning, and interest. Their development was unstable during a 3-year period in high school, and they were not aware of a preferred vocation. These same boys who were judged to be vocationally immature, however, turned out to be significantly successful as young adults. The obvious conclusion by Super was that ninth-grade vocational behavior does have some predictive validity for the future; boys who successfully accomplish developmental tasks at periodic stages tend to achieve greater maturity later in life. These early studies lead to the conclusion that career maturity has much to do with each individual's successful coping with requirements of life stages and his or her readiness to fulfill developmental tasks of each stage. In contemporary practice, the term a*daptability* is replacing the use of *career maturity*.

Finally, Super proposed six life roles that people are involved in, sometimes concurrently: (1) child, (2) student, (3) homemaker, (4) worker, (5) citizen, and (6) leisurite. The fact that individuals may be involved in multiple life roles suggests that success in one life role can facilitate success in another and that all life roles affect one another in the give-and-take of everyday life. The spillover effect from one life role to another is the subject of discussion in several chapters of this book. As mentioned at the beginning of our discussion of Super's many contributions to the career development movement, much of his work is very relevant today.

Circumscription, Compromise, and Creation: A Developmental Theory of Occupational Aspirations

This developmental-based theory of occupational aspirations emphasizes how people are attracted to certain occupations in early childhood. Similar to Super's theory, self-concept in vocational development is a key factor in career selection, but in this theory key determinants of self-concept development are one's social class, level of intelligence, and experiences with sex-typing. According to Gottfredson (2002), the author of this theory, individual development progresses through four stages:

1. *Orientation to size and power (ages 3–5).* The thought process during this stage is considered to be very concrete. Children do, however, develop some sense of self through sex roles and what it means to be an adult.

2. *Orientation to sex roles (ages 6–8).* During this stage, gender development significantly influences development.

3. *Orientation to social valuation (ages 9–13).* Preferences of work begin to develop through concepts of social class and awareness of self-in-situation.

4. *Orientation to internal unique self (beginning at age 14).* A greater self-awareness and perceptions of others are developed through introspective thinking. Crucial to this stage is a greater perception of vocational aspirations in the context of self, sex role, and social class.

There is a progression of self-concept development, from a child's rather simplistic and concrete view of life to the more comprehensive, complex, and abstract thinking of the adolescent and adult. During this period of physical and mental growth, assessments of occupational preferences are progressively based on sex typing, social class, and self-concept. According to Gottfredson, socioeconomic background and intellectual level greatly influence the development of self-concept. This theory places a major emphasis on the social self and external barriers that limit individual goals and opportunities. As Gottfredson sees it, people attempt to implement the social self in the choice process as they establish social identities; thus, satisfaction is primarily determined by a good fit between work role and self-concept.

A major position of this theory suggests that self-concept is composed of many elements, such as appearance, abilities, personality, gender, values, and place in society. (Keep this position in mind when you read Chapter 4.) According to Gottfredson, images of occupations or occupational stereotypes include personalities of people in occupations, the work that is done, and the appropriateness of work for different types of people. Cognitive maps of occupations constitute how adolescents and adults view occupations through major dimensions of masculinity–femininity, occupational prestige level, and field of work. An accountant, for example, has an above-average prestige level; the sex type is more masculine than feminine. In this way, the cognitive maps of occupations present areas of society that different occupations offer, hence providing one with a means of evaluating occupations as to their compatibility with the self.

The sociological aspects of career choice are also emphasized in the concepts of social space, circumscription, and compromise. *Social space* is presented as comprising zones of acceptable alternatives in each individual's cognitive map of occupations. As each person develops a sense of where he or she wants to fit in society, he or she establishes points of reference, or *territories*, that are acceptable in the career choice process. The process by which one narrows territories is referred to as *circumscription*. Finally, the term *compromise* as used by Gottfredson is the process of adjusting aspirations to accommodate external realities, such as availability of local educational programs and employment, hiring practices, and family obligations. Compromise also includes trade-offs in the process of career choice; people will generally abandon interests and sex type in favor of the prestige of occupational alternatives.

The scope of this theory was expanded to include a biosocial perspective. Primarily, what was added was a focus on the influence of genetic individuality and the interplay of genetic and environmental factors that contribute to behavior. The nature–nurture partnership approach to career development adheres to an inner compass from which one may circumscribe and compromise life choices. This perspective of career development differs from many other career development theories by focusing on inherited genetic propensities that shape individual traits. What is important for helpers to remember here is that behavior is shaped and influenced through an interaction of multidimensional and multifaceted factors. Gottfredson's theory has called more attention to the development of individuals in their young years and social aspects of one's development that can significantly influence career choice.

Developmental Theories of Career Choice in Perspective

Super's theory leaves little doubt that career development is indeed a continuous and discontinuous process over the life span. Developmental stages and tasks in career development provide windows of opportunity for counseling interventions. Of most importance in the career choice process is the idea of career maturity, which can be used to determine whether one is sufficiently prepared to make a career decision. The conclusion that a client's orientation to work, planning skills, and reality of occupational preferences are benchmarks for determining readiness for career choice is of major significance. Thus, helpers assist clients in focusing on developing an accurate picture of the self in multiple life roles. According to Super, self-concept is the driving force that establishes a career pattern.

Gottfredson's research has emphasized career education for the very young. Helpers are to be alert to how social issues, such as the socioeconomic status of one's parents, can influence career choice, especially constraints of career choice; social restraints of circumscription can limit career development. The goal here is that each child should feel free to choose any career. In Chapter 4, I highlight social restraints to career choice and development.

Person-in-Environment Perspectives

This perspective of career development includes career construction: a developmental theory of vocational behavior.

How one's life is influenced and shaped by contextual interactions over the life span is the major focus of person-in-environment theories. According to this view of human behavior, individuals are considered as products of environmental interactions that are very inclusive yet also unique. Furthermore, individuals are not only influenced by others but also influence others as they interact within environments; there is a reciprocity effect. In career construction theory, each individual's career development is influenced and constructed within environmental systems. Each individual builds a system of constructs that become his or her way of looking at life; constructs are formed from a wide range of interactions within ecological systems (Bronfenbrenner, 1979; Schultz & Schultz, 2005).

An ecological system is not in itself a career development theory but is a most inclusive method of understanding human development. The total ecological system is very inclusive: parents, other relatives, friends and acquaintances in one's neighborhood, schools, political parties, and employment systems, among many others. People develop in changing historical contexts and in sociocultural interactions and relationships; thus, many client concerns are embedded within person-in-environment experiences. Uniqueness emerges from individualized and shared experiences. Individual life stories unfold within changing ecological systems.

A constructivist's viewpoint of career development is quite a departure from other career development theories. According to constructivist theory, individuals define themselves as they participate in events and relationships in their environment; they develop personal constructs that are based on unique individual perceptions of events and situations. Different personal constructs and worldviews develop from different cultural contexts. Personal constructs continue to be modified over the life span. People's unique constructs are developed and modified through the way they interpret and view their lives (Kelly, 1955). The focus of this viewpoint is on individual behavior: "As individuals understand their environments and participate in events they define themselves and their environments" (D. Brown et al., 1996, p. 10).

Career Construction: A Developmental Theory of Vocational Behavior

Career construction theory embraces Super's (1990) basic principles of developmental tasks of Growth, Exploration, Establishment, Maintenance or Management, and Decline or Disengagement. In this section, I apply career construction theory to each developmental task. Savickas (2002) provided an insightful guideline when he suggested that careers are to be viewed from a developmental contextual position in which the focus is on one's adaptation to an environment through the development of inner structures. Within this framework, core roles are developed that in turn influence preferences for lifestyle and life roles.

What I am suggesting here is that the process of an individual's development includes integrated constructs that give clarity to purpose and role; roles interact to reciprocally shape each other. Thus, an individual's experiences in processing developmental tasks form the foundation for a greater understanding of self and subsequent vocational identity.

Similar to Super's theory, self-concept development is a major factor in career construction theory. *Growth,* the initial developmental stage, is addressed from early childhood experiences. Four major tasks of children are as follows:

1. Become concerned about one's future as a worker

2. Increase personal control over one's vocational activities

3. Form conceptions about how to make educational and vocational choices

4. Acquire the confidence to make and implement these career choices (Savickas, 2002, p. 168)

What I am emphasizing here is that one's self-concept is the filter through which one constructs numerous definitions of self that can affect all life roles, including the work role. Not surprisingly, there are an endless number of interactions, events, situations, and experiences that can influence one's conceptions about how to make a vocational choice. Some that are considered most important are interactions between parents and children that foster secure feelings and positive relationships. Another source of career confidence is success in school activities that encourages positive attitudes, beliefs, and competencies.

The second stage in constructing a career is *exploration*. One of the important processes in career construction theory is the search for congruent work environments in which to express one's vocational identity. During this stage, one is cognitively processing and assessing alternatives while searching for a clearer definition of self. Individuals who are able to integrate self-percepts into a stable structure are more able to crystallize their goals. Most important at this point in career construction is self-knowledge as well as knowledge of occupations.

The third career stage, establishment, suggests that an individual has made a career choice and is looking forward to a permanent work role. He or she is in the process of implementing self-concept into an occupational role. Characteristic of this stage are a greater self-understanding of and identification with the total system of a career field. A perspective growth is to be encouraged; one must learn to distinguish between real barriers to success and perceived barriers to success.

Maintenance and management, the fourth career stage, involves refinding the self and maintaining and preserving one's self-concept. Workers should avoid stagnation by updating their skills and developing new and innovative strategies in the work role. They should adopt a lifelong learning perception of being prepared for the future. In many respects, this is a time for renewal of career development.

The final stage, *disengagement*, is characterized by retirement concerns. This is a time when one gives up responsibilities and passes them on to others. There is a major adjustment during this stage as one adapts to accepting a reduced work role and a changing focus from a highly involved work identity. The vocational self-concept is in the process of recycling to retirement living; one is to adopt a different lifestyle.

Developmental constructivism is a means to discover how individual constructs are developed. Important to the understanding of the relevance of construction theory is the position that constructs are perceptions of events. As core roles emerge, one becomes aware of individual differences and gradually integrates constructs into systems that give clarity to one's purpose and role in life. It is an ongoing process through a series of stages in which one makes adjustments to an ever-changing society. In this context, each person creates personal constructs that can influence the direction of all life roles, including the work role. Finally, helpers can assist clients in learning to understand how constructs relate to career choice and development and how one can change or modify constructs into useful themes. Career construction theory suggests that each individual has unique sets of constructs that are continually modified; thus, each person may view the world somewhat differently.

Summary of Career Development Theory Perspectives

What we take away from our discussion of career development theories is that, not surprisingly, human and career development have many common elements. The interaction of life roles experienced by individuals over the life span suggests a connectedness that must be addressed in the helping process. The relationships between work roles and other life roles have significant implications for addressing both career and personal concerns. The commitment one must make to the case for the individual in the counseling process is underscored by various approaches to the practice of career development. The uniqueness of each individual provides clues for the development of tailored interventions that effectively address individual needs. Readiness for making a career choice is addressed aggressively in most career theories. The significant conclusion that some individuals are simply not ready to choose a work role has many implications for addressing the initial choice process.

The practical conclusions that are derived from theories have emerged from concepts, propositions, and ideas that provide insight into what is believed to be true about career development. One can also certainly conclude that the career development process can take many and different pathways. The career choice process, for instance, can take a rather stable, linear, progressive track, or it may be characterized by instability, uncertainty, and indecision, requiring one to recycle through developmental stages. The ability to think rationally and to effectively process information are the keys to success for all individuals who are making a career choice. The changing nature of the workplace and work requirements in the 21st century suggests that ongoing training, educational achievement, and skills development will continue to be most important. There appears to be a growing need for all clients to adopt a perspective of the future in which each person assumes responsibility for his or her career development; self-agency is to be fostered. In the next chapter, the discussion of career counseling models emphasizes the practical options that have evolved in current practices of career development.

Summary

Career development theories have evolved from the need to match worker skills with job requirements. Over time, however, career development theories have been expanded to include, for example, human development issues of self-concept, self-knowledge, and cognitive functioning. Career development research continues to expand its boundaries to include current social and economic conditions.

1. Trait oriented theories include trait and factor, person-environment correspondence counseling, and John Holland's typology

2. Social learning and cognitive theories include Krumboltz's learning theory of career counseling, career development from a cognitive information processing perspective, and social cognitive career theory

3. Two developmental theories include (a) the life-span, life-space approach and (b) circumscription, compromise, and creation: a developmental theory of occupational aspirations

4. Person-in-environment approaches include a career construction: a developmental theory of vocational behavior

_____ Supplementary Learning Exercises

1. Explain the role of trait and factor counseling approaches. Why and how has this approach to career counseling remained useful?

2. Explain the significance of learning as a means of expanding one's career options.

3. How has the interest in life roles influenced career counseling practice? Give examples.

4. In Holland's typology approach, the term *congruence* is used often. What is its significance?

5. What is a *personal construct*? Why and how is this term important to career counseling?

3

Career

ctices

Making an optimal career choice has been and remains one of the major objectives of career counseling. Over time, career counseling has broadened its scope and purposes to include career transitions of adults who make multiple career choices over the life span. In contemporary society, workers are to be lifelong learners, be prepared to make changes, adapt to new and different circumstances, and learn what happens in one life role affects others. Within this framework, helpers are to address all concerns clients bring to counseling. In essence, current practices in career counseling have become very inclusive. Helpers are not simply dealing with static states of human behavior but ever more with complex person–environment interactions that require sophisticated adaptive systems. The current interest in the relationship between career development and mental health is an example of a growing awareness that human development is multidimensional and multifaceted. Thus, career development can be both continuous and discontinuous. Current practices in career counseling therefore address the needs of the whole person.

This chapter focuses on current career counseling models developed from theoretical orientations of career development theories. The primary concerns in this chapter are major components of models such as the intake interview, use of assessment results, and effective interventions. First, however, a learning theory model of career counseling, adapted from Krumboltz and Sorensen (1974) and Mitchell and Krumboltz (1996), is presented in its entirety to provide an example of stages in the career counseling process. This model is representative of current career counseling practices that are very inclusive. This model not only includes the traditional concerns of interests, values, and personality variables but also focuses on career beliefs and obstacles, family life, emotional instability, and cognitive clarity. One should not be surprised to learn that current career counseling models have components similar to those used in personal problem counseling. As I discuss components of models, however, the content of the parameters of career counseling will clearly focus on the career choice process. Included in the discussion are some methods to address barriers that constrain career choice.

A Learning Theory of Career Counseling _____

The learning theory model of career counseling includes the following seven stages:

Stage 1: Interview

a. The client–counselor relationship is established.

b. The client is asked to make a commitment to the time needed for counseling.

c. Insightful and positive client responses are reinforced.

d. The helper and client focus on all career problems; family life; environmental influences; emotional instability; career beliefs and obstacles; and traditional career domains of skills, interests, values, and personality.

e. The client is helped in the formulation of tentative goals.

Stage 2: Assessment

a. Objective assessment instruments are used as a means of providing links to learning interventions.

b. Subjective assessment attempts to attain the accuracy and coherence of the client's information system and to identify the client's core goals and faulty or unrealistic strategies to reach goals.

c. Beliefs and behaviors that typically cause problems are evaluated by using an inventory designed for this purpose.

Stage 3: Generate Activities

a. Clients are directed to individualized projects, such as completing another assessment instrument or reviewing audiovisual materials, computer programs, and/or occupational literature.

b. Some clients may be directed to counseling programs that address personal problems or lack of cognitive clarity.

Stage 4: Collect Information

a. Potential intervention strategies are discussed.

b. Individual goals, including newly developed ones, are discussed.

c. A format for previewing an occupation is presented.

d. Clients commit to information gathering by making a job site visit or using computerized materials.

Stage 5: Share Information and Estimate Consequences

a. The client's difficulty in processing information is evaluated.

b. The client's faulty strategies in decision processing are evaluated.

c. Helpers and clients develop remedial interventions.

d. Clients may be directed to collect more information or recycle within the counseling model before moving to the next step.

Stage 6: Reevaluate, Decide Tentatively, or Recycle

a. Possibilities of success in specific kinds of occupations are discussed.

b. The helper provides the stimulus for firming up a decision for further exploration of a career, or for changing direction and going back to previous steps in making a decision.

Stage 7: Job Search Strategies

a. Client intervention strategies can include using study materials, learning to do an interview or write a resume, join a job club, role play, or participate in simulation exercises designed to teach the consequences of making life decisions. Concepts of career life planning are introduced, along with how decision-making techniques that have been learned can be used in future decisions.

The stages in this model suggest a progressive agenda that begins with establishing a working consensus relationship with the client before engaging in the process of gathering background information. Clients are active participants in the counseling process. Problem identification focuses on educational deficits that are considered as limiting the occupations one considers in the career choice process. The client and counselor address this issue by developing a learning plan that includes specific learning activities and a means of evaluating progress. Faulty beliefs and negative thinking that interfere with one's ability to think rationally and make optimal career decisions are aggressively addressed. Clients learn how to reframe their thinking process from negative thoughts to more positive ones. This model endorses the rationale that the way individuals view themselves and the world around them greatly influences what they believe about themselves. In addition, the learning model, along with other models discussed in Zunker (2006), focuses on the ability to process information, make rational decisions, increase one's self knowledge, and introduce career information resources and decision-making skills.

Interventions can take many forms; for instance, the client and counselor select appropriate assessment instruments for identifying specific needs. Some clients may be assigned to a computerized career information system to broaden their scope of occupational choices, while other clients may join a group who are exchanging career information or discussing career decision-making skills. Some clients may be assigned to a counselor who specializes in cognitive restructuring. These few examples of intervention strategies make the relevant point: Intervention components address a multitude of individual needs. Further discussion of career counseling procedures that have evolved from career development theories, along with the use of example cases, have been provided by Sharf (2002), Swanson and Fouad (1999), and Zunker (2006).

The differences between counseling components developed from different theoretical orientations reflect somewhat of a different emphasis in the use of assessment, diagnostic procedures, and intervention components. The trait-oriented theories are considered to focus on a *differential* approach, which emphasizes matching occupational requirements with client traits or values, interests, personality, and aptitudes. The *developmental* approaches promote tasks that are used to move the client through a series of developmental stages. The social learning and cognitive theories are labeled as *reinforcement-based approaches* to career (Osipow, 1990) and, as such, focus on how social learning is reinforced and influences self-perceptions and one's worldview. Differential, developmental, and reinforcement-based approaches also have distinct similarities, as one would expect considering the major goal of all theories is an optimal career decision. Within the practice of career development, helpers have also been known to use technical eclecticism in order to meet the needs of their clients; interventions used in different career counseling models are selected on the basis of individual concerns. Thus, helpers should be committed to making an in-depth analysis of other model components. Keeping this recommendation in mind, the remainder of this chapter is devoted to counseling suggestions that have evolved from career development theories presented in Chapter 2. The following discussions focus on the intake interview and problem identification, use of assessment, and other intervention strategies. Less emphasis will be placed on the theoretical orientations of counseling techniques. The reader should be able to recognize theoretical orientations of some of the suggested interventions and strategies. For example, even though almost all career counseling models have an assessment component, the use of assessment results may vary. As mentioned in Chapter 2, career development theories offer some different approaches to career counseling, but all have contributed to current career counseling models.

Intake Interview

In most counseling models the intake interview is used to collect background information, such as social history; educational level; work history; family information; behavioral problems; affect; medical history; and, in the case of career counseling, problems that can interfere with career choice. Presenting problems in all helping situations are carefully evaluated. The sequence and content of the intake interview usually follow the outline listed below. Be aware, however, that one should be thoroughly trained in interview techniques that include appropriate communication skills for all clients including multicultural groups. Helpers should also be aware of the many suggestions and specific techniques for interviewing multicultural groups provided by Ivey and Ivey (2003), Okun (2002), and Zunker (2006).

1. Background information

    This information can be attained through a structured form that the client is to fill out and discuss with the helper, or it can be obtained through a face-to-face opening session.

2. Presenting problems (the reasons given by the client for coming to counseling)

3. Current status information (affect, mood, and attitude)

4. Health and medical information (including substance abuse)

5. Family information

6. Social/developmental history

7. Life roles (e.g., homemaker, leisure, citizen, and interrelationship of life roles)

8. Problems that can interfere with career choice (e.g., work identity, career maturity, faulty thinking, lack of information-processing skills, and educational deficiencies, among others)

9. Problems that interfere with career development (e.g., work-related dysfunctions, work maladjustment, faulty cognitions, psychological disorders)

10. Clarification of problems (state problems clearly and concretely)

11. Identification of client goals (e.g., determine feasibility of goals, create subgoals, and assess client's commitment; Brems, 2001; D. Brown, Brooks, & Associates, 1996; Cormier & Nurius, 2003).

This rather straightforward format is considered to be very inclusive and indeed provides categories of basic information that is considered essential in the counseling process. However, because of its inclusive nature, helpers will often need more than one session to complete the intake interview. Ivey and Ivey (2003) pointed out that counselors should and must strive to build a trusting relationship with their clients. It should not be considered unusual to temporarily end the interview to administer assessment instruments, for example. Presenting problems could also be so complex that the client is referred to a counseling professional who has specialized training. Helpers should focus on important psychological dimensions of functioning, such as need satisfaction, stress and coping strategies, attainment of developmental tasks, social skills, and many other characteristics and attributes. Problems that impede effective functioning may include indecisiveness, poor self-esteem, faulty cognitions, psychological disorders, and substance abuse, among many others. Finally, helpers will find that many client needs can emerge at any time during the counseling process.

It is during the intake interview when helpers make tentative appraisals of the client's personality type. Thus, subjective as well as objective appraisals of clients are made concerning such traits as personality, intelligence, and values; the focus of the interview is on individual traits. A client's goals, interests, and talents provide insights into vocational identity. Appraisals during the interview include the client's social networks, support systems, stages of development with an emphasis on career maturity, and vocational identity. During the interview, the helper assists the client in developing an accurate picture of the self and life roles. One of the unusual elements in the developmental approach is that social space is addressed as a pervasive influence in the career choice process. The position that one may limit one's career options or compromise them because of one's social status has far-reaching implications. At some point in the interview, the helper and client should address barriers to career choice.

Self-efficacy is a most important variable in most career counseling models; therefore, in-depth appraisals are made. Clients who do not view themselves as competent will greatly limit their career choice prospects. Potential barriers to career choice and development include educational deficits and negative cognitions. Personal beliefs are evaluated in terms of their influence on outcome expectations. Clients are encouraged to verbalize their expectations of a future work role. Interviewers use their listening skills to evaluate their clients' perceptions of outcome goals and self-efficacy deficits.

Clients may be asked to tell their life story. The helper uses the way the client perceives events, situations, and environmental interactions to provide clues to the development of personal constructs. A client's unique life role development is thought to give meaning to the client's personal constructs. Of most importance are the client's core values, which can lead to an understanding of an individual's career choice and commitment. The accomplishment of life's task and progression through life stages also are of major importance. Interviewers take the position that people are active participants in their own development; they construct meaning from decisions they make (Kelly, 1955). A client's description of career concerns can be used to emphasize how vocational self-concepts are most important in selecting work roles. Finally, it is most important to establish a culturally appropriate relationship in which the client's needs and worldviews are discussed. The continuation of the interview depends heavily on client assessment results.

Throughout the interview, helpers should be alert to any clues that provide insights into a client's personality, mood, social functioning, and other characteristics. General appearance, behavior, affect, hygiene and dress, eye contact, and speech and attitude, among other characteristics, provide important information. Within this context sets of needs should emerge. Intervention strategies may be used to confirm concerns that have been tentatively identified. Before deciding on client goals and/or intervention strategies, the client's concerns are conceptualized. Later in this chapter and in other chapters that follow, examples of counseling cases will illustrate the conceptualization process.

_____ Using Assessment Results for Career Counseling

Standardized tests and inventories, as well as nonstandardized methods, are used in career counseling models. Standardized tests in particular have been identified with the career counseling movement over time. The importance of tests to the practice of career development is emphasized by the following seven career counseling goals of assessment results: (1) identify career beliefs; (2) identify skills, proficiencies, and abilities; (3) identify academic achievement; (4) discover personality variables; (5) identify and confirm interest levels; (6) determine values, including work values; and (7) explore career maturity variables. In most career counseling practices, the use of assessment results is determined by the needs of each client, although some helpers routinely use some inventories for the purpose of enhancing the client's self-knowledge and/or to identify and discuss barriers to career choice.

Nonstandardized or self-assessment has recently received more attention (Healy, 1990; Subich, 1996). Examples of self-assessment procedures include the following:

- Writing a structured or unstructured autobiography followed by an analysis and discussion with helper
- Interest identification through a variety of exercises that may include listing 20 things you like to do followed by a discussion of them (Goodman, 1993)
- Card sorts in which the individual sorts occupations into categories of "would not choose," "would choose," or "no opinion," followed by a clarification of choices
- A structured career life planning experience exercise, referred to as *lifeline*, in which the individual develops more self-awareness by selecting an occupation as if he or she were free of identified roles and responsibilities. Each individual eventually reformulates goals when reassuming originally identified roles; goals are then modified.
- Guided fantasy, in which the individual learns relaxation techniques, then establishes a fantasy of a day on the job in the future, and eventually discusses reactions to this fantasy with the helper. Clients who achieve a high degree of self-awareness are thought to have a better chance of making an optimal career choice.

- Skill identification by focusing on previous experiences of both work and nonwork experiences, such as hobbies and volunteer work. The client compares skills learned with job requirements of occupational interest (Zunker, 2006).

Nonstandardized tests offer options for clients when techniques, content, and norms used in standardized tests are not applicable.

The level of readiness for career counseling can be assessed with the Career Thoughts Inventory (Sampson, Peterson, Lenz, Reardon, & Saunders, 1996), a measure of primary factors that are thought to reveal levels of readiness. Examples of primary factors are as follows: capacity to think clearly, motivation to learn about options, and commitment to carry out a plan of actions. Another dimension of readiness is labeled *complexity* and generally refers to contextual factors that may make it more difficult for an individual to focus on career decision making. Other measures of cognitive functioning include ability to process information and to think rationally. The Career Beliefs Inventory (Krumboltz, 1988) and the Career Thoughts Inventory (Sampson et al., 1996) are often used. Assessing a client's level of information processing can be accomplished by evaluating the following: (1) *encoding*, or the client's perception of information; (2) *goal setting*, the client's ability to recognize procedural requirements to reach goals; (3) *effective plan development* and pattern matching (i.e., the ability to establish alternative solutions and/or several means of reaching goals); and (4) *action step*, the client's ability to select appropriate behaviors to solve problems exposed in previous steps (Rounds & Tracey, 1990). In sum, the client's level of readiness for decision making and the client's ability to effectively process information are two important factors that should not be overlooked in career counseling models.

One of the most important key concepts in career decision making is *self-knowledge*. This concept is very inclusive, representing numerous traits and characteristics, including self-concept, self-perceptions, self-awareness, self-efficacy, and self-esteem. In this context, there is a sense of self that is most important to the development of all life roles, including the work role. Assessment results that provide the stimulus that encourages the process of self-discovery therefore can be very productive for most clients in the career decision-making process. One widely used method of clarifying self-knowledge is an informative discussion of the client's attitudes, interests, personality, and values. Other goals include increasing the client's awareness of his or her needs, something that can be used for the purpose of enhancing one's motivation to change.

It is generally agreed that a comprehensive evaluation of each client's cognitive abilities, values, interests, and personality is a necessary part of the career decision-making process. These traits are used with other data to determine an individual's needs and/or fit in an occupational environment. Needs are used to determine the potential of job satisfaction in certain occupations that offer need reinforcers. Work environments are also matched with personal styles as measured by interests and personality inventories. Some specially designed tests include the Minnesota Importance Questionnaire (Rounds, Henly, Dawis, Lofquist, & Weiss, 1981), which provides a means to evaluate individual needs for the purpose of determining potential congruence with certain occupations. The Self-Directed Search (Holland, Powell, & Fritzsche, 1994) and the Strong Interest Inventory (Harmon, Hansen, Borgen, & Hammer, 1994) are used to match a person's responses with Holland's RIASEC typology: Realistic, Investigative, Artistic, Social, Enterprising, and Conventional. The matching process is made easier by publications listing abilities and interests according to Holland types. Both the Self-Directed Search and the Strong Interest Inventory provide concrete examples of occupations for each Holland type.

Measures of a client's uniqueness can also be fostered by assessment instruments that assess a variety of trait characteristics, including assets for securing goals, self-concept, career maturity, vocational identity, interests, values, and beliefs about problem resolutions. Level of ability is also considered to be a most important characteristic in the choice process as well as in career development. The *career development and assessment model* comprises four phases of assessment. The first involves *life structure* (social elements that constitutes a person's life) and *work salience* (a measure of five life roles). The Salience Inventory (Nevill & Super, 1986) is used for this purpose. The second phase measures a client's perception of the work role with the Adult Career Concerns Inventory (Super, Thompson, & Lindeman, 1988). In the third phase, aptitudes (Differential Aptitude Test; Bennett, Seashore, & Westman, 1974), interests (Strong Interest Inventory; Harmon et al., 1994), and values (Work Value Inventory; Super, 1970) are assessed. In the fourth phase, self-concepts and life themes are assessed by adjective checklists (Johansson, 1975) or card sorts (Hartung, 1999), or by a repertory grid technique (Neimeyer, 1989). The results of these instruments are used to evaluate a client's career development and to determine interventions that promote career development.

Finally, in *construction career theory*, assessment is very inclusive and focuses on client concerns, career adaptability, vocational self-concept, and vocational identity. Career narratives that include an individual's life story are used to relate vocational self-concepts to work roles. To assess career adaptability, the Career Maturity Inventory (Crites & Savickas, 1996) is used for high school students, and the Career Development Inventory (Savickas & Hartung, 1996) is used for college students. These two inventories generally measure competencies for making educational and vocational choices. Assessing vocational self-concept and career themes is accomplished by the use of the adjective checklists just described, card sorts, or a repertory grid technique. In addition, career themes are assessed through either an autobiography or interview. Measures of interests include the Self-Directed Search and the Strong Interest Inventory; these two instruments also are used to assess vocational identity.

Interventions

In this section, examples of interventions will make it clear that there is the potential for a wide range of helping procedures that could be used in the practice of career development. As in the immediately preceding section, there are differences in approaches to the career counseling process that influence the content and use of interventions as well as the use of assessment results. Nevertheless, there are also similarities in intervention strategies. Most career counseling models that have evolved from career development theories support the importance of identifying client problems and needs that give direction to the development of the content of intervention strategies. Some career development theories may place a greater emphasis on self-concept development and the need to address life stages, for instance, whereas others may emphasize cognitive functioning, learning that broadens one's career perspectives and career beliefs. Within these two approaches to career choice and development are other numerous interventions that are most plausible and worthy of consideration. What this means to helpers is that there is no shortage of intervention strategies, but the process of choosing effective ones is of utmost importance. At this point, we revisit the case for the individual; client need identification should focus on the uniqueness of each person. It is from the position of individual uniqueness that tailored interventions are developed. Because of the variety and potentially large number of interventions that can be used in career counseling, they are limited in this section to those that have evolved from career development theories.

Interventions that enhance a client's knowledge of the self through identified traits are indeed an important focus of the trait-oriented theories. One of the purposes of intervention strategies is to match client needs to groups of occupations that offer the prospect of satisfaction and fulfillment. A logical intervention resulting from this perspective would involve discussions that identify measured traits and their significance. Ideally, the client is able to summarize how the knowledge of certain traits is important in the career choice process and how one matches needs with reinforcers found in the work environment; thus, job satisfaction factors are considered important not only in the initial choice process but also in career decisions that follow over the life span.

In the very popular scheme of matching personality types with occupational types in Holland's RIASEC typology, the focus is on the strength of the client's personality type. In the Holland system, decisive individuals are thought to have a strong and consistent personality pattern. Clients who have inconsistent personality patterns may be undecided or indecisive and not fully committed to pursuing a career choice. Thus, one major purpose of counseling sessions is helping clients find occupations that are congruent with their personality types. A lack of discovery of a congruent occupation suggests several alternatives in the counseling process. Counselors may choose to engage clients in values clarification, a more in-depth analysis of interests and attitudes, and/or discussions of past experiences (e.g., past work experiences, hobbies, and extracurricular activities). Intervention strategies may also include discussion of personal problems that may need to be addressed as a part of the career choice process.

In both career developmental and career construction theories that emphasize life-span development the focus is on tasks and stages of development. Self-concept is a major component in life-span developmental theories. In Super's (1990) view, self-concept develops through a variety of events and experiences in one's environment as well as physical and mental growth. One's observations and identification with working adults also are considered most important. What I am suggesting here is that a more sophisticated vocational self-concept evolves from a greater awareness of the work world. In addition, internal factors, such as aptitudes, values, and personality, become a vital and functioning part of one's total self-concept. Interventions can be most relevant at different stages of life throughout the life span. As Super saw it, self-concept is a vital part of a continuous developmental process.

Current national career guidelines recommend certain competencies and indicators of competencies relevant to one's career development over the life span. As one would expect, the importance of self-concept is touted as a part of the competencies and indicators, beginning with students in elementary school. The developmental tasks for students include interventions that will increase their self-knowledge and help them learn more about occupations and educational requirements and developing planning skills. Interventions that focus on one's ability to identify personal interests, abilities, strengths, and weaknesses, for example, are to be initiated in early childhood development. As a part of a continuous process of one's development, an increasingly sophisticated range of competencies and indicators is provided as measures of self-concept development.

The centerpiece of career construction theory are personal constructs, which are modified in a continuous process involving one's interpretation of events and circumstances experienced over the life span. Learning experiences are thought to be bidirectional, however; thus, an individual who is influenced by others, events, and experiences can also influence others—and, possibly, the outcome of events and experiences; there is reciprocity. Constructivists support the belief that individuals define themselves as they participate in events and relationships in their environment. As a person develops personal constructs, his or her view of the world differs from the views of others. One is the product of cultural contexts; hence, interventions are indeed individualized and concentrate on helping clients identify and understand the meaning that unique personal constructs give to one's purpose and life roles. As in life-span developmental theories, vocational self-concepts are enhanced through discussions of abilities, interests, strengths, and weaknesses. In addition, career interests measured by interest inventories are used to identify occupations that appear congruent when compared to one's vocational self-concept. Thus, clients develop a clearer understanding of their vocational self-concept in discussions of significant events in their life story. Some clients may find that writing an autobiography, followed by an in-depth discussion, is more effective.

In social learning and cognitive theory interventions the focus is on the here and now. A faulty career belief is addressed by interventions that focus more on cognitions that are faulty or distorted and less on insights or potential causes. The client concentrates on how to reconstruct a faulty career belief through cognitive reconstruction, which is discussed further in Chapter 12. One of the key concepts in this theory is *self-efficacy*. Following the lead of Bandura's (1986) social learning theory, helpers show clients how personal performance accomplishments are keys to improving one's self-efficacy. Thus, outcome expectations are regarded as personal beliefs. In this context, an individual who believes he or she can successfully perform well in an activity has a better chance of doing just that. What is most important to helpers is to recognize that self-efficacy can be improved. Major interventions include skills training programs that provide the opportunity to experience positive performance outcomes. People conclude that they have the ability to perform correctly when faced with certain tasks and, in fact, have a good chance of performing well with other tasks that are encountered; their self-efficacy has been enhanced. Self-efficacy is discussed in several chapters that follow. In the next section of this chapter, career and personal concerns are viewed as inseparable. Suggestions for integrating career and personal counseling are introduced. Interventions are focused on four domains: (1) career, (2) affective, (3) cognitive–behavioral, and (4) culture.

Whole-Person Approach to Career and Personal Concerns

Over time, a number of prominent career development researchers have suggested that there is a connectedness between career and personal concerns that should be addressed. Osipow (1979), for example, suggested that career and mental health concerns could be approached from an occupational mental health position. He suggested a blending of vocational development with the mental health of working adults. More recently, Krumboltz (1993) and Betz and Corning (1993), among others, have suggested that career and personal concerns are intertwined and need to be addressed in the counseling process. Historically, however, career and personal domains were thought to be separate entities and, as such, should be approached as distinctly different domains (Spokane, 1991). Following this logic counselor training programs were established from the position that career and personal concerns were separate domains.

In contemporary society there has been considerable attention directed to the changing nature of work accompanied by uncertainties of the future world of work and the decline of the American dream. New technology and the restructuring of industrial organizations that promoted outsourcing have impacted entire families and their lifestyles. The spillover effect from one life role to another has given credence to addressing the personal concerns of adults in career transition. The position that work is a major factor in each person's life story suggests that personal concerns can significantly influence one's career development; thus, a greater emphasis on life role development has emerged as a prominent counseling goal. There now is an increasing awareness of interplay between work and personal concerns and all life roles. The concern for the mental health of workers is not a new phenomenon but rather a growing awareness of factors that can influence behavior. A whole-person counseling approach is one suggestion for integrating career and personal concerns in the practice of career development. In the next paragraphs, I introduce some suggestions for managing sets of career and personal concerns.

The following is a summary of relevant information from an intake interview presented to a helper: Jan grew up in the suburbs near a large metropolitan area. Her family has lived in this area for several generations. She is now in her late 20s, has not been married, and lives alone in an apartment not far from her family's home. She has been employed in a local department store for 3 years after completing 2 years of college. Jan told the helper that she has difficulty controlling her temper at work and has been involved in several "misunderstandings" with fellow employees. She is trying to decide whether she should find another workplace. Jan complains that she is never able to relax. She states, "This job is going to ruin everything for me!" and "I can't even get along with my family!"

Helpers may find that some clients express feelings of distress associated with their work role for a variety of reasons. No doubt there are indeed workplaces that can contribute to one's anxiety and subsequent problems associated with work stress, for example. The fact is that work stress is currently a very viable subject of discussion by workers as well as industrial managers and psychologists; Chapter 11 is entirely devoted to a discussion of work stress. In Jan's case, however, sources of her anxiety hold the key to effective interventions that can moderate feelings of distress. Helpers must be aware that sources of anxiety can come from many situations and events in the workplace as well as from experiences in one's personal life. In Jan's case, it was determined that she did experience high levels of anxiety associated with all life roles. The fact that Jan is "never able to relax" does suggests that her anxiety could be self-generated.

The helper's tentative conclusions from Jan's intake interview were thoroughly discussed with her in a working consensus counseling relationship. It was mutually agreed that assessment interventions could reveal and confirm some sources of anxiety from several factors, including career beliefs and self-knowledge (abilities, interests, personality, and values). The rationale for assessment here was to confirm tentative conclusions reached earlier that faulty beliefs could be one important factor that influences Jan's disruptive behavior patterns and low self-esteem. In addition, the discussion of variables associated with self-knowledge can provide relevant information about Jan's view of herself and her confidence level. Potential work stressors in the current work environment were also to be assessed. The overarching goal was to evaluate a broad range of contributing factors, including self-esteem, self-concept development, and self-efficacy deficits. The helper in this case was acutely aware that anxiety can be triggered by many situations, and in the case of Jan there needed to be an evaluation of her perceptions of events and her subsequent interpretation of them. Someone who is highly anxious tends to focus on what could go wrong in the future; he or she fears not being able to control future events. When one is overly sensitive to perceived threats, the intentions of others, including coworkers, can be misinterpreted. In essence, all life roles can be affected by feelings of anxiety.

In a whole-person approach to helping, one of the keys to success is learning how to manage sets of needs that clients bring to counseling. The case of Jan is a good example of multiple needs associated with career choice and development as well as numerous personal needs. One way of addressing sets of needs is by observing them in four domains: (1) career, (2) affective, (3) cognitive–behavioral, and (4) culture, as illustrated in Box 3.1. Each domain contains representative strategies and typical client concerns. In the career domain, strategies are derived from the theoretical orientation of career development theories discussed in Chapter 2 and this chapter. The concerns listed include examples of associated problems from indecisiveness to retirement. The affective domain includes a broad range of emotionally driven problems, from mood disorders to a lack of insight and awareness. The cognitive–behavioral domain focuses on faulty thinking, cognitive distortions, and problems in decision making. The culture domain includes concerns ranging from deficiencies in the use of English language to discrimination and oppression. The examples of strategies and concerns in each domain are not to be considered as inclusive but are representative of numerous strategies and concerns for each domain. In the following paragraphs, the four domains described in Box 3.1 are used to illustrate how multiple needs can be addressed.

Jan's concerns are conceptualized in four domains, as follows:

Career: Jan's faulty beliefs about her work role could be a causal influence that is responsible for her failure to identify with a work environment. She is currently experiencing poor relationships with fellow workers, extreme stress, and work impairment.

Affective: Jan appears to be experiencing significant anxiety and anger, is emotionally unstable, and is subject to panic attacks. She is likely to overreact to the give and take of a work environment.

Cognitive–behavioral: Jan's anxiety is self-generated and appears to be influenced by faulty thinking, feelings of insecurity, and overgeneralization of negative experiences. Self-destructive behavior is a likely consequence of faulty thinking and reasoning.

Box 3.1   Representative Strategies and Client Concerns in Four Domains

CAREER

Strategies

Trait-Oriented counseling, Developmental counseling, Social Learning and Cognitive counseling, Person-in-Environment counseling

Assessment of traits, clarifying interests, self-concept development, vocational identity development, awareness of developmental stages and tasks, rational decision making, self-directed career maintenance, interpersonal skills development, sources of job satisfaction, work adjustment variables, coping with job loss, and preparing for retirement

Concerns

Indecisive, deficiencies in basic skills, career maturity issues, poor work identity, work impairment, work maladjustment, deficiencies in basic skills, adjusting to career transitions, balancing life roles, job loss, stress, violence in the workplace, relational problems, failure to adapt to changing work requirements, loss of work identity, and adjustment to retirement

AFFECTIVE

Strategies

Client-centered therapy, Gestalt experiments, Existential therapy, Psychodynamic therapies

Empathy, active listening, awareness techniques, dignity and worth of individual, ventilation and catharsis, self-regulation, wholeness of individual, insight and awareness, meaning in life, positive regard, and internal frame of reference

Concerns

Emotional instability, sad, anxious, angry, panic attacks, impulsivity, poor self-esteem, feelings of inferiority and helplessness, depressed mood, lethargy, fatigue, and poor personal relationships

COGNITIVE-BEHAVIORAL

Strategies

Behavioral *counseling, Cognitive restructuring, Rational-emotive therapy, Reality therapy, Beck's cognitive therapy*

Counter-conditioning, bibliotherapy, refraining, A_B_C_D_E analysis, systematic desensitization, modeling, contingency management, homework assignments, assertive training, problem-solving techniques, contracting, and social skills training

Concerns

Faulty thinking, inappropriate behavior, self-destructive behavior, cognitive distortions, maladaptive behavior, faulty beliefs, overgeneralizations of negative experiences, poor information processing skills, and problems in decision making

CULTURE

Strategies

Culturally based interventions, Multicultural counseling

Focus on level of acculturation and worldview, cultural identity, cultural orientation, work-related values, culturally appropriate assessment techniques and resources, adjustment techniques to new socioeconomic system. Use indigenous helpers, alternative counseling procedures, and expanded repertoire of helping responses

Concerns

Deficiencies in the use of English language and basic skills, poor adjustment to the dominant cultural values, collectivist worldview, cultural shock, lack of job skills, difficulty with assimilating new lifestyle, restrictive emotions, level of cultural identity; effects of discrimination and oppression, and relating to others

SOURCE: From *Career Counseling, A Holistic Approach*, 7th edition by V. Zunker, 2006. Reprinted with permission of Wadsworth, a division of Thomson Learning: www.thomsonrights.com. Fax 800 730-2215.

Culture: Jan was born into a middle-class family and has primarily adopted an individualistic worldview. She endorses the position that through self-determination one can find an acceptable role in society and is aware that she has failed to accomplish this goal. She is also aware of the importance of recognizing and appreciating cultural differences.

Observing client problem identification in these four domains suggests an interrelationship of concerns that can be addressed simultaneously. In Jan's case, her reaction to anxiety is very inclusive and has negatively affected all life roles. At this point in her life, Jan's perception and interpretation of situations and events are distorted to the point that she feels threatened and distressed. In the workplace, misunderstanding the intentions of coworkers has created a dysfunctional working environment. Relationships with family and friends have likewise been affected. What is suggested here are problems with faulty thinking and perceptions within the cognitive–behavioral domain. Helpers can offer cognitive-reconstruction techniques among other cognitive–behavioral approaches that provide methods of modifying a faulty thinking process. In this case, the helper can use the work environment as an example of how faulty reasoning can create not only problems with coworkers but also with others in different social situations. Most significant here is for Jan to recognize that how she perceives and reacts to situations and events in her life is an important factor for her own mental health and, subsequently, her ability to function on a job. Helpers should recognize the importance of consistent patterns of intervention strategies they choose to use. In Jan's case, career and personal interventions involve an emphasis on cognitive processes. Social learning and cognitive career development theories stress the need to identify a client's faulty beliefs and address them through enhancing positive self-talk and cognitive restructuring and reframing. Although how and why a person has developed feelings of anxiety may be important, cognitively oriented interventions address the here and now rather than discussing past background and experiences to gain insight and awareness. Thus, interventions focus on how to change negative thoughts to more positive ones. It was important for Jan to recognize that faulty beliefs affected not only her ability to function appropriately in a work environment but also her personal life. The major goal was to modify her thinking process.

In subsequent chapters, the discussion of barriers to career choice and development will make it clear that choice and development are a complex, multidimensional, multifaceted process. In Chapter 6, I revisit the information presented in Box 3.1 with a case that involves the mood disorder of depression. In Chapter 11, I discuss coping strategies to reduce the effects of stress, including addressing self-efficacy, self-esteem, and social support. How to generate self-enhancing thoughts also is discussed and illustrated in Chapter 7. In a whole-person approach to career counseling helpers need to be alert to all mental health concerns that could affect a client's ability to think rationally.

Summary

1. A learning theory model of career counseling contains the following sequence: interview, assessment, generate activities, collect information, share information and estimate consequences, reevaluate, decide tentatively or recycle, and job search strategies.

2. The intake interview includes background information, presenting problems, current status information, health and medical information, family information, social and developmental history, life roles, problems that interfere with career counseling and development, clarifying problems, and identifying client goals.

3. The use of assessment is determined by client unique needs. Both standardized and nonstandardized methods are used. A wide range of tests and inventories is used, including measures of ability, acculturation, career beliefs, career maturity, educational achievement, interests, personality, and values.

4. Intervention strategies include enhancing self-knowledge, discovering specific needs, job satisfaction factors, strength of personality type, identity needs, learning more about occupational and educational requirements, modifying faulty beliefs, understanding the meaning of personal constructs, clarifying understanding of self-concept, how to process career information, and learning career decision-making skills.

5. The rationale for a whole-person approach to career and personal counseling emphasizes the awareness of interplay between career and personal concerns and all life roles.

6. Integrating career and personal concerns in the practice of career development addresses sets of needs by four domains: (1) career, (2) affective, (3) cognitive–behavioral, and (4) culture.

Supplementary Learning Exercises

1. In your future job setting, how would you see yourself managing sets of needs that clients bring to counseling?

2. How would the learning theory of career counseling differ from models developed from the theoretical orientation of life-space, life-span approach, and John Holland's typology? Provide examples.

3. What does the label *reinforcement-based approach to career development* mean? Give examples.

4. Under what conditions would you use nonstandardized methods of assessment? Explain your rationale.

5. What has career maturity to do with career counseling? Explain the significance of this concept.

4 Constraints Affecting Career Choice and Development

The study and refinement of procedures to enhance career decision making has been an ongoing effort for several decades and remains a viable concern today. The processes involved in making a career choice have been addressed by career development theories that include a trait-oriented approach, a social learning and cognitive approach, a lifelong developmental approach, and a person-in-environment perspective. The key characteristic of the trait-oriented approach is the assumption that individuals have unique patterns of ability and traits that can be objectively measured and correlated with the requirements of various types of jobs. In the social learning and cognitive approach, social conditioning, social position, and life events are thought to significantly influence career choice. Developmental approaches stress that individuals make changes during developmental stages and adapt to changing life roles: Individual development is unique, multifaceted, and multidimensional. One's career development in the person-in-environment perspective is thought to be influenced and constructed within several environmental systems, such as family, church or synagogue, neighborhood, school, neighbors, friends, workplace, and the culture and customs of the larger environment (Zunker, 2006).

Each group of career development theories discussed in Chapters 2 and 3 was developed to better understand the process of making an optimal career choice. Each theory has similar priorities but focuses on different aspects of human traits, growth, and development; thus, all theories contribute to our understanding of the career choice process. The various positions of career development theories have also uncovered problems and constraints in making a choice. Two areas of concern that have received attention from researchers have been constraints of career choice associated with gender and with minorities. Sociologists, on the other hand, have primarily focused on constraints of career choice by a number of factors, including status of parents, labor market demands, and structure in organizations. Not surprisingly, sociologists have studied the relationships between social class and choice and placement in a career; their studies have been longitudinal and comprehensive. In order to grasp a fuller understanding of constraints affecting career choice and development, in this chapter I explore the work of some prominent sociologists. Let's begin with an introduction to American class structure.

Model of American Class Structure

The American class structure depicted in Table 4.1 includes six class rankings (Gilbert, 2003). Each rank is based on sources of income, including income of the main earner, typical education, and typical household income in the year 2000. The top two groups, *capitalist* and *upper middle class*, are considered to be the privileged classes. The capitalist class includes families that were in the upper 1% of income in the year 2000. The capitalist class is composed of a very small group of people who are top executives, own substantial enterprises, and are heirs to family fortunes. They have tremendous political power. The next group, the upper middle class, has grown in number and importance in the last two decades. The key to success of this group is access to a university education, which usually includes graduate study. This group consists of managers, professionals, and medium-sized business owners. The next two groups, *middle class* and *working class*, are considered to be the majority class that includes about 60% of society. The middle class, 30%, often overlaps with the working class; for example, if a worker's income level drops, then he or she shifts to the working class. The middle class are semiprofessionals, lower level managers, and nonretail salespersons. The working class of 30% is defined by occupational groups such as low-paid craftsman, clerical workers, and retail sales workers who typically have a high school diploma. The *working poor* (15%) and *underclass* (12%) are also classified as lower class. The working poor are characterized as laborers and service workers; many people in this group have not earned a high school diploma. The underclass may be unemployed or have only part-time jobs, and many depend on public assistance (Andersen & Taylor, 2006; Gilbert, 2003).

This very brief introduction to class structure provides reference points when discussing concerns of particular groups of people. It also points out the growing disparity between the wealthy and poor. It is most instructive to recognize that class structure is primarily determined by one's earnings and occupation.

Also emphasized by sociologists is that upward mobility is associated with level of education; therefore, helpers are indeed correct in pointing out that staying in school has much to do with one's future. In the next paragraphs, I briefly review the relevance of socioeconomic status (SES). The focus will continue to be on some factors that constrain career choice.

Socioeconomic Status

The measure of an individual's status in society includes sources of income, typical education, and typical household income. As pointed out in Table 4.1, people of privilege have significantly higher incomes; usually attend very

Table 4.1   Model of the American Class Structure: Classes by Typical Situations

Class, Percent of Households	Source of Income, Occupation of Main Earner	Typical Education	Typical Household Income, 2000
Privileged Classes Capitalist 1%	Investors, heirs, executives	Selective college or university	$2 million
Upper-Middle 14%	Upper managers and professionals, medium-sized business owners	College, often post-graduate study	$120,000
Majority Classes Middle 30%	Lower managers, semi-professional, nonretail sales workers	At least high school, often some college	$55,000
Working 30%	Operatives, low-paid craftsmen, clerical workers, retail sales workers	High school	$35,000
Lower Classes Working Poor 13%	Most service workers, laborers, low-paid operatives, and clerical workers	Some high school	$22,000
Underclass 12%	Unemployed or part-time workers, many dependent on public assistance and other government transfers	Some high school	$12,000

SOURCE: Gilbert, D. (2003). *The American Class Structure in an Age of Growing Inequality* (6th ed.) p. 276. Copyright Wadsworth 2003 a division of Thomson Learning. Printed with permission.

selective universities; and may be heirs who own businesses, upper level managers, and professionals. Some have inherited fortunes, and some have gained wealth after spending years studying at college and/or professional schools. Upward mobility for many people in the upper middle class was gained through an extensive educational program. This brings up the important question of who goes to college.

To answer this question one must reflect on research findings from the 1950s to more current times. In 1957, nine thousand high school graduates in Wisconsin were followed to determine their chances of attending college. The findings revealed that IQ, SES, and gender were strong determiners of who attended college among the high school graduates in Wisconsin at that time (Sewell & Shah, 1977). Some other conclusions were most significant, such as that the chances were fairly good that a boy from a high-status family and with a low IQ might go to college. A boy from a low-status family, however, had better chances of attending college if he had a high IQ (Gilbert, 2003). This research was repeated with a larger national sample 25 years later and yielded approximately the same results, with one exception: Gender was no longer a strong deterrent to college admission. One should note that minority status was evidently not a variable used in these studies; however, in 1957 the chances were good that minorities were not afforded equal access to education.

Yet another study involving college attendance was conducted in the 1980s for the U.S. Department of Education by the University of Chicago. Gilbert (2003) reviewed the data from this study to determine the level of influence social class and mental ability had on individuals who were admitted and attended college. He found that "nearly all the high ability graduates from high-status families, but very few low-ability graduates from low-status families went to college (83 versus 13 percent)" and that "Among top SES school grads with below average abilities, 57 percent were in college, compared to 33 percent of bottom SES kids with above average intelligence" (pp. 165–166). Class differences in those who attended college were very revealing, however: Mental ability and SES were strong independent determinants of who goes to college. In a more recent study, Mortenson (2001) confirmed that class disparities in actual completion of college were even greater in the year 2000 than in the 1970s.

Another interesting question is where high school graduates are going to college. As one would expect, students from high-income families tend to go to highly selective universities, whereas students from low-income families tend to attend 2-year community colleges. One should also recognize, however, that the American university systems have attempted to include all talented youth regardless of SES. Some private universities are offering qualified students free tuition if the parent's income is less than a certain amount per year. Drucker (2002) suggested that access to educational opportunities will definitely increase in the next decade; for example, educational programs available via the Internet will grow. The spiraling costs of a higher education, however, may restrict many students from low-SES families from attending a 4-year university. The message to gifted prospective students from low-SES families is that there is more to getting in college and finishing a 4-year program or higher than mental ability alone; the lack of economic resources can have a powerful effect on people's lives.

Research findings suggest that the extent of social mobility for many people (moving from one social class to another) is greatly influenced by educational level. The following sociological perspective of limited social mobility is taken from Anderson and Taylor (2006, p. 233).

Debunking Society's Myths

Myth: The United States is a land of opportunity where anyone who works hard enough can get ahead.

Sociological perspective: Social mobility occurs in the United States, but less often than the myth asserts and over shorter distances from one class to another: Most people remain in their class of origin.

The major point here for helpers is that social mobility is not just about individual effort; sociologists' view is that upward movement is influenced by factors that affect the whole society, that is, class status, changes in occupational systems, economic cycles, and demographic factors. This does not mean that helpers do not encourage clients to move ahead, because mobility does occur in this country. What it does mean, however, is that there are barriers and restraints that will offer challenges to people who seek upward mobility through educational attainment and subsequent careers. It may require the collective effort of family, kin, and community (Higginbotham & Weber, 1992). Finally, it has been observed that downward mobility has increased because of the declining value of the dollar and cost-of-living increases; people in the middle class are now experiencing a decline in income as well as status (Mishel, Berstein, & Schmitt, 2001). It is important that each individual be thoroughly informed of existing barriers to social mobility; individual situations and conditions should be carefully evaluated. Helpers can display evidence of the close relationship between years of schooling and status level of parents and between years of schooling and success at work (Hotchkiss & Borow, 1996).

Social Class and Socialization

People absorb their culture through *socialization*, the process by which one learns the expectations of society (Anderson & Taylor, 2006). Following this logic, socialization is the process in which one develops a basis for identity and establishes a personality. People internalize cultural expectations, which can be powerful influences on how each person views and interprets the everyday give and take of life as well as self-perceptions, self-esteem, and self-concept. Through socialization people learn to act in socially acceptable ways; they learn to internalize beliefs and behaviors of their culture that are modified and/or reinforced over the life span. Socialization agents include one's ecological system, such as family, friends, relatives, teachers, church or synagogue, school, recreational programs, and government organizations, among others.

The ecological system provides helpers with the opportunity to view all aspects of a person as a whole. According to Bronfenbrenner (1979), there are four systems that make up the environment: (1) the *microsystem*, or the person; (2) the *mesosystem* of family, peer group, and schoolmates, among others; (3) the *exosystem* of friends of family, extended family, neighbors, and workplaces; and (4) the *macrosystem*, which is the sum of the broad ideologies expressed and modeled by the sociocultural group. Within this view of human development uniqueness emerges from individualized and shared experiences and one's unique interpretation of those experiences. Each individual life story unfolds within changing ecological systems. Core assumptions may well be embedded in the learning experiences within ecological systems.

The growing disparity between the wealthy and poor also means that people live in distinctly different neighborhoods. Many of the affluent live in gated communities and associate with neighbors who are also of equal status and class. Their social backgrounds (e.g., family income, father's occupation) can be very similar. There has been an increasing trend of residential isolation of the rich since 1970 accompanied by a greater concentration of the poor (Massey, 1996). There are some exceptions to this trend, especially among affluent African Americans; they are leaving the urban ghettos and moving to Black communities in the suburbs (Gilbert, 2003).

What this all means for helpers is that contextual interactions can greatly influence how each individual views his or her future lifestyle, including options for careers. This process begins in early childhood. In a review of studies conducted on children's conception of social class, Gilbert (2003) concluded that "even preschool children are aware of class differences. . . . By the time they reach 12 years of age, children are not very different from adults in their thinking about class" (p. 113). These conclusions were based on studies by Kohn (1969, 1977), Leahy (1983), the National Opinion Research Center (1953), Simmons and Rosenberg (1971), and Tutor (1991), and in general are supported by research conducted by Berns (2004), Galliano (2003), D. F. Roberts (2000), and Warner and Steel (1999). By observing the roles of others in context, children internalize values, beliefs, and expectations of the future.

Be aware, however, that socialization is a process that continues over the life span. In adolescence, patterns of socialization experience can vary by race and social class. As one would expect, there are significant class and race differences in how people view the world around them. In a national study of adolescents, Csikszentmihalyi and Schnieder (2000) found that young people who are most economically privileged tend to define their activities more like play than work, whereas those with less economic resources define their activities as work. Thus, adolescents whose families are working class view the world as more work-like when compared to others their age who are more privileged (Anderson & Taylor, 2006). This conclusion reinforces the position that class and race differences in perceptions of life and work are a reality; however, socialization is multidimensional and multifaceted, and each client should be viewed as an individual. One cannot always be certain of the environmental sources that affect an individual's worldview. Individual differences should be recognized; views can be modified by a variety of experiences and situations in one's environment. The forces of a changing society can alter socialization influences.

Keeping individual differences in mind, note that tendencies of behavior by class and status are thought to be internalized through influences during childhood and adolescence. A number of studies by Kohn (1969, 1976,

1977; Kohn & Schooler, 1983) have examined class differences in the values of parents that are thought to be passed on to their children. Parents in higher class positions, for example, stressed the values of self-control, curiosity, and consideration. According to Kohn, these values influence capacities for self-direction and empathic understanding of others and, most importantly, are oriented toward the internal dynamics of the person. Working-class parents focused on obedience, neatness, and good manners. These values are thought to instill behavioral conformity, that is, the assumption of fixed standards of behavior. In addition, Kohn suggested that parents at higher class levels value self-direction more than conformity to fixed standards (Gilbert, 2003). Interestingly, these value systems are thought to be primarily developed from occupational experiences. Kohn, for instance, based his conclusions regarding the higher class on demands of professional and managerial positions that require individual initiative and judgment and, as such, are more self-directed than highly structured blue collar jobs of the working class (Gilbert, 2003).

What we have here is the position that life experiences, especially work experiences, shape social values. People who occupy managerial and professional jobs generally favor self-direction, whereas people in highly structured jobs at the blue collar level value conformity. A self-directive approach suggests that one values self-empowerment to meet challenges head on; one takes positive action for self-improvement. Those who value conformity tend to feel that they have little power over events in their lives and adhere to authority. These differences in social values between class structures that are imparted to the young can influence career choice. Gottfredson (2002) stressed the importance of social space in career choice; each person's view of where he or she fits or would want to fit into society should be thoroughly explored. Self-concepts, according to Gottfredson, are primarily influenced by SES and intellectual level. Thus, in the process of decision making one narrows his or her territory according to an acceptable social space. This process is referred to as *circumscription*. In a broader sense, Gottfredson suggested that an interplay of genetics (mental ability) and environmental factors contributes to behavior. Furthermore, individuals and their environments are involved in a continuous state of dynamic interaction that can lead to change in individual aspirations. Therefore, the individuality of all clients should be respected.

Potential Career Choice Constraints

There is general agreement that class and status provide pathways to better jobs for some people and barriers for others. It should not be surprising that most sociologists agree that children from privileged families are more likely to land desirable jobs than children from the working class. There are certainly exceptions to this conclusion, however; each one of us could probably tell the story of someone who has achieved social mobility through persistence, hard work, and educational attainment. Therefore, individual differences are the mainstay in the case of an individual when addressing potential career choice constraints. The sociologists' view of career constraints nevertheless has an important message that helpers should incorporate for a fuller understanding of the career choice process. Helpers should adhere to the sociologists' perspective of human development, social mobility, class structure, SES, and the socialization process.

It is generally accepted that people who are born into the privileged class have a good chance of remaining there. As a member of the privileged class, one can expect to attend a well-established university; that is, the chances of being admitted are good. People of the privileged class usually live in segregated communities and mainly associate with other members of their group. Thus, their friends have similar backgrounds and, for example, enjoy similar events at the local country club. Status is mediated from one generation to another through access to higher education (Gilbert, 2003). As mentioned earlier in this chapter, there are exceptions to these rules; social mobility does indeed occur.

Just as the privileged have friends with similar backgrounds, so too do members of the working class. They share their neighborhoods with other members of the working class, attend events with them, and socialize with them. Children therefore grow up in ecological systems that are dominated by the mores of the working class. Their characters are shaped by indigenous values associated with the working class. One's work may be the centerpiece of his or her existence, whereas others may despise their work role. Individual interpretations of experiences and situations may be quite different within groups; the general rule to follow should be that there are differences within groups as well as between groups. When conceptualizing a client's concerns, background data, including family SES, should be used along with other data. Scores from a personality inventory, for instance, may indicate that a client may indeed be open to considering a wide range of careers and is receptive to new ideas. Clearly, clients may restrict or circumscribe their choices to their perceived social space (working class) and resist consideration of alternatives because they may have been conditioned to think that this is their role or place in life. Although I have emphasized family background as a strong influence on career choice, one must also recognize influences within the context of the ecological system. Teachers, coaches, friends, peers, and business owners in the neighborhood are all a part of the equation. What may appear to be a simple connection—working-class parents produce working-class children—can be much more complex and intertwined with other variables. The role of the helper is to assist clients in sorting out all possibilities.

One important piece of the puzzle may be to determine whether a client is internally or externally oriented. I now turn to Rotter's (1982) work on internal and external locus of control. As defined by Schultz and Schultz, (2005), an internal locus of control is "a belief that reinforcement is brought about by our own behavior," and an external locus of control is "a belief that reinforcement is under the control of other people, fate, or luck" (p. 436). One of Rotter's basic assumptions was that he believed most behavior is learned through experiences with other people. People who have learned to be internally oriented expect reinforcement when they display certain skills. On the other hand, externally oriented people see no connection between their behavior and reinforcers; life events are viewed as matter of fate, luck, or the result of powerful others. Furthermore, internally oriented people contribute their success to ability and hard work, whereas externally oriented people have the tendency to contribute their success to good luck or an easy task (Ryckman, 2004).

Rotter focused on the differences between externally oriented and internally oriented people. Externally oriented people believe that their role in life is a matter of luck or fate, whereas internally oriented people believe that through hard work they are capable of determining their fate. Internally oriented people are optimistic about the future and tend to have confidence in their ability to succeed. Externally oriented people tend to have low self-efficacy and little confidence in their ability to change their future. Important to our understanding of this subject is that Rotter did not suggest that people fall into one category or the other as in a typology but simply that they may be more internally oriented than externally oriented, or vice versa. Thus, it is very probable that people may have characteristics of both external and internal orientation. This position is similar to how helpers evaluate personality characteristics—by degree or strength of a characteristic.

Research involving academic performance and an internal or external locus of control has revealed that internally oriented people outperform the externally oriented. Researchers suggest that internally oriented people are more focused on the task and are more persistent, flexible, and cognitively active than those who are externally oriented. Internally oriented people were viewed as willing to make the necessary effort to control outcomes (Ryckman, 2004). These characteristics are important to career development as well. Kirkcaldy, Shephard, and Furnham (2002) found that internally oriented people are more satisfied with their jobs; they tend to be assertive, independent, efficient, and confident. Also, internally oriented people report less stress and experience the comfort and satisfaction that are associated with more control on the job (Ryckman, 2004). Finally, internally oriented people tend to have better mental health than the externally oriented. It appears that internally oriented people cope with stress more effectively than externally oriented people (Liu et al., 2000). These conclusions provide supporting information concerning influences on behavioral development and especially as to how cognitive processes influence behavior. In the next paragraphs, I evaluate more research that is associated with career choice and development and mental health.

Bandura (1986), known for his work on observational learning, suggested that our behavior is influenced by social and environmental forces and cognitive processes. This position is referred to as *triadic reciprocality*. Bandura contends that one's interpretation of social and environmental events is unique according to each person's expectations; therefore, one interprets the potential effects of actions by determining which behaviors are appropriate in a given situation. One of the important factors in Bandura's work is that the cognitive processes one uses when interpreting an event or situation are based on unique learning experiences that have been reinforced. Furthermore, individual expectations are uniquely learned from a variety of sources and people; thus, some behaviors learned in one's childhood ecological system can be either reinforced or unlearned in new and different environments. Most relevant to our discussion, however, are Bandura's views on efficacy expectations.

According to Bandura, effective performance is a result of high and realistic efficacy expectation; that is, individual beliefs and convictions can produce certain behaviors. Conversely, people who have self-doubts and feel inadequate will not necessarily perform well. Therefore, it is not the acquisition of skills that determines adequate performance but rather the acquisition of good skills accompanied by the belief that one is capable of performing a task that permits competent functioning. Hence, efficacy expectations can influence choice of individual activities as well as the environmental settings in which activities occur (Ryckman, 2004). A related study of efficacy expectations conducted by Betz and Hackett (1981) revealed that male and female students differed in their beliefs about their ability to complete educational training programs required for various occupations. Men were more confident they could prepare for traditional masculine occupations, whereas women were more efficacious in preparing for traditional female occupations. Thus, self-efficacy was considered an important factor in why women eliminated certain career choices.

Finally, the relationship between mental health and self-efficacy is most instructive. Bandura (1997) suggested that people with low self-efficacy are unable to cope with stress, which, could result in physiological problems (see Chapter 11). Inferred here is that low self-efficacy can tend to negatively influence one's capability to cope effectively. Negative influences can also affect all life roles to the point that one develops severe mental health concerns; for example, depression, anxiety, and neuroticism have been associated with low self-efficacy (Muris, 2002).

The discussions concerning constraints of career choice and development and its connection to mental health began with differences between values by social class. Making the assumption that values are learned through socialization in ecological systems, it was suggested that people in the privileged class tend to be internally oriented, whereas those in the working class are externally oriented. It was suggested that contextual interactions greatly influence how people view their future and life roles. The point was also made, however, that there are differences within social groups as well as between social groups, leading to the assumption that differences in values by social class alone cannot account for variances observed in making a career choice and attaining a desirable job. People of the privileged class, for example, have important connections that can be used for obtaining a top-notch job. In this case, the most important factor for career choice was a matter of who you know and had very little to do with differences in values. The primary premise of *happenstance approach theory*, developed by Mitchell, Levin, and Krumboltz (1999), suggests that chance events do happen and can have positive or negative consequences; that is, by chance the person in the right place at the right time gets the good job.

Social class does matter when it comes to higher education. Although through sacrifices and hard work some people have attained a college degree or have graduated from a professional school, the people who are born into families with high status and the accompanying high level incomes are in a much better position to finish a higher education degree. Higher education perpetuates differences in social class by facilitating the relatively higher income levels of graduates as opposed to persons with less education. High school graduates from working class families who have limited funds may restrict their career choice to occupations that can be attained through community college programs, even though there are available scholarships at 4-year colleges, federally backed loans, and work-study programs that assist needy students. These high-stake decisions require a commitment from parents and prospective students that neither is willing to take or cannot take. Both parents and prospective students may see their limited work role as a matter of fate or luck.

In sum, career choice constraints are thought to develop from early childhood experiences that include SES and influences from ecological systems, among other variables. Children reared in families that are considered as working class tend to be more externally oriented than children who are reared in higher status families. Children from working-class families tend to perceive a greater restriction on future opportunities in the work world than do children from higher status families. Efficacious expectations also tend to be different. Children from higher status families tend to be more optimistic and have more confidence that they will attend college and obtain an optimal job than do children reared in working-class families. Although there are exceptions to these assumptions, research tells us that most people remain in the class status of their origin.

What we have here is the need to address false beliefs and assumptions and cognitive processes that are primarily negative. Helpers must look for individual sets of needs that are unique for each client and respect individual client needs regardless of social class. The case for the individual is a simple, straightforward concept that aids helpers in maintaining the position of individual uniqueness. This concept is very relevant to this chapter's focus on potential career choice constraints. The uniqueness of each client suggests that there are similarities and differences between people from different social and cultural backgrounds. Worldviews, for example, may differ between cultural groups as well as within cultural groups. Beliefs, attitudes, interests, as well as how one interprets events and situations, may be conditioned and shaped in one's ecological system, which includes class and status of family. One would expect to find differences in worldviews between the privileged and the poor. The importance of background information to helpers, however, is to conceptualize individual needs in collaboration with the client. In this process the degree and kinds of individual constraints can bring clarity to perceived and real barriers to career choice, work, and mental health. In the next section, Bandura's modeling techniques for increasing self-efficacy are recommended as one method of addressing false beliefs and negative thinking.

Self-Efficacy for Effective Behavior

Each client's perception of his or her ability to effectively function in a variety of given situations is indeed a most relevant concern for helpers. Positive thinking about the self in situations, accompanied by positive self-talk, is a good indication of an attitude of optimism; a strong sense of self-esteem; and most important, self-efficacy. Self-efficacious people have expectations to succeed through their own initiative, skills, and knowledge. I have referred to people with strong feelings of self-efficacy as being *internally oriented* and to those who see no connection between behavior and reinforcers as *externally oriented*. Externally oriented people are thought to think differently and draw different conclusions such as "This is beyond my control" or "I am just an outcast" when faced with a difficult situation. One effective way to change negative thinking is through the development of self-efficacy; according to this unifying theory of behavioral change one can effectively learn to cope with career choice constraints.

Performance accomplishments, vicarious experiences, verbal persuasion, and emotional arousal are the means through which people build perceptions of self-efficacy (Bandura, 1986, 1997). Bandura considered personal mastery of experiences as a most effective method of improving one's feelings of self-efficacy. Clients who perform well on a test or demonstrate effective work skills are reinforced by their efforts. A worker who receives recognition for job accomplishment develops confidence that other tasks can be learned and mastered. Thus, a series of successful accomplishments fosters an attitude of optimism that can carry over to other tasks. Schultz and Schultz (2005) pointed out that "the higher level of self-efficacy, the wider the range of career possibilities and the stronger interest in them" (p. 425). Therefore, low self-efficacy can contribute to a more restrictive consideration of careers and can lead to indecisiveness.

Vicarious experiences, or simply the visualizing of other people performing successfully, has the potential to instill positive expectations in observers, who can thus believe they can effectively perform the tasks being observed.

Observational learning is one of the key methods thought to develop self-efficacy. *Verbal persuasion* is an expression of confidence that one has done a good job and has performed well; it is simply a verbal reinforcement by important others of a task well done. *Emotional arousal* concerning an event or situation can either debilitate performance or prove that one is capable of performing well under pressure. People who perceive that they have done well when faced with challenges under pressure are strongly reinforced to meet other challenges. Be aware that the procedures used for building efficacy expectations focus on the client's belief systems and thinking process.

Modeling techniques are similar methods used in vicarious experiences that encourage the development of efficacy expectations. Clients are given the opportunity to observe selected behaviors—for example, the behavior of another person (model) completing a work task. Specifically, the step-by-step procedures are observed, as is what happens to the model as a consequence of his or her actions and behavior. The rationale is that one can learn through observing the actions of another person and as a result build confidence that he or she too could accomplish such a task. Job shadowing is one technique that has been used to help prospective workers learn work tasks by observation. The key result of modeling techniques is the belief or perception that one is capable of completing tasks observed; thus, the client's efficacy expectations are enhanced by the level and kind of behaviors that are demonstrated.

As the reader has learned from the previous discussion in this chapter and in other chapters, the causes of low self-efficacy observed in some clients is multidimensional, that is, the result of combinations of influences. Thus, helpers search for specific concerns that are problematic. In the helping process a comprehensive conceptualization and assessment of client issues, concerns, and contexts should be fostered. The use of an interview assessment and other client data is used to identify, define, and evaluate outcome goals. Helpers may want to use methods developed by Cormier and Nurius (2003) to determine specific areas of concern. Goals are identified through the use of written and oral instructions; clients are instructed in how to state long- and short-term goals. Clients eventually develop a list of goals and sub-goals. Each client estimates what he or she would like to accomplish in the way of improving efficacy expectations. The following example of goals that involve different concerns was adapted from Cormier and Nurius (2003, p. 629). For each goal, clients are to indicate levels of confidence that can be used as quantitative measures of their success.

Goal 1 for Career Choice

Confidence in decreasing doubts about career opportunities (40 to 80)

0	10	20	30	40	50	60	70	80	90	100

No Confidence   A Great Deal of Confidence

Goal 2 for Career Choice

Confidence in my ability to master the requirements of a selected career (30 to 70)

0   10   20   30   40   50   60   70   80   90   100

No Confidence   A Great Deal of Confidence

Goal 3 for Career Choice

Confidence that I can be successful in a job that is very demanding and of high status (50 to 80)

0   10   20   30   40   50   60   70   80   90   100

No Confidence   A Great Deal of Confidence

Goal 4 for Career Choice

Confidence in seriously considering alternative career options by studying three to five different careers a week

0   10   20   30   40   50   60   70   80   90   100

No Confidence   A Great Deal of Confidence

Goal 1 for Class in Learning English

Confidence in decreasing anxiety when pronouncing English words in class (50 to 70)

0   10   20   30   40   50   60   70   80   90   100

No Confidence   A Great Deal of Confidence

Goal 1 for Work

Confidence in decreasing doubts about succeeding in a higher level job than my father has (30 to 50)

0   10   20   30   40   50   60   70   80   90   100

No Confidence   A Great Deal of Confidence

Goal 2 for Work

Confidence in decreasing doubts about the value of my opinion concerning work tasks (50 to 70)

0   10   20   30   40   50   60   70   80   90   100

No Confidence   A Great Deal of Confidence

Goal 1 for Education

Confidence in decreasing doubts about succeeding in college (50 to 70)

0   10   20   30   40   50   60   70   80   90   100

No Confidence   A Great Deal of Confidence

Goal 1 for All Situations

Confidence for increasing positive thinking through self-talk (50 to 70)

0   10   20   30   40   50   60   70   80   90   100

No Confidence   A Great Deal of Confidence

These examples permit clients to designate specific personal goals that can be self-monitored. Even small increments of success are thought to build confidence in one's ability to learn and perform. Helpers should assist clients in establishing realistic goals that require specific behaviors and actions. Morrow, Gore, and Campbell (1996) suggested that improved willingness to engage in belief about one's ability to learn can enhance willingness to learn about occupations. It is generally agreed that self-knowledge and increased occupational knowledge can increase the number of alternative options in the career choice process.

Self-management programs that help clients develop self-directed behavior also may be helpful. The following are steps of a self-management program developed by Watson and Tharp (2002):

1. *Selecting goals.* Clients are to specify changes they wish to make. Helpers are to make certain that expectations are realistic. Goals are to be stated in a positive manner and are measured quantitatively.

2. *Translating goals into target behaviors.* Target behaviors, such as increasing one's confidence in the ability to perform a specific task or increasing confidence in skillfully expressing one's opinion, are specified.

3. *Self-monitoring.* Clients learn to observe their own behavior through self-monitoring by recording specific behaviors in a behavioral diary. They are to evaluate their behaviors by frequency of occurrence and the consequences of each behavior.

4. *Working out a plan for change.* An action plan is developed to bring about desired changes. Such a plan includes the necessary actions to bring about change, behavioral contracts, and social support available. Methods for self-reinforcement are also specified.

5. *Evaluating an action plan.* Each action plan is evaluated in terms of effectiveness of the change process. Some plans may need to be revised or adjusted. Clients are to understand that evaluation is an ongoing process of lifelong change.

Effective self-management programs employ combinations of strategies. Clients learn to establish goals and evaluate their own progress. They learn to monitor their progress and to self-reward when they experience success. Clients become aware of the consequences of their behavior in different contexts. They learn that gradual progress can enhance their confidence level and build self-efficacy. They also learn that environmental support can be most helpful in overcoming obstacles; thus, social support as an effective tool used in the current situation can also be an effective tool for accomplishing other goals in the future (Cormier & Nurius, 2003). Other methods that can be used for helping clients develop a more open and positive view of the world are problem solving, assertiveness training and rehearsal, and cognitive restructuring (see Chapter 12).

Summary

Perceptions that one has limited career options may evolve from influences in one's socialization process. Sociologists have focused on limited career choice factors by status of parents and between social classes and choice and placement in a career. High school graduates from lower status families generally do not have the financial resources to attend college; thus, these young people may view their upward mobility as constrained. Career choice constraints can evolve from multidimensional influences; therefore, helpers should conceptualize each client's needs from an individual perspective.

1. A model of the American class structure is reported as follows:

    There are six class rankings: (1) capitalist (upper 1%), (2) upper middle class (14%), (3) middle class (14%), (4) working class (30%), (5) working poor (13%), and (6) underclass (12%). Class structure is determined by income and occupation.

2. Socioeconomic status (SES) is determined by sources of income, typical education, and typical household income. There are class disparities in the actual completion of college: More students from high-status families graduate from high school, and graduates from high-income families tend to attend highly selective colleges. The increasing cost of a college education may restrict some low-SES high school graduates from attending. Social mobility (upward movement) is greatly influenced by educational level. Helpers should point out to clients the potential barriers to social mobility but should also display evidence between years of schooling and success at work.

3. Social class and socialization have interesting connections. Through socialization, individuals absorb their culture, develop a basis for identity, and establish a personality. Socialization takes place in ecological

systems. Uniqueness emerges from individualized and shared experiences. Contextual interaction greatly influences how each person views the future. Socialization is a lifelong process that begins in early childhood. Children internalize values, beliefs, and expectations of the future. Research suggests that in adolescence there are different worldviews between class and race. Because the socialization process is considered to be multidimensional and multifaceted, helpers should respect the case for the individual.

4. According to Kohn (1977), parents in higher SES classes stressed values of self-control, curiosity, and consideration. These values influence the young to be self-directed and internally oriented. Lower status parents focused on obedience, neatness, and good manners, which are thought to influence behavioral conformity and an assumption of fixed standards. In essence, social class values imparted to the young can influence career choice options.

5. Potential career choice constraints include the following:
   - Clients from lower status families may restrict or circumscribe their career choice according to perceived social space.
   - Rotter (1982) suggested that people can be observed as either externally or internally oriented. Externally oriented people tend to believe that their role in life is a master of luck or fate. Internally oriented people tend to believe that hard work and self-determining will ensure their future.
   - Bandura (1986) suggested that effective performance is a result of high and realistic self-efficacy expectations. Competent functioning involves good skills and the belief that one is capable of performing a task.
   - Negative thinking can influence all life roles; thus, helpers should address clients' false beliefs and assumptions.

6. Self-efficacy is thought to be essential for effective behavior. One effective way to change negative thinking is through the development of self-efficacy:
   - Clients can learn to cope with career choice constraints.
   - Clients can increase self-efficacy through performance accomplishments, vicarious experiences, verbal persuasion, and emotional arousal.
   - Clients can observe the behavior of others to develop the perspective that they can accomplish tasks.
   - Goal identification by clients is used to provide estimates of improving efficacy expectations in a variety of contexts.
   - Other methods that can be used to increase self-efficacy are self-management programs, problem solving, assertiveness training and rehearsal, and cognitive restructuring.

Supplementary Learning Exercises _____

1. What role does socioeconomic status (SES) play in constraints on career choice? How is SES determined?

2. Give at least five reasons why most people remain in their social class of origin. What can helpers do to assist clients in attaining social mobility?

3. What constraints on career choice do the working class experience?

4. Explain the significance of the socialization process on career choice. What interventions would you use in the helping role?

5. Explain the difference between externally and internally oriented clients.

Career Choice and Development and the Changing Nature of Work

5

This chapter focuses on career choice and development constraints that have emerged from changes in the workplace, how work is being restructured, and how the nature of work is changing. For the past 30 years, the changing organizational context of careers and new concepts in career development have received considerable attention. Economic restructuring, demographic changes, globalization of the economy, external markets, and technological changes have dominated the dialogue. What has happened to work in America has significant consequences for many families and especially for individuals who experience constraints in career choice and for those who find barriers to their career development. There appears to be a consensus of opinion that many adults will make multiple career choices over their life spans (Drucker, 2002; Feldman, 2002). This suggests that adults will be challenged to meet the demands of changing technology and other changing work roles. Changes in the workplace may be accompanied by individual problems associated with mental health concerns or faulty beliefs that were discussed in Chapter 4.

As helpers, we must recognize that the changes in how, where, and when people work reflect ongoing complex changes in most aspects of our society. Changes, however, are not new for the American workforce; changing work roles have been ongoing since our country's inception. Thus, most workers recognize that there have been significant changes in the nature of work over a period of time. New careers and work procedures have been developed on a fairly regular basis throughout U.S. history. Currently, however, one of the major concerns is the restructuring of the U.S. economy and extensive and rapid ongoing changes that require individual workers to change their career development plans. Some people view the ongoing restructuring of organizational changes as significantly limiting their freedom of choice. This perspective is quite different from traditional beliefs; most Americans believe in the right to choose, which has been an underlying principle of the American dream. In this chapter, I discuss changes in the workforce brought about by economic restructuring, technological advances, and external market demands. Although changes in the workplace are discussed separately, extensive restructuring of the workplace and economy are considered to be interrelated and intertwined. Within each of these contexts potential individual reactions to career choice and development are discussed, as are the accompanying mental health problems. In addition, an identity crisis may present significant barriers for some adolescents while they are in the process of making an initial choice. The first part of this chapter focuses on initial career choice. This overview of how initial career choice is shaped provides a backdrop for later discussions on constraints. The rationale here is that the better one is informed about the career choice process, the greater understanding one will have of potential barriers that can deter initial career choice and those that follow. Thus, an overview of career choice perspectives of some career development theorists is also very instructive. In the final part of this chapter, career choice is viewed as the central component of a person's identity, followed by influences of economic restructuring, loss of internal career ladders, the boundaryless career model, implications of contract breach, and a summary of career barriers.

Initial Career Choice: The Shaping Process

There are good reasons why the process leading to initial career choice has been elusive and responsible for realms of research and speculation. Initial career choice involves decisions that are based on each person's background, traits, culture, and numerous other factors that have shaped a unique individual. "Human development is a holistic enterprise" (Shaffer, 2002, p. 618). Many social forces shape development. People may share some experiences and characteristics with others, but interacting situations and events are uniquely interpreted, evaluated, and internalized. Viewing clients as unique individuals, however, does not rule out the use of valid interventions that have helped others. The point here is that there are differences in the effectiveness of interventions; what works well for one client may not be as effective for another. Normal and idiosyncratic development are both important, however. Thus, researchers continue to look for additional clarification to determine how adolescents and young adults formulate their initial career choice. In the next paragraphs, I introduce some observations from studies of human and personality development related to the formulation of initial career choice process.

A logical connection between identity development and initial career choice has been pointed out by both human development researchers (Newman & Newman, 2003; Shaffer, 2002; and Sigleman & Rider, 2003) and personality development researchers (Ryckman, 2004; Schultz & Schultz, 2005). The basic concepts of identity formation, for example, can be considered a unifying factor. The major focus of most studies involving identity formation has involved the puberty and adolescence stages of identity cohesion versus role confusion (Erikson, 1968). This stage in life is a time when one is faced with certain developmental tasks, such as autonomy from parents, gender identity, internalized morality, and career choice (Havighurst, 1972). Erikson, on the other hand, views this stage of personal identity development as a time when one is developing a single, unified concept of the self and a sense of personal identity in order to answer the age-old of question of "Who am I?" (Nairne, 2003). Erikson's eight stages represent an order of ascendancy based on the epigenetic principle that development occurs in a series of stages and that psychosocial strength has a special time or period of importance (Kail & Cavanaugh, 2004).

Much has been written about identity cohesions versus role confusion centering around what has been appropriately labeled an *identity crisis*. This can be a difficult time for many adolescents, who may be experimenting with different roles and ideologies in an attempt to find a compatible fit. Those who emerge from this period with a strong sense of self-identity are better prepared in terms of the self-knowledge that is so necessary in making an initial career choice. Those who fail may experience what Erikson (1968) referred to as an *identity crisis* and subsequent role confusion. Withdrawal from normal life sequences and what one wants to become is the likely reaction of individuals who exhibit confusion of roles (Schultz & Schultz, 2005). Role confusion can result in a tendency to procrastinate and influence one to delay making important life decisions for as long as possible.

According to Ryckman (2004), Erikson suggested that the most disturbing part of this period of life for adolescents is an inability to find an occupational identity. This contention is supported by Violato and Holden's (1988) research on a large sample of adolescents; they concluded that the areas of greatest concern among the group surveyed were careers and grades. Identity development has been approached by observing stages of identity status. James Marcia's (1980) research has identified different stages of confirming identity in the form of the following four identity status groups (Shaffer, 2002):

1. *Identity diffusion.* Persons in this stage have given little thought to resolving identity issues. At this time they are not questioning who they are, and they have not committed to a career. Example: "I don't exactly know what I want to do in the future, and so I haven't thought too much about a career."

2. *Foreclosure.* Persons in this stage have made a premature commitment to career but with little thought given to their alleged commitment. They have yet to experience an identity crisis. Example: "My brothers are working at that company, so I guess I will go there, too."

3. *Moratorium.* Persons in this status are currently experiencing what Erikson identified as an identity crisis. They are actively searching for answers to life commitments. Examples: "I don't really want to go to work in that plant. I think I should decide what's right for me instead

of just following what my brothers did"; "I have been looking into courses in community college to see what they might have to offer."

4. *Identity achievement*. Persons in this status have made insightful considerations of identity issues and have made firm commitments to goals, values, and a career. Examples: "I spent a lot of time in the community college counseling center, and I finally decided which career is best for me"; "I believe I have found something that really interests me, and now I know what it is I want."

Marcia (1980) suggested that the process underlying identity development requires adolescents to be proactive, to self-assess, and to use personal agency to work through solutions for life commitments. This is a complex process that requires mature perceptions and assumptions on the part of the adolescent. It should not be surprising to find that some adolescents will delay commitments and others will resist making any decisions altogether. Some may adopt a negative identity and resort to disruptive acting-out behaviors. Some may decide to enter college but not declare a major, or they take a job and plan to decide on a career later. Super (1963) concluded, after following the career development of high school students through adulthood, that *career maturity* is essential for making a career decision. The important traits of career maturity are planning skills, accepting responsibility, and an awareness of various aspects of a preferred vocation. It is generally agreed that career maturity takes place during certain periods of the life span (adolescence through young adulthood) within a range of ages; that is, the age of the person can vary. Some people may resist making serious commitments until well into adulthood. Currently, there are an increasing number of young adults who are delaying career commitment (Feldman, 2002).

The current labor market that I referred to earlier in this chapter, and which I discuss further in the next part of this chapter, may reward individuals who make early commitments with better opportunities in the workplace. College students, for example, who have committed to major fields of study may find opportunities for internships and other work-related educational programs early in their degree programs. Some important considerations are discovering skills and interests, gathering information, and eliminating some possible choices to create a realistic set (Feldman, 2002). At this point, individuals may select work environments that reinforce their interests and perceived skills. This process is driven by individual initial predispositions and has been termed *cumulative continuity* (Kokko & Pulkkinen, 2000). Likewise, in what is referred to as *interactional continuity*, an individual's choice of careers may be shaped by feedback from important others, such as members of his or her peer group. Self-perceptions of abilities are most strongly reinforced by feedback received from an environment that is honest and realistic (Feldman, 2002; Kokko & Pulkkinen, 2000). In the next paragraphs, I summarize some career development theories' perspectives of career choice. These perspectives should help consolidate the position that the career choice process is complex and involves factors associated with both human and career development.

Career Choice Perspectives
From Career Development Theories

Super's (1974) developmental approach to the career choice process includes six dimensions: (1) orientation to vocational choice (an attitudinal dimension), (2) information and planning (a competence dimension), (3) consistency of vocational preferences, (4) crystallization of traits (forming a self-concept), (5) vocational independence, and (6) wisdom of vocational preferences (realistic preferences). Super emphasized that career development occurred through stages over the life span. In Healy's (1982) developmental model the client's individuality is of the utmost importance in career decision making. He stressed that individuality can be established by helping clients understand the meaning of their goals, obstacles, assets for securing goals, beliefs about problem resolution and counseling, action already taken, learning style, and goal impediments.

In a learning theory model proposed by Krumboltz, Mitchell, and Gelatt (1975), the following observations are made: career decision making is a learned skill, clients come from a wide array of groups, clients need not feel guilty if they are not sure of a career to enter, and no one occupation is seen as the best for any one individual. This group of researchers felt that individuals choose poor career alternatives because of faulty beliefs. Unique learning experiences over the life span formulate the primary influences that lead to career choice. In their cognitive information-processing perspective, Peterson, Sampson, and Reardon (1991) suggested that career choice results from an interaction of cognitive and affective processes. Furthermore, making career choices is a problem-solving activity. They suggested that career identity is highly dependent on self-knowledge.

The choice model in a social cognitive theory (Lent, Brown, & Hackett, 2002) contains the following five components: (1) self-efficacy and outcome expectations promote career-related interests; (2) interests, in turn, influence goals; (3) goal-related actions lead to performance experiences; (4) the outcome of performance experiences determines future pathways, that is, whether self-efficacy is strengthened or weakened; and (5) efficacious expectations can influence people to make a career decision or redirect goals. This model supports the rationale that social beliefs and expectations are the mechanism through which self-efficacy deficits are developed, especially for women. Self-efficacy is strengthened when success is experienced within a performance domain, whereas it is weakened when there are repeated failures. Thus, individual influence situations ultimately affect one's thoughts and behaviors.

According to Gottfredson (1981), individual development progresses through four stages: (1) orientation to size and power (ages 3–5): some sense of what it means to be an adult; (2) orientation to social situations (ages 9–13) in which self-concept is influenced by gender development; (3) orientation to social valuation (i.e., awareness of social class and self-in-situation; ages 9–13); and (4) orientation to the internal, unique self (beginning at age 14) that includes a growing perception of others and increased self-awareness. This theory addresses career choice from the position that choice is actually a process of eliminating options and a narrowing down of choices. Important aspects of careers are thought to be prestige, interest, and gender type. Individuals may compromise their goals by selecting a career that fits their gender rather than pursuing their interests.

John Holland (1992) believes that career choice is an expression of, or an extension of, personality into the world of work, followed by subsequent identification with specific occupational stereotypes. The rationale is that individuals are attracted to a given career primarily because of their particular personalities. As discussed in Chapter 3, Holland proposed six personality styles (Realistic, Investigative, Artistic, Social, Enterprising, and Conventional) with matching occupational environments. The stability of a career choice depends on the dominance of personal orientation. Holland suggested that individuals are products of their environment; that is, environmental experiences greatly influence personal orientation and subsequent career choice. Self-knowledge is a key ingredient in making an optimal career choice.

In sum, how one forms an initial career choice is a multidimensional process of development that is very inclusive. One can conclude that people play an active role in the formation process of initial career choice though participation in activities in their environment. There may be some stage-like changes as well as gradual ones. The shaping process is both continuous and discontinuous. Some key factors that can influence career choice include the following: competency in planning, attitudes, consistency of choice, crystallization of traits, the person's individuality, socioeconomic status (SES), faulty beliefs, self-knowledge, self-efficacy, freedom of choice, prestige of career, interests, career gender types, and personality types. The career choice process is thought to be a learned skill and a problem-solving activity (Zunker, 2006).

Career Choice: A Central Component of a Person's Identity

The work role is a major part of most people's life stories. A person's work not only provides financial security but also provides one with a social identity; associates; friends; and, in most cases, a workplace. Through one's work role, a person meets other people who have similar interests, and we strongly identify with shared work roles. Most Americans spend a considerable part of their lifetimes involved with their work and work-related activities. Initial career choice, therefore, has always been a most important decision, but current conditions driven by an external market may require some workers to make multiple career choices. In addition, an uncertain and unpredictable job market may have a significant influence on the initial career choice process of many prospective workers. Career paths other than some professional ones are less clear, and there is an increasing number of new work roles. I discuss economic restructuring in more detail later in this chapter, but in the meantime the discussion will continue to focus on relevant influences on the career choice process itself.

For a more thorough perspective of how initial career choice is influenced, helpers should observe biological, psychological, and social/cultural influences that interact to shape behavior. What is being suggested is an integrative approach that is very inclusive yet straightforward. In Box 5.1, some negative factors that can influence career choice are listed in three groups. These factors are not all inclusive, but they do represent some issues discussed in this chapter and in Chapter 4. The importance of this perspective, however, is to point out the multidimensional nature of human development per se and some important factors that can influence initial career choice. In the biological domain, inherited characteristics are thought to influence predispositions of intellectual functioning, personality traits, and temperaments (Eysenck, 1967; Eysenck & Eysenck, 1985; Holland, 1992; Kail & Cavanaugh, 2004; Plomin & Petrill, 1997). Intellectual ability may also be influenced by speed of neural transmissions (Nairne, 2003). Although the extent of influence genetic predispositions have on the development of personal characteristics has been questioned, there is evidence to support the position that inherited genes do indeed influence intellectual functioning and suggest a predisposition toward certain personality traits and temperament.

Box 5.1   Negative Factors That Influence the Development of Career Choice Constraints

Biological Influences

Genetic predispositions toward less than desirable intellectual ability, personality traits, and temperament

Psychological Influences

An external orientation that suggests individuals have no control over life events

Failure to self actualize and to enhance self-knowledge, including skill development

Identity crisis that leads to role confusion

Lack of decision-making and problem-solving skills

Lack of openness to new ideas, methods, and procedures

Low self-esteem

Mental health concerns, including mood and personality disorders

Self-efficacy

(Continued)

(Continued)

Social/Cultural Influences

Changing work roles

Contextual experiences that can discourage some individuals from considering upper level work roles.

Difficulties faced in achieving social mobility

Discrimination against and oppression of career ideals

Insufficient knowledge of the world of work

Lack of access to educational institutions

Lack of access to occupational opportunities

Lack of quality educational experiences

Poor role models

Racial discrimination

Sexual harassment

SES disadvantages

Supply and demand of jobs

Uncertainty of external labor markets

Unstable familial experiences

The psychological domain could have an almost endless list of problems, value structures, personality traits, and mental health issues, among other psychological factors. Be aware that the influences listed in these domains considered are not inclusive but rather a format for adding other relevant issues. The function of all domains, especially the psychological influences domain, makes the point that initial career choice is an integrative process in which there is an interaction within and between domains; it is multidimensional and multifaceted. Thus self-efficacy, for example, may be partly influenced by genetic predispositions, faulty beliefs and assumptions, and contextual experiences. This position allows helpers to effectively conceptualize client concerns by domains and between domains. An individualized conceptualization promotes the uncovering of unique specific concerns that can be addressed by tailored and valid interventions.

One of the important psychological factors in decision making is self-knowledge, a topic that has occupied the attention of most career development researchers. One major focus has been on methods to evaluate each client's perception of the self, including perceived strengths and weaknesses as well as measured characteristics and traits. Adolescents and young adults in particular search for a clearer definition of the self in order to establish a sense of career identity. People generally evaluate career fit by projecting into work environments. An oversimplified rationale is that people who have a realistic perception of their own abilities, interests, and personality traits, for example, have a much better chance of appropriately evaluating career opportunities. What is behind this interest in self-knowledge? Plenty! Self-knowledge is a very inclusive concept that involves the total person: core values and beliefs, basic assumptions, contextual interactions, self-concept, self-esteem, self-efficacy, and many other complex factors. The process of knowing oneself is a lifetime event.

In adolescence, self-perceptions are particularly significant for providing pathways to form a career identity. Failure to crystallize one's knowledge of self can lead to an identity crisis (Erikson, 1968), which may be embedded in genetic predispositions, psychological issues, faulty cognitions, and salient messages from contextual experiences. Culture, race, gender, and SES disadvantages, especially in early childhood, could influence the development of a self-perspective of low self-esteem and a lack of openness to career selection. The belief that fate and luck control one's future (i.e., an external orientation) has many negative consequences for both life and work roles. The development of skills, for example, is one way to improve self-efficacy (Bandura, 1986), but an individual who is externally oriented may not conceptualize how individual effort can lead to a clearer pathway for career selection. Over time, skill development can have a significant impact on career selection (Feldman, 2002).

The increasing awareness of the connection between mental health issues and career choice and maintenance is a refreshing development. The whole-person approach of helpers who offer career counseling include significant emotional and cognitive influences that have an effect on how each person approaches the initial choice process. Mood disorders, which usually include anxiety, depression, and emotional instability, are logical concerns of helpers who are assisting clients in the decision process. Negative cognitions can seriously alter an individual's ability to make an optimal career decision. Self-referent beliefs and assumptions that are demeaning can influence feelings of being inadequate, incompetent, and inefficient. Negative cognitions can lead to indecision and/or negative overgeneralizations about the world of work and one's future goals (see Figure 5.1).

The environment continues to be recognized as a major force in human development. Contextual experiences can be a positive force for influencing initial career choice; unfortunately, they can be a negative influence as well. As we learned in Chapter 4, some adolescents develop faulty beliefs about their ability to determine their future; their family and other members of their community have unwittingly passed on the belief that fate and luck are of major importance in determining one's future. The oppression of career

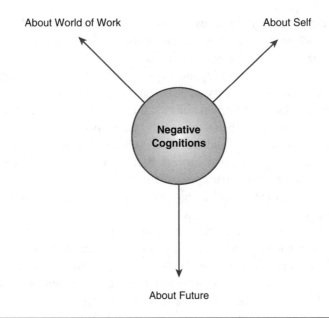

Figure 5.1   The Pervasive Role of Negative Cognitions
SOURCE: Adapted from Barlow and Durand (2005).

ideals influences some people to accept the fate of low-level jobs and sup-
presses their motivation to move upward through personal initiative. In a
very realistic way, the environment may not provide access to educational
and occupational opportunities, although more community colleges are being
constructed. The realism of work commitments, however, means that for
some people a full-time job during the week and a part-time job on the weekends are required to pay the bills. Under these conditions, many people in
low-end jobs cannot find the time or resources to enroll in training programs. Finally, the external market has impacted supply and demand for
jobs, especially for the working class. Many manufacturing jobs have been
moved to other locations, resulting in fewer traditional jobs for the working
class. Insufficient knowledge of the changing workforce has left many people
searching for information about the world of work. In the next section, I
provide some information about how the nature of work is changing and
being restructured.

Economic Restructuring

The U.S. economic system, which is in the process of being restructured, has
brought about significant changes in production and distribution of goods
and services. According to Drucker (2002), economic restructuring will continue for 50 years or more, and there will be significant transformations in the
basic structure of work. External markets have had a significant impact on

most aspects of careers in the working world of organizations. Most organizations have shifted from an internal career ladder approach to a performance–rewards approach. These changes have influenced employers to focus the hiring process on how much an employee can immediately contribute to the goals of an organization. Although careers based on market demands have always been an important element of working in an organization, in the current environment practically all workers are exposed to the risks of losing their jobs when there is a change in demands for products or services. The social consequences could be as significant as, but also somewhat different from, those of the Industrial Revolution, which greatly impacted families. Before the Industrial Revolution, for example, most members of the nuclear family were involved in production on farms and in artisan workshops. During the Industrial Revolution, an increase in the number of factories located in urban areas took work and the workplace away from the home (Drucker, 2002). Thus, the changing nature of work and a changing location of the workplace had a significant impact on family members; the rise of industrialism in the late 18th century created vast social change.

There now exists what many have labeled a *global economy*, which is the driving force of economic restructuring. Markets have opened around the globe, resulting in more world trade. Nations have increasingly become interdependent. Multinational corporations have grown to be a very powerful force in that they have significant political influence worldwide (Andersen & Taylor, 2006). In the meantime, U.S. industries have faced severe competition around the globe; in many countries, the wages for workers are significantly lower. To meet the competition from countries that can manufacture goods at a cheaper price, U.S. industrial organizations have made significant changes in work itself and in the workplace. These changes have had a tremendous impact on the lives of workers and their families.

What we have here is *deindustrialization*, which has shifted work from production of goods to delivery of services. Although some organizations continue to have assembly lines, they have downsized their workforces and have outsourced most manufacturing jobs to overseas locations where labor is much cheaper. The delivery of services has been fostered by technological advances. Electronic information, for example, can be transferred globally in less that one second. Many firms have offshore data entry locations, because again, the hourly wage is much cheaper. Robots have replaced some workers, especially in the automobile assembly plants. Thus, it appears there are new forms of work for some people and no work for others. Although there should always be some jobs at the lower end of the pay scale that do not require educational or technical skills, it is generally agreed that a good educational or skill development background will be essential in future job markets.

In this very brief review of economic restructuring there is clearly a changing job market that is expected to continue to change for some time. The most recent job market changes have affected both white collar and blue collar jobs. By 1995, forty-three million jobs were eliminated in the United States, and the casualties at that time were white collar jobs (Uchitelle &

Kleinfeld, 1996). In the early 2000s, the American workforce had the smallest proportion of factory workers in all the developed countries (Drucker, 2002). As mentioned earlier, many of the jobs lost were outsourced to other countries where labor is cheaper. In other situations, organizations downsized their workforce to cut costs. The traditional pathway of the "organizational man" has been virtually eliminated. Workers have lost many guarantees that previously existed in the workplace and, with it, the loss of job security.

Loss of Internal Career Ladders

One of the keys to fully understanding what is currently going on in the job market is recognition of what the pervasive nature of changes in organizations means for the worker. Previously, industrial organizations provided job security, tenure, and a lifetime job. This concept was often referred to as an *internal career ladder* (Leana, 2002). Employees would select job opportunities with an organization that was committed to advancing their career development through a variety of in-house and off-site educational programs. This position on the part of the organization helped individuals in the decision-making process by marginalizing concerns about short- and long-term interests. The internal career ladder was viewed by employees as a systematic method of achieving job security and, most important, it promoted feelings of well-being.

Current market forces have resulted in significant changes concerning the relationship between the individual and the organization. Fiercely competitive external markets have created an almost completely different approach in the way that organizations do business and form relationships with individual workers. In previous years, organizations hired people and put them in the system for growth; they assumed considerable responsibility for their employees' career development. Currently, organizations hire and pay individual workers on the basis of what they can immediately contribute to the firm. Compensation is usually based on performance. Under these conditions, organizations have taken much less responsibility for an individual worker's career development. There are no guarantees for a lifelong job. Individual effort to stay up to date in terms of job skills is essential. Along with the loss of job security, benefits, and training opportunities, individual workers are more at risk and can lose their commitment to an organization and, with it, the loss of motivation and their feelings of well-being.

It should be mentioned here that the people most affected by the current job approach changes have been higher level workers, such as managers. Managers and professional members of organizations had reaped the greatest benefits of job security and career development training when compared to lower level workers (Jacoby, 1999). As Leana (2002) pointed out, however, there was much more lost than training programs; an ideal career and the career development of each worker are important parts of the American dream. A career was, in many respects, a psychological contract of commitments between employee and employer and thus met the expectations of the American worker. Leana characterized it as the traditional career ideal. Career management systems were set up by organizations to foster the career development of each employee. The changes in relationships between organization and employee have indeed undermined stability and security and replaced them with job insecurity and high turnover rates. It should not be surprising to learn that workers' commitment to organizations has significantly declined in the last 20 years. Prospective employees are now facing new approaches to work roles and greater responsibility for their career development. In the next section, I introduce the evolving perception of career and career development in organizations.

A Prevalent Career Model: Boundaryless Careers

The focus on a relatively new career model in organizations suggests a different and changing perception of the nature and structure of work in organizations that continues to evolve. It also suggests that one can expect further and continuing changes in the future. *Boundaryless careers*, as the name implies, suggest that a worker is not bound to any organization or segment of an organization but is prepared to use her or his expertise in different work sites and teams. Furthermore, one's work may cut across functions and workplaces and may require multiple skills. Some have labeled such workers *free agents*, people who offers their skills to the highest bidder (Arthur & Rousseau, 1996). Thus, the evolving career model highlights differences in the structure of work in organizations and how individual workers are to function, be evaluated, and be paid. Clearly, workers in the 21st century will assume greater responsibility for their career development.

In the midst of changes that involve the nature and structure of work in organizations, job expectations and perceptions of work per se will need to be addressed. The boundaryless career has been touted as a welcome challenge for a more diverse work role. The perception of work from this point of view suggests that one is freed from pursuing the interests of an organization in a step-by-step fashion; career development is more individually oriented (Feldman, 1985). In this respect, career development reinforces a career identity. One is not just a Company B employee but a professional data analyst who happens to be working for Company B. As a free agent, the data analyst offers services to the highest bidder and in doing so learns that there are opportunities for personal rewards in the workplace; one can become more accepting of a new system of working. What it comes down to is that each worker will be required to evaluate his or her comfort level and ability to function when working in an environment that has high risks as well as substantial rewards (Leana, 2002).

The boundaryless career model is a good example to illustrate the differences in the way work has been restructured in 21st-century organizations.

Other changes in established work patterns include independent contractors, self-employed individuals, contingent workers, consultants, and freelance workers. An information technologist may begin her or his career by working for an independent contractor, or he or she may be employed as a contingent worker (someone who agrees to work for a specified period of time). What stands out here is the insulation from risks in the current work environment. The ability to perform, backed by a strong knowledge base, is the essence of job security in the workplace. The winners in the boundaryless career model will be those who have signed on as lifelong learners and, most important, learn to tolerate problems associated with risks in a competitive workforce.

Contract Breach

Over the last 20 years, workers in organizations have viewed downsizing and restructuring as a breach of contract. The have acted accordingly, and this is reflected in high turnover rates, lower job performance, and in general a negative attitude concerning their employers (Robinson, 1996). It is not only organizations that have changed in the way they view employer–employee relationships; employees have, too: They have lost their sense of trust in organizations. How prospective workers and current employees view their future with an organization may be summarized as follows: *Linear development has shifted to perpetually changing work roles and careers.* It is increasingly common for workers to experience uncertainty of job tenure and to know that one must be flexible in a new employment relationship (Cappelli, 1999; Werner, 2002). One would suspect that individuals in the initial choice process have some of the same reactions as current or previous employees. Thus, individual career decision making within organizations has been affected by uncertainties as well as by individuals contemplating an initial career choice; there are legitimate concerns about their long-term interests.

The changing nature of work in organizations has it proponents. One view of the influence of external markets is that organizations need self-directed continuously learning workers who find new work roles challenging and exciting. Managers in organizations are including novel learning experiences for employees in order to encourage them to recognize developmental opportunities (London, 2002). New technologies require continuous expansion of knowledge in order to stay abreast with global competition. What is being stressed here is that workers are being encouraged to take responsibility for their own careers; they are to adopt the role of self-developer (Sullivan, 1999). One of the long-time major purposes of training in organizations has been to encourage individual career motivation. Workers who develop self-efficacy, identity, and resilience will be in a much better position to cope with the uncertainties in current organizations (London, 2002).

Some Career Barriers

In this final section of the chapter, some career barriers are identified from discussions in this chapter and Chapter 4. Career barriers are grouped into four categories, in alphabetical order as follows: (1) contextual experiences, (2) external market forces, (3) mental health issues, and (4) negative cognitions. Sources of constraints are listed under each of the four headings as shown in Box 5.2. These four categories are to be viewed not as discrete but rather as interacting forces that influence the development of career choice constraints. Sources of deficits in self-efficacy, for example, can evolve from contextual experiences, subsequent faulty beliefs, and/or a personality disorder. SES disadvantages may restrict one's ability to compete for work roles in organizations that require an extensive educational background; some individuals lack the financial resources for obtaining a higher education degree. Box 5.2 is not meant to oversimplify the nature of career barriers and sources of constraints, but just the opposite: Helpers should view sources of influence as being multidimensional. Although there are definite connections that overlap categories, the four categories are meant to provide a whole-person approach to conceptualizing sources of constraints. The consequences associated with a variety of external and internal constraints may be uncovered in locus of control problems and self-efficacy deficits that need to be addressed, as in the example of Jill, a client described in the next paragraph.

Box 5.2   Some Career Choice Barriers

Contextual Experiences

Limited access to educational opportunities

Limited access to occupational opportunities

Gender discrimination

Lack of financial resources

Locus of control

Negative perceptions of life and work

Racial discrimination

Socialization process

SES disadvantages

(Continued)

(Continued)

External Market Forces

Changing organizational structure

Downsizing of workforce

Loss of internal ladders

Loss of job security

Work role changes

Uncertainties of short- and long-term interests

Mental Health Issues

Anxiety disorders

Mental retardation

Mood disorders

Personality disorders

Schizophrenia

Somatoform and dissociative disorders

Substance-related and impulse control disorders

Negative Cognitions

Faulty beliefs and assumptions

Identity crisis

Low self-esteem

Self-concept deficits

Self-efficacy deficits

Demeaning self-talk

A client named Jill was currently experiencing the mood disorder of depression, even though she had made a career commitment and planned to enter a particular education program. Further probing by the helper uncovered a locus of control problem that had not been addressed. Jill had grown up believing that getting a good job was a matter of luck, but more recently she had been encouraged by a friend to take aggressive action to upgrade her skills so that she could get a better job. She was not able to cope with the stress associated with opposing positions and developed symptoms of depression. Faulty beliefs influenced by contextual experiences were addressed through cognitive restructuring, and career barriers were approached as a problem-solving activity (see Chapter 12). In this case, the helper viewed Jill's self-efficacy deficits as constraint problems that could be overcome by observational learning and development of realistic goals.

What stands out in Box 5.2 is the category of external markets. Helpers should be familiar with the psychological sources of career choice constraints as listed under contextual experiences, mental health issues, and negative cognitions, but to think in terms of external market forces as career choice constraints requires a somewhat different approach to career barriers. One might suspect that we will hear more about the growing recognition of influences from market forces in a global economy that affects the nature of work in the United States and other countries. Career development theory has been heavily dominated by psychologists who believe that one can control her or his own destiny (A. G. Watts, Super, & Kidd, 1981). T. Watts's (1995) observations, however, suggest that the career choice process must address more than just psychological variables; in current changing conditions, social and economic factors may be equally important. Will helpers end up counseling about a market-driven workforce (Cappelli, 1999)? This position will more than likely become of greater interest to workers as well as to helpers in the future social, economic, and political transformations we are expected to experience.

Summary

This chapter is a continuation of the discussion of career barriers and sources of constraints. Psychological influences from career constraints have many sources. Of major importance in this chapter have been the influences that shape behavior and, subsequently, the initial career choice. Career barriers are viewed as having both internal and external sources of constraints. Interacting sources of constraints are viewed as complex influences that are multidimensional and multifaceted.

1. In initial career choice, the shaping process includes many social forces that mold development.

   Normal and idiosyncratic development are both important. Personality identity development involves issues of identity cohesion versus role confusion. An identity crisis delays important life decisions.

   Inability to find an occupational identity is a major concern for adolescents. Four identity status groups identified by Marcia (1980) include identity diffusion, foreclosure, moratorium, and identity achievement. Currently, an increasing number of young adults are delaying career commitment.

2. Career choice perspectives from some career development theories were summarized. A developmental approach suggests that career development occurs through stages over the life span. Career decision

is viewed as a learned skill. Faulty beliefs may result in poor career alternatives. Career choice is a problem-solving activity. Self-knowledge is essential for initial career choice. Self-efficacy deficits are addressed to improve future expectations. Important aspects of careers are prestige, interests, and gender type. Individuals may compromise goals by selecting a career that fits their gender type rather than pursuing interests. Career choice is an expression of or an extension of personality into the world of work. Individuals are attracted to careers because of their personality.

3. Career choice is viewed as a central component of a person's identity. External markets may require that some workers make multiple career choices. Uncertain and unpredictable job markets are barriers faced by many people in the initial career choice process. Initial career choice is influenced by biological, psychological, and social/cultural factors that shape behavior. Inherited characteristics in the biological domain influence one's predisposition toward intelligence, personality, and temperament. The psychological domain contains a broad array of mental health issues and self-referent deficits. Environmental experiences are a major driving force in human development. Contextual experiences can exert both negative and positive influences on development. Socioeconomic status disadvantages can be very influential in one's perception of the self and the world of work.

4. Economic restructuring is a major driving force in the changing nature of work, and it is expected to continue for several decades. External markets have also changed the nature of work.

   U.S. industry has changed from production to the distribution of goods and services. Workers are hired on the basis of what they can immediately contribute to an organization. Nations have become interdependent.

   Multinational corporations have increased in number and are more powerful worldwide. Many manufacturing jobs have been outsourced. Workers have lost the guarantee for a lifetime job.

5. Loss of internal career ladders has proven to be very disturbing for many workers. Organizations no longer provide stages of promotion and career development through career ladders.

   Job security has been lost in many work environments. Organizations are now less responsible for career development of workers. Workers' commitment to organizations has declined.

6. A prevalent career model is known as boundaryless careers. In the current job market, the boundaryless career suggests that a worker is not bound to any organization or segment of an organization.

   A *free agent* is a worker who offers his or her skills to the highest bidder. Workers must take responsibility for their career development.

7. Contract breach reflects workers' concerns about downsizing in the workforce. Workers have lost their sense of trust in organizations. All employees are being encouraged to become self-developers.

8. Some career barriers are grouped as contextual experiences, external market forces, mental health issues, and negative cognitions. Sources of constraints are included in each category. The four categories are not to be considered discrete. They provide a whole-person approach to conceptualizing career constraints.

Supplementary Learning Exercises

1. What is the significance of identity formation to career choice and development?

2. Explain the significance of negative self-talk in the career counseling process. How would you address concerns associated with negative self-talk?

3. What is meant by the term external market? What is the external market's role in career choice constraints?

4. Explain the concept of career ladders. How were they used, and why have they disappeared in most organizations?

5. Select one of the barriers to career choice found in Box 5.2 and describe its role in constraining career choice.

PART II

Mental Health Issues
and Solutions

6 Depression and Its Impact on Career Development

Part II of this book is about integrating career and personal counseling. Its chapters focus on how helpers view clients from a whole-person perspective of concerns that clients bring to counseling. Helpers address not just career concerns or just personal ones, but both, as well as how they interrelate. A holistic philosophy of counseling suggests that client concerns are inseparable and intertwined. Helpers do not limit their ability to understand that a client's belief systems and interests are interrelated. What we have here is the position that helpers are alert to personal concerns that might interfere with a client's ability to adequately process information and make optimal decisions and/or a worker's ability to perform at work. Helpers also address how reactions to work stressors can limit a client's ability to function in other life roles. The relationships between career and mental health concerns suggest links that should be addressed in intervention strategies in a holistic or whole-person counseling approach (Zunker, 2006).

A holistic perspective of helping is particularly relevant for clients who present a combination of career concerns and symptoms of psychological disorders. Clients with a mood disorder, or a personality disorder, or both, for instance, more than likely experience serious functional problems in all life roles. Thus, mental health concerns of a personal nature present potential problems for clients in the initial career decision-making process and decisions that follow as well as in interpersonal interactions in the workplace and the ability to perform appropriately. On the other hand, workers who experience severe reactions to work stressors more than likely will also present work–family conflicts and other relationship problems. Counseling progress for clients with both career and personal concerns may be limited unless helpers address the interrelationship of concerns, recognizing that clients appraise life situations in similar ways, that is, they overgeneralize negative feelings to most life situations. The interactive relationship between career and personal concerns is integrated and fused in a whole-person counseling approach (Zunker, 2006).

The call to integrate career and personal counseling was heightened in the 1990s (Betz & Corning, 1993; Krumboltz, 1993). The growing interest in the relationships between career and mental health suggests that helpers are to fuse career and personal concerns as an extension of career counseling. Integrative counseling and psychotherapy, however, have been used for several decades by counseling psychologists, licensed professional counselors, mental health counselors, and clinical psychologists, among others (Corey, 2005; Trull, 2005). Integrative approaches to counseling include the following:

- A *transtheoretical* model, which consists of constructs and techniques from established counseling theories from which users create new or modified ones to effectively address specific client problems that need changing
- A *theoretical integration* model, which may be composed of two or more counseling theories that create a systematic consistent theoretical integration or conceptual framework, such as cognitive and behavioral or humanistic and cognitive
- A *technical eclecticism* approach, which consists of a collection of valid techniques from different schools of thought that are based on theoretical positions not necessarily subscribed to by the user (Corey, 2005; Sharf, 2004)

These approaches of integration are instructive in that techniques and interventions are carefully selected from empirically supported theoretical domains that provide opportunities for systematic and consistent plans and actions. Integration of career and personal concerns, however, suggests (1) that technical eclecticism involving valid techniques from different approaches to personal concerns would be used with (2) career counseling techniques from career development theories that provide consistency of procedures.

The focus in this chapter is on both human growth and development and career development as being multidimensional and multifaceted. Concepts of integration are introduced that suggest that biological, psychological, and social influences together are determinants of how individuals think and behave. Helpers are most effective when they are able to illustrate how one life role can affect another. In this chapter, I introduce the rationale for an integrated approach to uncovering interactive influences that lead to psychological disorders. From this perspective, clients are exposed to significant links between personal and career concerns. One way to view the connection between career and personal concerns is to observe how psychological disorders develop as an interactive process in a biopsychosocial model (Trull, 2005).

Biopsychosocial Model

The biopsychosocial model depicts how biological, psychological, and social influences interact to be the underpinnings of a psychological disorder. The interplay of these three dimensions have led researchers to uncover some interesting findings; for example, positive thinking and subsequent behavior have increased the tendency for the immune system to be more effective (Barlow & Durand, 2005). Unfortunately, the opposite is also true—negative thinking can negatively impact a person's physical and mental health. Helpers must remember that this model is an integrative one in which three dimensions play a role in an interactive process of influence. Thus, psychological disorders in this context are considered to be multidimensional. Helpers may also find that the biological dimension is referred to as a *physiological dimension* and that the social dimension may also include cultural aspects and is sometimes referred to as the *social/cultural dimension*.

Figure 6.1 illustrates the interactive process of a biopsychosocial model in an integrated approach to psychopathology from the three dimensions of this model. As shown, stressful events trigger responses in three dimensions. In the biological dimension, a stressful event can cause physiological responses, including cardiovascular system reactions such as an increased heart rate and high blood pressure. One's inherited genetic vulnerability and/or chemical imbalances also contribute to severe reactions to a stressful event. Learned conditioned responses, such as negative cognitions and self-defeating thinking, influence individual emotional responses in the psychological dimension. In the social dimension, unique social and cultural experiences influence each person's reaction to stressful conditions. What is important here, however, is the interaction of the three dimensions as contributing influences to the causes of psychological-related disorders.

A similar position was taken by Sulsky and Smith (2005), who used a stimulus–response model; they defined stress as "any circumstance (stressor) that places special physical and/or psychological demands on an organism leading to physiological, psychological, and behavioral (social) outcomes" (p. 6). The stimulus–response model and the biopsychosocial model both suggest that the causes and effects of stress should be approached from a whole-person multidimensional perspective for moderating the concerns clients bring to counseling.

A stressful life event is purposely used to illustrate the rationale of an integrative theory in the biopsychosocial model and the stimulus–response model. Stressful life events are not only a reality but also they tend to happen often. You have probably observed that some people are able to quickly overcome stressful events while others react quite differently and become depressed. People who develop self-defeating thoughts may very well overgeneralize negative feelings to the point that they affect other life roles, including the work role. An integrative approach can be used to determine specific influences that have contributed to a psychological disorder, particularly those that disrupt an individual's ability to function on a job and live a satisfying life. More information about the biopsychosocial integrative approach to helping is included in the discussion of the development of mood disorders in the next section. A three-dimensional diagnostic format will be used to determine effective interventions.

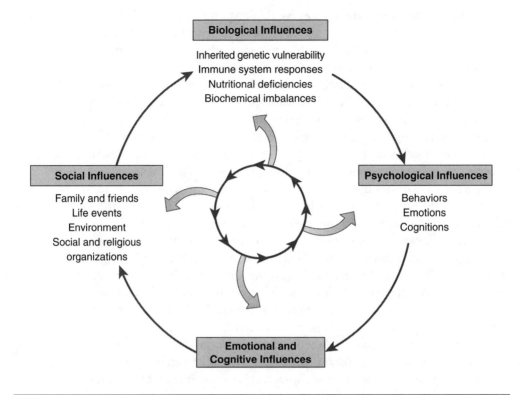

Figure 6.1   An Integrated Approach to Psychopathology

SOURCE: From *Abnormal Psychology, An Integrative Approach* (with CD-ROM and InfoTrac®) 4th edition by Barlow/Durand. 2005. Reprinted with permission of Wadsworth, a division of Thomson Learning: www .thomsonright.com. Fax 800-730-2215.

Development of a Mood Disorder: Depression _____

The mood disorder of depression can disrupt one's work role and have a spillover effect on other life roles. *Episodic cycling*, in which individuals can experience depression while at other times experiencing manic episodes, is characteristic of many mood disorders. Combinations of depression and manic episodes are identified by symptoms and structure of mood disorders for classification and treatment. The ways in which biological, psychological, and social dimensions influence the development of a depressive mood disorder are illustrated in the paragraphs that follow.

Symptoms of depression are very pervasive in the lives of individuals who experience them. Difficulties with common life situations increase the chances that the person will feel alone and helpless and/or socially isolated. Feelings of hopelessness and isolation tend to promote and increase depressive feelings that can be long lasting and general. Depressive reactions can result in the above-mentioned *spillover effect* that can disrupt relationships with family, friends, and work associates. The loss of interest, lack of motivation, and poor concentration that characterize depressive episodes often result in pervasive dysfunctional behaviors in the work-place; workers with symptoms of depression usually have difficulty in ful-filling the requirements of a work role. Workers in great despair may start the search for another job or workplace without recognizing that they are not addressing their underlying problems. Helpers assist clients to sort out the underlying causes of depression in a three-dimensional format to deter-mine the most effective courses of action in the form of interventions. In the following paragraphs, I evaluate symptoms and causes of depression in three dimensions. Keep in mind that it is the combination and interaction of three dimensions that are thought to contribute to the causes of mood disorders. A biopsychosocial integrative perspective developed by Barlow and Durand (2005) is used to uncover the interplay of three dimensions as illustrated in Figure 6.2.

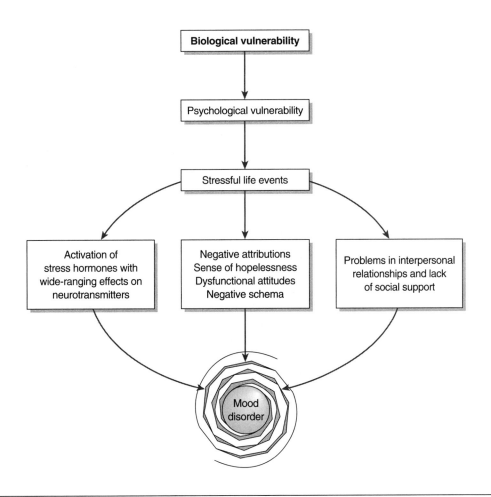

Figure 6.2   Development of Mood Disorder of Depression

SOURCE: From *Abnormal Psychology, An Integrative Approach* (with CD-ROM and InfoTrac®) 4th edition by Barlow/Durand. 2005. Reprinted with permission of Wadsworth, a division of Thomson Learning: www.thomsonright .com. Fax 800-730-2215.

Biological Dimensions

These factors include genetic influences as well as physiological functions. Familial and genetic influences, for example, have been studied to determine the propensity of family members to inherit mood disorders. Some findings have been significant; for example, some evidence suggests that there are indeed higher rates of depression found in relatives of individuals who have experienced mood disorders. Furthermore, there appears to be a greater chance of passing on mood disorders to a relative when an individual has experienced severe mood problems (McGuffin et al., 2003). The important link for helpers to remember is that individuals may inherit a genetic vulnerability or a pervasive predisposition to experience mood disorders. Genetic vulnerability also raises some interesting questions: Why is it that some relatives do not develop a predisposition for a mood disorder? Is it because of other biological and health factors? Is it because of differences in psychological and social influences, especially in early childhood? These questions point out that not all answers to causes of a mood disorder can be found in a single dimension; one must consider the interaction of all three dimensions to elucidate specific causes. An important point to remember is that what one inherits are dispositions or tendencies, not certainties or destinies (Schultz & Schultz, 2005). Helpers begin by focusing on their client's historical data for relevant information.

Studies of biological influences on mood disorders are ongoing. Some studies have suggested that mood disorders are related to two things: (1) neurotransmitter imbalances—that is, chemicals that transit impulses from one neuron to the next—and (2) structural problems of the brain, including brain wave activity that is present in depressed clients (Nairne, 2003). The ongoing study of these complex systems and their relationship to psychopathology is currently in the process of uncovering some underpinnings of mood disorders. *Neurohormones* (hormones that affect the brain) are the focus of an increasing number of studies involving causes of psychopathology. Researchers increasingly have found more evidence of potential specific links between neurotransmitters and neurohormones with certain mood disorders. In the meantime, there is an increased focus on the imbalances of neurotransmitters and their relationships to psychopathology. Some of the latest information we have from this ongoing research suggests that it is most difficult to specify relationships with certainty. This problem is much more understandable when one recognizes that there are literally thousand of neurohormones (Barlow & Durand, 2005).

Schultz and Schultz (2005) reported that the immune system's defenses, such as T-cells and natural killer cells, which resist viruses, bacteria, and tumor cells, have been studied to determine a physiological explanation of reactions to negative beliefs associated with depression. One study, involving 105 first-semester law students, found that individuals who held more negative beliefs about life had significantly lower numbers of T-cells and natural killer cells than those who were optimistic (Segerstrom, Taylor, Kemeny, & Fahey, 1998). This study is used here as an example to illustrate the potential affects of negative thinking and other depressive reactions on general health.

The preceding example of terms and the study involving the immune system's defenses should make it clear to helpers that there is much to be learned about psychopathology through biological research. Second, research that involves the functions of the brain, the autonomic nervous system, the cardiovascular system, and the immune system, for example, is extremely complex and time consuming. Third, the results of this research should eventually provide us with very relevant information for better understanding of human behavior from a biological point of view. Finally, helpers should remain alert to the findings of the research community and be open to suggestions for integrating new concepts into helping interventions.

Psychological Dimensions

The psychological dimension is viewed as a very broad-based force that "includes all internal perceptual, cognitive, emotional, and personality factors that affect development" (Kail & Cavanaugh, 2004, p. 9). Our focus on the causes of mood disorders, and especially depression, suggests that we closely examine psychological experiences that are thought to be key causes of depressive reactions; it is estimated that 60% to 80% of depression is caused by psychological experiences (Barlow & Durand, 2005). First, recall that psychological experiences are considered to be unique for each individual. This position suggests that each person interprets life events from a frame of reference that is uniquely his or her own. Thus, helpers should be alert to their clients' vulnerabilities, such as negative self-evaluations. It is the client's *interpretation of the meaning of an event* that is most relevant. Stressful life events are considered to be major contributors to all psychological disorders.

What I am suggesting here is that helpers should try to uncover the context of an event to fully understand the meaning it has for the client. To illustrate, consider the example of a person who has been laid off from his job because of downsizing. There is no doubt that job loss, however it happens, has a significant affect on workers and their families. However, if job loss is combined with other stressful situations, such as losing one's home, then the negative impact on feelings of well-being and security is increased. It is the context of the immediate situation that clarifies the meaning of stressful events (Barlow & Durand, 2005).

Researchers have discovered that severe events usually precede all types of depression (G. W. Brown, Harris, & Hepworth, 1994). As stated earlier, in most cases of depression it is the *meaning* of the event that is most significant, but in some cases it is the nature of the event that is of utmost significance.

The breakup of a relationship is one example of an event that in itself has the potential impact to cause depression. Once again, however, understand that it is the interaction of stressful life events with vulnerability, such as genetic influences and self-defeating thinking, that leads to a greater potential for depression (Barlow, 2002).

Learned Helplessness and Depression

The concept of *learned helplessness* has direct implications for causes of depression. Learned helplessness was derived from a study of the reaction of dogs that were placed in containers that contained two compartments divided by a low wall. The dogs were given occasional shocks. Seligman (1975) observed that the control group of dogs, who were able to easily escape the "shock" compartment, eventually jumped to the other compartment, where they received no shock. They learned to cope well with shock; that is, they could do something about it. The experimental group of dogs did not have a way of escaping to the second compartment, and so they could not avoid the shocks. When the experimental group of dogs received a shock, they jumped about but quickly gave up and dropped to the floor, whimpering, and never learned to escape, *even when the experimental setup changed and they were able to physically escape the shocks.* Similar experiments were conducted with humans using loud noise, with similar results from the experimental group. One of the major conclusions Seligman reached was that humans respond in a similar manner—they become anxious and depressed when they feel that they have no control over a stressful condition. The residual affect is that negative events support negative feelings one has across a wide variety of future stressful conditions. Thus, when a person feels helpless in future situations there is the distinct possibility that he or she could develop symptoms of depression (Schultz & Schultz, 2005).

The more recent thinking regarding the concept of learned helplessness suggests that a *sense of helplessness* is the more appropriate term that can be attributed to the cause of many forms of depression. This suggestion is based on the assumptions that an individual may feel a sense of helplessness when reacting to a stressful life event, but only in depression does one feel hopeless about the future. You will discover in the next chapter that control and predictability are most important to positive feelings of well-being.

Finally, the cognitive vulnerability aspect of depression has received considerable attention from the research community. Most frequently addressed are negative cognitive styles of some individuals who have the tendency to interpret life events in a negative manner. Negativism is directed toward themselves, for instance, "I am a failure on this job"; "I'll never amount to anything"; "I'm too dumb to get this done."

Thus, these individuals view themselves as failures, think negatively about the immediate world, and have a negative view of the future (Beck, 1976).

This kind of distorted thinking can easily trigger emotional distress that can lead to depression. Cognitive vulnerability, irrational beliefs, and self-defeating thoughts are discussed further in Chapter 7.

Social and Cultural Dimensions

According to Barlow and Durand (2005), marital relationships, gender, and social support are most prominent in the social and cultural dimension. The fact that the United States has a divorce rate of approximately 1 million a year gives credence to the suggestion that marital relationships are a significant factor in the lives of many citizens in this country and in others (Goldenberg & Goldenberg, 2002). Divorce rates in developed countries have also increased over the past decades, but compared with the United States, they are considerable lower in Canada, Austria, France, and Germany. Ethnicity also offers some interesting facts: African American divorce rates are higher than divorce rates of European Americans. Among the Hispanic population there is considerable variability. Mexican Americans and Cuban Americans have about the same divorce rate as European Americans, but the Puerto Rican American divorce rate is much higher (Kail & Cavanaugh, 2004).

Disruptions of marital relations can lead to depression. Studies of 695 women and 530 men who experienced a marital split revealed that almost 21% of the women experienced severe depression, and 17% of the men had a similar experience (Bruce & Kim, 1992). In addition, it was found that almost 17% of men in this study who had not experienced a previous depressive episode became severely depressed, while only 5% of the women did. These findings suggest that more men than women develop a mood disorder for the first time after a marital split. Thus, men may be more vulnerable than women to a first-time severe depressive episode after a divorce is final.

There is general agreement that in most divorce cases men and women both feel deeply disappointed, misunderstood, and rejected (Brodie, 1999). These feelings can last for significant periods of time. Walther (1991) referred to the time after divorce as a period known as *divorce hangover*. Developing new relationships and making new friends are difficult, and there are usually feelings of hostility toward the former spouse as well as feelings of poor emotional well-being. All of these are potential stressors that could lead to mood disorders.

Reactions to divorce also differ by gender. More women than men develop major depressive episodes worldwide as a result of the divorce process and its aftereffects (Hankin & Abramson, 2001). These differences in reactions between men and women are partially attributed to the possibility that men have been encouraged to be more independent and women to be more passive and sensitive. Women have been subjected to more discrimination than men, and many women have experienced sexual harassment. Helpers also must remember that traditional parenting styles tend to encourage traditional gender roles in which the women's role is to take care of family and home while men are the primary breadwinners. When marital relationships are disrupted, women are faced with additional responsibilities and associated stressful conditions. Women who assume nontraditional roles in cultures that encourage traditional gender role stereotypes may also experience severe stressors. One's cultural background is also a significant factor in the development of a mood disorder.

Culture-related behavior is learned; thus, one can expect differences in reactions to divorce both between cultures and within cultural groups. In many cultures, social forces restrain women. They learn to not be assertive and follow unique roles of their ethic group. The social restraints of some cultural groups place women in a lesser secondary role. They may have little in the way of autonomy and are isolated. Yet most women from different cultural groups feel a strong devotion to their family. Family relationships are of the utmost concern and primary focus. Unique roles of ethnic groups shape family identities that are typically traditional. Therefore, disruptive marital relationships can be a major cause of very strong sources of stress and subsequent depression.

Barlow (2002) suggested that there is a stronger perception of uncontrollability among women that contributes to a higher rate of depression of women worldwide. He suggested that the sources of this perception are the result of cultural influences in societies that promote gender-stereotypical thinking. Although women have made significant gains with problems that interfere with their development, they are still at risk for developing emotional problems that stem from feelings of helplessness and uncontrollability in societies that promote stereotypic gender roles. Social factors are indeed relevant influences on feelings of well-being.

The positive side of social support has received increased attention for its role in moderating the effects of depression. Several studies have suggested that a socially supportive network of friends and family can speed one's recovery from depression, as highlighted by Johnson, Winett, Meyer, Greenhouse, and Miller (1999). Social support has also been recognized as a good buffering effect against stressful life events. It appears that social support is more effective in moderating stressful events when it is used in combination with other interventions (Rice, 1999). In the 1980s, House, Landis, and Umberson (1988) suggested that a large number of friends and high frequency of social relationships can extend an individual's life span. It appears that the willingness and ability to confide in friends and feel that those friends are caring and supportive is a good buffer against onset of mood disorders.

A major goal of this chapter has been to build an understanding of a biopsychosocial integrative theory that addresses causes of mood disorders from three dimensions: (1) biological, (2) psychological, and (3) social. A client's vulnerability or general tendency to develop depression has major implications for both career development and mental health. In our discussion of the biological dimension it was observed that a general tendency to develop depression could be attributed to an overactive neurological response to stressful life conditions. Also recognized was that depression can be a genetically determined biological vulnerability. Significant indications from research findings suggest that women have a stronger biological vulnerability to develop depression than men do. Finally, genes are thought to account for about 20% to 40% of the causes of depression (Barlow, 2002).

Evidence also suggests that stressful life events can serve as a trigger for onset of a depressive episode. Stressful events activate hormones, which in turn activate neurotransmitter systems that could seriously affect an individual's feelings of well-being especially if the stressful condition occurs over the long term. Of great significance is the interaction of biological and psychological dimensions that heightens an individual's vulnerability for onset of depression; individuals are likely to develop feelings of helplessness and hopelessness (Seligman, 1975). Negative cognitions that result in negative self-evaluations and negative self-talk make one even more vulnerable.

In the social dimension, family members and friends can provide buffers that moderate reactions to stressful life events and shorten the recovery time of a depressive episode. Unsatisfactory marital relationships have the potential to trigger stress responses that could lead to depression. Cultural social forces form barriers that block women from fully participating in a society. Women of almost all cultures are relegated to a lesser secondary role in societies that promote gender role stereotyping. Frustration and stress reactions make these women vulnerable to developing mood disorders. Family relations are particularly important to women of many cultures. When relationships are disrupted, strong stressful reactions can be expected. Women in particular are subject to developing feelings of frustration and lack of control in societies in which they have experienced discrimination (Barlow & Durand, 2005).

The Career Counseling Connection

A whole-person approach that assists clients with career choices and maintenance over the life span suggests an extensive and a most inclusive perspective of helping. Helpers recognize that a mood disorder such as depression can negatively impact all life roles, including the work role. A person who is depressed has difficulty in processing information and the meanings associated with life events that are critically important to the decision-making process. Negative self-appraisals so common in depression can disrupt job performance and career development. The interplay of interacting influences suggests that combinations of intervention strategies are most effective in addressing multidimensional problems that are both personal and career-related. Using the biological, psychological, and social dimensions to comprehend the interplay of causes of depression, helpers address those relationships and concerns through *technical eclecticism*, that is, interventions derived from four categories or domains: (1) career, (2) affective, (3) cognitive–behavioral, and (4) culture (see Chapter 3).

Career domain strategies include domain-specific concerns that help individuals make optimal career decisions and adjust to career transitions over the life span. A whole-person approach, however, recognizes that career concerns are intertwined with personal concerns found in each of the other domains. Thus, in the case of a depressed client career domain concerns such as indecisiveness, poor work identity, work impairment, and balancing life roles, for example, are impacted. There is an interrelationship of concerns that are addressed by intervention strategies that cut across domains such as in cognitive–behavioral approaches.

An example of a depressed client could include the following concerns by domains:

Career: work stress, indecisiveness, work impairment, and relational problems

Affective: feelings of helplessness, sadness, anxiety, depressed mood, and lethargy

Cognitive–behavioral: inappropriate behavior, negative self-evaluations, overgeneralizations of negative experiences

Culture: discrimination and oppression, difficulty in assimilating new lifestyle, cultural identity

The obvious interrelationships of concerns provide the helper with a perspective to conceptualize client concerns for the purpose of developing appropriate intervention components. The conceptualization process provides the rationale for addressing the severity of concerns to determine whether some concerns can be addressed simultaneously. In some cases, however, helpers refer clients to other, more specialized professionals, when they do not have the training to offer appropriate interventions (Zunker, 2006). Helpers begin by conceptualizing issues that describe what the person does in a variety of stressful situations. The client is asked to explain his or her meaning of *depression* in terms of his or her thoughts, actions, and feelings within the environment and/or situation in which stressors occur. Thus, specific thoughts, feelings, and actions are identified in context—that is, in the environments, situations, and with whom they occur. Clients are also asked to identify any physiological changes and reactions they experience in each situation, such as headaches and elevated blood pressure (Cormier & Nurius, 2003).

The social and cultural contexts in which depressive feelings are experienced are most important connections to include in the development of interventions. Finally, helpers are to identify antecedent sources that elicit emotional and physiological reactions. Certain *antecedent events*, also referred to as *stimulus events*, can trigger feelings of anxiety and, in some cases, just the opposite: feelings of being relaxed. Role overload in the workplace, for instance, can trigger feelings of anxiety and body-related sensations. For purposes of clarity, helpers should ask the client to describe specifically how a work overload problem is stressful. Relaxed feelings may be triggered by positive reinforcing events or the presence of a friendly, supportive work associate. Specific information from positive and negative stimulus events adds depth and meaning to the purpose of tailored intervention components (Cormier & Nurius, 2003).

In the career domain there are many potential sources of stress associated with the workplace that could lead to depressive reactions. Examples of stressors include the physical environment of the workplace, requirements of jobs, role ambiguity, shift work, and downsizing. A client's vulnerability to depression may also be associated with negative self-evaluations of his or her work performance. A worker's concerns can be very pervasive indeed and require interventions that address both work and personal problems. Affective domain concerns, which frequently are emotionally driven and promote feelings of inferiority and helplessness, are addressed through strategies that enhance self-development, self-efficacy, and self-actualization in the workplace. Affective strategies are helpful for clients who are unable to express their emotional feelings and have difficulty with developing personal relationships. Cognitive–behavioral strategies are largely verbal and are based on the premise that faulty thinking must be addressed to change behavior. Cognitive restructuring, for example, is an effective method used to address irrational beliefs and negative self-talk; it can be designed to address career and personal issues as well as their interrelationships (see Chapter 8). Culturally related concerns require techniques and interventions that have been modified and structured to address culture-specific variables. "Each culture has meaningful ways of coping with problems" (Okun, 2002, p. 152).

Depressed clients may exhibit the above-described symptoms and more, but what the examples of symptoms suggest is that client concerns are often interrelated and intertwined. Overgeneralizations of negative experiences and negative thinking, for example, are associated not only with depression and feelings of helplessness but also with work performance and interpersonal interactions. In essence, clients with depression can experience symptoms that cut across domains. Intervention strategies therefore can be selected on the basis of individual needs from one or more of the four domains of career, affective cognitive–behavioral, and culture. The key to selecting strategies includes knowledge of their effectiveness, theoretical underpinnings, and experience in their use.

To determine appropriate interventions for depressive episodes, helpers trace causes of depression in three dimensions: biological, psychological, and social. The biological dimension is the most complex, with ongoing research and innovations that may not be familiar to many helpers. Effective medications have been used to treat depression, and more combinations of medications should become available in the future. Some of the new medications have been effective in altering levels of neurotransmitters that correct chemical imbalances. Thus, clients who have experienced severe depression may also need drug therapy. Combining drug therapy with interventions designed to address psychological causes of depression has proven to be effective. Of great significance are the early findings that psychological interventions can alter brain chemistry (Barlow & Durand, 2005). Helpers should learn more about these exciting subjects in the future.

Cognitive–behavioral techniques, especially cognitive restructuring, have been very popular interventions for addressing the underlying causes of depression. Their use has also been recommended for addressing work stress reactions, which are covered in Chapter 11. This does not rule out the use of affective techniques when helping clients moderate the affects of depression. As mentioned previously, modified forms of cognitive–behavioral and affective techniques can also be used to address culture-related problems. Helpers should recall that psychologically related problems are most powerful in causing depression.

Social interactions are a large part of daily existence. People influence, and are influenced by, others. When a person becomes depressed, social support can be very helpful. This social support may come from friends, family, and social and religious institutions. It is a part of the healing process that, when combined with other interventions, is most effective. Social support can be especially effective for individuals of different cultures who interact with others of their ethnic background in supportive ways. Interventions may include training to become more assertive, interpersonal training in general, and cognitive restructuring, among others.

Mental health concerns discussed in the preceding paragraphs can affect workers in many ways, especially those who are experiencing a depressive episode. Efficiency of performance, attention span, demeanor, interpersonal relations, and response time are examples of potential problems. The suggested interventions can include discussions and homework that includes the workplace and work requirements. Specific references to how distorted thinking can affect job performance and relationships with other workers and supervisors are good examples. Self-efficacy and self-esteem usually associated with depressive episodes are two variables that are linked to work motivation, adjustment, maintenance, and career development. These and other variables that strongly affect career choice and maintenance are discussed in the chapters that follow.

The three-dimensional biopsychosocial model of potential causes of psychopathology also is referred to in most of the chapters that follow. This model suggests that mental health disorders be viewed as multidimensional rather than one dimensional. Mental health disorders that emerge from interacting influences significantly affect the career choice process and work adjustment and maintenance. Work role and other life roles do not escape the negative affects of mental health disorders, and in fact they become a part of the dynamics of individual problems that need to be addressed by helpers who assume a whole-person approach to helping. In the next chapter, I introduce other mental health issues, which have received increasing attention for their pervasive effect on the lives of individual workers.

Summary

This book is about how to integrate career and personal concerns in counseling. Career choice, development, and personal concerns are viewed as intertwined and connected. Integrative approaches are used to observe relationships between career and personal client concerns.

1. The *biopsychosocial model* is an interactivist position that supports the proposition that biological, psychological, and social influences interact in the development of psychological disorders. These three dimensions are the focal point of interest in determining the development of a psychological disorder and its relationship to career concerns in what is also known as an *integrative approach*. An integrative approach is used to determine specific influences that have contributed to a psychological disorder.

2. The development of mood disorders is illustrated by symptoms of depression. An integrative perspective is used to uncover the interplay of three dimensions: (1) biological, (2) psychological, and (3) social/cultural. The *biological dimension* consists of the inherited genetic vulnerability to develop mood disorders. Neurotransmitter imbalances and structured problems of the brain significantly contribute to the development of a mood disorder. The *psychological dimension* is a very broad based force that includes cognitive, emotional, and personality factors. Marital relationships, gender, and social support are most prominent in the *social cultural dimension*.

3. The career and work connection is demonstrated by the nature of a depressive episode. Mood disorders such as depression can affect all life roles, including the work role. The relationship of career and personal concerns are addressed through technical eclecticism in four categories: career, affective, cognitive–behavioral, and culture. The interrelationship of concerns provides the helper with a perspective from which concerns are conceptualized. Interventions are developed from client information about specific events and situations.

Supplementary Learning Exercises

1. What is meant by the interactive process of a biopsychosocial model? Describe the significance of the process.

2. Identify the concept of learned helplessness. How is it connected to depression?

3. Describe how you would address the needs of a client who is depressed. Limit your answer to identifying concerns and proposing effective interventions.

4. Describe some symptoms you would expect to find in a worker who is depressed.

5. What is meant by the term *spillover effect*? Describe consequences.

7

Other Mental Health Issues and Career Concerns

This chapter reviews and summarizes some selected mental health issues that can have significant influence on all life roles, including the work role. I continue to use an integrative approach to discover potential influences on the development of psychological disorders; biological, psychological and social/cultural factors are conceived as interacting influences that contribute to the development of each disorder. How each mental health concern can disrupt one's ability to function in the society in which he or she lives and works is the major focus of this chapter. From the position of a whole-person approach to helping, helpers are interested in the most efficient methods of conceptualizing each client's unique concerns. Helpers can be most effective when they address underlying causes of dysfunctional behavior from the perspective that client concerns are intertwined and interrelated. Influences, causes, and solutions to disorders, instead of the procedures and methods used to establish labels for psychological disorders, will occupy this chapter's discussions.

Symptoms of behavior that can lead to work impairment will be highlighted as concerns that are also associated with everyday living. It is the interrelationships of concerns that give meaning to intervention strategies that address them. The focus is on client concerns associated with

1. Apprehension and fear—an example of an anxiety disorder

2. Fear of social situations and/or being around others—an example of social phobia

3. Fear of serious health problems that are nonexistent—an example of a somatoform disorder

4. Substance-related disorders—alcoholism and drug abuse have been hot topics over several decades

5. Disruptive symptoms of schizophrenia—an example of a psychotic disorder

These client concerns are representative of an inclusive group of psychological disorders. They were chosen to represent a significant number of anxiety disorders, a large number of phobias, a group of somatoform disorders, a very pervasive psychotic disorder, and an overview of significantly disruptive substance-related disorders. Even though I have also discussed mood disorders (Chapter 6) and 10 personality disorders (Chapter 9), there are, of course, many more psychological disorders that could be used to illustrate the connection among career, work, and mental health. The general pattern of discussion for all disorders includes a summary of symptoms and causal influences from biological, psychological, and social/cultural factors; consequences of symptoms; and suggested interventions.

Concerns Associated With Apprehension and Fear _____

Everyday life can include anxiety and feelings of fear and apprehension. Some people, for example, may be apprehensive about a dental appointment, meeting a new friend, interviewing for job, or accomplishing some established goal. *Anxieties* produce physical and psychological responses, some of which may be unpleasant, but as one learns to adapt to anxiety responses the chances of surviving them increases. Ironically, it is generally agreed that some feelings of anxiety are necessary, for example, for a peak performance on a test or in a basketball game. Persistent and intense anxiety, however, may interfere with an individual's ability to function on a job and in other life roles. Excessive anxiety can result in intense fear and/or panic attacks.

Fear is considered an immediate emotional reaction to a real or perceived danger. The fear response is thought to be a strong escape reaction tendency: The person wants to be removed from a situation or simply get out of the way of danger. Panic attacks, however, include intense fear and extreme discomfort that usually is accompanied by a rise in blood pressure, increased heart palpitations, and shortness of breath. There could be sweating, chest pain, nausea, fear of dying, and trembling, among other symptoms (American Psychiatric Association, 2000). These symptoms can come about very suddenly in a panic attack; impending danger causes an instantaneous reaction. The emotional state during a panic attack may involve the feeling that one has lost control of a situation; in this sense, anxiety is future oriented in that the major concern is what will happen in the future. Panic attacks may be characterized by an immediate alarm reaction that is a part of strong escape tendencies caused by reactions to the perception of a very serious emergency. Individuals can develop a variety of cues that trigger panic attacks. The sensing of possible future threats, for example (even though danger is not present), can increase the likelihood of a panic attack. Anxiety and panic are closely related (Barlow & Durand, 2005).

People with *generalized anxiety disorder* (GAD) are consumed with worry to the point that they constantly feel on edge, easily become fatigued, have difficulty in concentrating, and experience muscle tension and sleep disturbance (American Psychiatric Association, 2000). As with other psychological disorders, it is the persistence of symptoms over a period of time (6 months or more, in this case) and the intensity of symptoms that distinguishes a person with GAD from someone who worries about daily events on occasion. People with GAD cannot set their worries aside but constantly ruminate about potential future problems; under these circumstances, anxiety and worry are difficult to control. The consequences of GAD are many, including the development of both physical and mental health problems. Interpersonal relationships, ability to perform at work, high blood pressure, a constant state of irritability, and poor family relationships are examples of relevant concerns. Box 7.1 presents an example of how GAD can monopolize a person's life in the case of Fern.

Box 7.1   The Worry World of Fern

The yardman was due in 2 days, but Fern was already worried that he would cut down her mother's flowers. "He doesn't like for me to tell him what to do," she thought. She was also worried that he would not be on time. Fern planned to shop for groceries but was concerned that she would not remember what to buy. Thus begins Fern's day of worrying. She goes from worrying about one situation to another and never stops feeling apprehensive. It is typical of her to ruminate about pending events, appointments, and most other matters of daily living. For example, she constantly worries whether she will be fired from her job in a grocery store or whether she can pass the courses she is taking at a local community college. She has dropped out of classes on two other occasions, stating she was not sure she could meet the standards despite having good grades in high school.

Fern is 28 years old and is living at home, looking after her aging parents. After graduating from high school she delayed going to college and took a job in a grocery store near her home. After 3 years, she enrolled in the local community college and attended classes for several days before she decided to withdraw. Two semesters later she enrolled in college again, but once more she only attended classes several times and withdrew. What soon followed was a brief depressive episode before she enrolled for the third time.

Fern has other worries. She is very concerned about her health. She is also monitoring her weight but is reluctant to weigh herself because, as she puts it, "I just know that I am going to be overweight." Long before each meal, she worries about overeating. Fern cannot relax. Even when eating a meal, she experiences anxiety, with thoughts that something is bound to go wrong at any time.

Not surprisingly, Fern worries about personal relationships. She has a few friends and has dated on several occasions. Before each date, however, she is concerned about what she would talk about and whether she would be able to impress her date. Whether her date would consider her to be naive and not ask her out again are examples of Fern's worried thoughts. These thoughts may not be considered highly unusual, but when her first date was considered successful and enjoyable, Fern just knew that the next one would be a complete failure. She did not have a friend at work and was generally considered to be loner by most other employees. Although some found her to be somewhat friendly, there seemed to be a barrier that prevented her from establishing closer relationships. Fern also worried about her relationship with her supervisor. Although he has never raised his voice to her and is most always cordial, Fern thought the ax could fall any day and that she would be without a job. Fern's anxiety would increase whenever the supervisor was around. Anxiety made everything in life difficult for Fern; even when initial experiences were pleasurable, she just could not stop worrying.

In the case of Fern, the career–work connection is clearly about people with anxieties that severely affect the ability to successfully function in a work role. Clients who express concerns and symptoms of worry and feelings of anxiety similar to Fern's indicate that negative and distorted thinking should be aggressively addressed. People who have chronic and excessive fears of the future may find that they are unable to cope with anxiety apprehension. The alert helper will focus on interventions that moderate the client's fear of the future and enhance the client's self-efficacy through the use of combinations of techniques that include assertiveness and behavioral rehearsal, systematic desensitization, cognitive restructuring, and homework assignments illustrated in Chapter 12.

Some Causes of Anxiety Disorders

There is increasing evidence that the causes of anxiety are also influenced by biological factors. Anxiety, for example, has been associated with specific brain circuits and neurotransmitter systems. Currently, researchers expect to be able to use imaging procedures to uncover more specific factors of brain involvement with anxiety and panic attacks (Charney & Drevets, 2002). It has also been suggested that people inherit vulnerabilities to being tense and anxious (Gray & McNaughton, 1996). Thus, the tendency to experience panic attacks is more than likely inherited (Barlow, 2002). More evidence is expected to support the heritable contribution of a negative mood state that can lead to physical tensions and feelings of apprehension (Barlow & Durand, 2005). Helpers should be aware that anxiety, panic, and fear tend to influence the development of psychopathology.

The psychological influences on the development of anxiety involve a variety of factors. Freud (1946), for example, traced the presence of anxiety to infantile fearful situations. Bandura (1997), a researcher known for his contributions to social learning theory, suggested that anxiety was the result of models observed in early childhood. Children, for example, discover that events are not always in one's control, and the loss of control has different consequences. For some, uncertainty of control may lead to danger-laden beliefs, whereas others are not as troubled by the perception that one is not in total control of one's future. Individuals who are most vulnerable to developing anxiety disorders are those who develop a general sense of uncontrollability that negatively affects their total lifestyle (Barlow & Durand, 2005). As pointed out in Chapter 6, people who lack self-confidence and have low self-esteem are unable to cope with stressful events.

Social/cultural influences are thought to be largely interpersonal stressful life events that are sources of stress, which leads to anxiety. Such events may be divorce, death of a loved one, severe problems at work, physical injury, illness, and social pressure to succeed at work. What we have here are the following three things: (1) stressful life events that interact with (2) generalized biological vulnerability, such as inheritable traits that trigger physical reactions, and (3) psychological vulnerability from which the individual has developed a general sense that life events are out of control. Barlow (2002) labeled this process of anxiety development *triple vulnerability theory* (p. 125).

Intervention Strategies

Generalized anxiety has been addressed by the use of a variety of drugs, with mixed results. One class of the drugs used is the *benzodiazepines*, which have proven to be best as a short-term relief strategy only. The disadvantage of using benzodiazepines is associated with side affects that can interfere with one's ability to perform on a job; also, prolonged use could be addictive. Antidepressants, some of which are currently being observed for their effectiveness, are predicted to be the drugs of choice for the future (Brawman-Mintzer, 2001). Ongoing research is designed to find more effective antidepressants to combat symptoms of GAD. It should be noted that drug therapy is often combined with psychologically oriented interventions.

There are a number of promising psychological interventions to treat anxiety. The use of brief therapy, for example, has focused on helping people gain more awareness of what is actually threatening when they experience an increase in anxiety. Clients can learn to recognize the significance of muscle tension, shortness of breath, and level of emotional reactions. Helpers assist clients in processing threatening images and information for the purpose of understanding how and why they feel anxious. Relaxation techniques are also used to help clients combat tension (Barlow & Durand, 2005; Borkovec & Costello, 1993).

Cognitive–behavioral techniques, discussed in Chapters 6 and 12, have also been used effectively to counteract anxiety-provoking thoughts (Wetherell, Gatz, & Craske, 2003). Mediation techniques have also been used with clients who have difficulty dealing with stressful feelings; these procedures have focused on the client's acceptance of threatening thoughts rather than attempting to avoid them (Barlow & Durand, 2005; Roemer, Orsillo, & Barlow, 2002). Cognitive–behavioral approaches combined with family therapy have been very helpful in treating children with generalized anxiety (Barrett et al., 2002). Helpers should be aware that GAD can be very debilitating, as illustrated by the case of Fern in Box 7.1. GAD can negatively affect all life roles, including career choice and development. Other anxiety disorders include specific phobias, posttraumatic stress disorder, and obsessive–compulsive disorder. The effects of excessive anxiety are illustrated in the case study of John, presented in Chapter 12.

Concerns Associated With Fear of Social Situations and Being Around Others

Fear of social situations and/or being around others is known as *social phobia*. It should be made clear, however, that fear associated with one or more social and performance situations must be extreme and persistent; for example, it is not unusual for people to fear public speaking. People with social phobia, however, have an extreme fear of performing in front of others, such as in public speaking, because they are fully convinced they will be judged harshly or experience embarrassment in front of an audience of strangers. Furthermore, exposure to feared social situations causes anxiety that is excessive and unreasonable to the point that one could have a panic attack. People with social phobia usually avoid feared situations, but when they cannot they endure them with intense anxiety and distress. Social phobia understandably can interfere with one's ability to function in all life roles, including the work role and the forming of normal relationships (American Psychiatric Association, 2000).

In the mid 1990s, 13.3% of the U.S. population, estimated currently at 35 million, have or had experienced social phobia (Barlow & Durand, 2005; Kessler et al., 1994). One can expect to observe an extreme case of fear of social situations in the form of extreme shyness. Again, as in most psychological disorders, extreme reactions separate full-blown cases of social phobia from individuals who may tend to be somewhat shy and introverted. Other situations that tend to produce anxiety are eating in restaurants or signing a paper in the presence of an observer (Barlow & Durand, 2005). It is worth noting that when people are extremely inhibited in most all social situations, they fit into a subtype labeled *social phobia, generalized type* (American Psychiatric Association, 2000).

It is also important to remember that shyness may not be extreme enough to be labeled social phobia but may indicate that some interventions used in full-blown cases of social phobia could be helpful as early interventions. Helpers are likely to see clients who have early symptoms of social phobia that can be effectively addressed. Clients with shyness problems, for example, would more than likely be indecisive, inhibited, and experience low self-esteem. Adolescents can be very vulnerable to the development of social phobia; for example, some adolescents can develop severe anxiety when they think others are watching them. In fact, social phobia usually begins during adolescence and tends to be prevalent in young adults who are undereducated, single, and from families of low socioeconomic status (Barlow & Durand, 2005).

Influences That Can Lead to Social Phobic Behavior

As usual, we observe biological influences first. Kagan (1997) suggested that as early as 4 months after birth the tendency toward shyness and inhibition can be observed; infants react differently to facial expressions, especially those that depict anger. Thus, there appears to be an inherited vulnerability to social phobic behavior, especially if excessive behavioral inhibitions are observed. According to Barlow and Durand (2005) and Hirschfield et al. (1992), excessive behavioral inhibition increases the chance one will develop phobic behavior. A combination of biological vulnerability to develop anxiety and the presence of social inhibition increases the risk that a person will develop phobic behavior disorder.

As with many psychological disorders, vulnerability can be traced back to early childhood experiences. It is speculated that during early development children learn to fear social evaluations from their parents and/or relatives. Learned fear of being evaluated by others is thought to be more prevalent in children whose parents have exhibited symptoms of social phobia (Lieb et al., 2002); children observe and adopt their parents' reactions to events. As children advance in age, development of phobic behavior can be greatly influenced by traumatic experiences in early adolescence, especially for children who are severely challenged and mocked by peers. What we have here is the interaction of biological vulnerability, psychological and social development, and stressful life experiences.

Effective Interventions

Drug therapy has been shown to be an effective treatment of severe social anxiety. Researchers have used antidepressants and combinations of other drugs with some effectiveness. There continues to be ongoing research with current and newly developed drugs for the treatment of phobias. Thus far, drug therapy has shown some promising results; however, when drug therapy was compared with psychological interventions, the latter was superior and more enduring (Barlow & Durand, 2005).

Cognitive–behavioral group therapy has been touted as an effective tool for addressing symptoms of social phobias. Clients learn to role play and rehearse situations that tend to produce phobic behavior while the remainder of the group observes as an audience. Group procedures are followed by individual therapy that is designed to help clients reveal unique perceptions of danger that are assumed to exist (Heimberg, Salzman, Holt, & Blendell, 1993). This process provides the helper with general and specific situations that can be addressed with cognitive restructuring designed to challenge the client's negative cognitive schemas. Helpers who recognize early symptoms of phobic behavior can be very instrumental in modifying problems that could lead to serious consequences. Box 7.2 presents a case study of Sam, a man with social phobia.

Helpers will probably see various degrees of social phobia in their clients. Keeping Sam's case in mind, counselors should recognize that full-blown cases of social phobia can severely affect an individual's ability to work and

Box 7.2   The Case of Sam

Sam is a 26-year-old White man; he has never been married and lives alone in an apartment complex. He graduated from high school but never attended college. He has worked for short periods of time at a hardware store, for a landscape designer, and in a service station. Sam is now employed by a local manufacturing company.

No one paid much attention to Sam during his first 2 months at work. He got his job done on time, worked by the rules, and was very quiet and reserved. He was considered by his work associates as a good worker who caused no problems in the workplace. As a result of Sam's desire to keep his distance from fellow workers, his private life was unknown. That in itself does not necessarily mean that someone has a psychological problem, but in Sam's case there was none of the usual chatter that goes on between workers. Sam was most difficult to engage in a meaningful discussion. Although he attended sports events and concerts and went to movies, he had no friends—Sam was always alone. Those who tried to converse with Sam usually got only a "yes" or "no" response. Almost everyone who worked with Sam just left him alone.

Eventually, Sam was called on to make recommendations for improving work procedures. When the time came for Sam to present to his small group of fellow workers, he called in sick. When more pressure was placed on Sam to offer suggestions for improving production of goods, he resigned from his job. During a visit to his home by his supervisor, Sam was found hiding in a closet. It was discovered that he had been in the closet for several days, eaten very little, and appeared very unstable. Sam reluctantly agreed to go to a mental health facility for help. After several interviews Sam was diagnosed as having a severe case of social phobia. Sam told his counselor that he could not take the chance of being humiliated in the presence of his fellow workers. The focus of his anxiety appeared to be perceived events that involve social evaluations. Sam claimed that he recognized that his fear of social situations is excessive but, as he put it, there was little he could do about it; he could not stop feeling intensely anxious around others.

actively participate in other life roles. Sam's case also illustrates how stress emerging from life events can result in very debilitating anxious apprehension. What we have here is an opportunity to point out one of the most important counseling skills that helpers develop over time: Early detection of psychological symptoms that can result in full-blown cases of severe disorders should be immediately addressed. In Sam's chronic disorder of social phobia, considerable effort will be required for him to moderate his current view of the world. On the other hand, if early symptoms of extreme shyness are addressed during adolescence, for example, then clients can learn to cope successfully with stressful events.

The career work connection in this case is fairly straightforward. People who develop social phobic reactions may find it very difficult to maintain gainful employment. The pervasive nature of anxiety and excessive focus on worry can be addressed through cognitive restructuring, and the development of effective coping skills can be accomplished through stress inoculation. Helpers can also expect to find that clients who seemingly have given up hope are more than likely to have inadequate problem-solving skills; they may indeed have limited ability to effectively process career information.

_____ Fear of Health Problems That Are Nonexistent

Somatoform disorders involve intense preoccupation with one's health or appearance. One of the best-known somatoform disorders is *hypochondriasis*; hypochondriacs are individuals who constantly go to a medical doctor for physical complaints that are unfounded. Some individuals are fully convinced that they have a serious disease even when a physician assures them they do not. In the extreme, this disorder gets out of control when one's life is dominated by the fear of a serious health problem that is nonexistent. Preoccupation with unfounded medical conditions is another example of how distorted thinking can be incapacitating; a person with this preoccupation would have difficulty in meeting his or her commitments at work and in other daily activities. Other somatoform disorders include conversion disorder, pain disorder, and body dysmorphic disorder.

The symptoms of hypochondriasis are rather specific and precise so that helpers can be certain that one's preoccupation with bodily functions is not better accounted for by another disorder. What is emphasized is that an individual has misinterpreted bodily symptoms and is preoccupied with unfounded medical conditions for at least 6 months. The person experiences intense distress, and there is impairment in social, occupational, and other important functioning. What all this implies is that there are indeed similarities between hypochondriasis and other disorders, such as generalized anxiety disorder. Thus, a helper might encounter people who are experiencing a preoccupation with unfounded medical conditions over shorter periods of time and intermittently will not meet the criteria for a diagnosis; however, they could be experiencing similar but less intense and persistent impairments observed in people with true hypochondriasis. It is more than likely that helpers will see both people with full-blown hypochondriasis as well as clients who experience the same symptoms for shorter periods of time but also have difficulty in keeping a job or meeting their obligations in other important roles.

There appears to be general agreement that hypochondriasis is a disorder of cognition and perception with an emotional component that heightens the reaction intensity; people with hypochondriasis have a perceptual sensitivity to illness cues. They interpret what is happening to their body as threatening. If their stomach is upset, for example, they believe that they have cancer, or if they have a headache, it is because they have a brain tumor. Hypochondriacs are never free from the possibility of becoming gravely ill. The onset of this disorder can happen at any time over the life span. Peak periods are during adolescence, middle age, and after age 60 years (Barlow & Durand, 2005). Like most mood and anxiety disorders, it is chronic in nature.

Effective Interventions

Helpers can focus on misinterpretations of body sensations or other signs that indicate a severe illness and ask clients to identify and challenge these perceptions. Clients are instructed to create symptoms such as the sensations they experience in certain parts of the body that have convinced them they are seriously ill. Clients are then persuaded that they do indeed have control and can take steps to help solve their own problems. Reassurance and support on the part of mental health professionals is very helpful. *Explanatory therapy*, in which the client's concerns are detailed and carefully explained, did indeed reduce fears and beliefs associated with hypochondriasis (Fava, Grandi, Rafinelli, Fabbri, & Cazzaro, 2000). Cognitive–behavioral and stress management interventions, which are discussed further in Chapter 8, also have been effective (Warwick, Clark, Cobb, & Sailovskis, 1996). Difficulties in living associated with hypochondriasis are illustrated in the case of Corrina, presented in Chapter 12.

Substance-Related Disorders

One of the well-known "problems in living" concerns has been associated with substance abuse. Helpers have primarily focused on assisting clients to be drug free and thus in a better position to solve other problems. It has been well recognized that establishing a therapeutic relationship is difficult with substance abusers, because they can be involved in criminal activity; also, they often are unwilling to discuss their involvement in drug use. The major problems, however, are the severity of withdrawal symptoms and a strong desire to experience the pleasure associated with their drug of choice. To begin to understand the complexity of this disorder, one can categorize drugs according to Nairne (2003) as follows:

Depressants	*Opiates*
Ethyl Alcohol	Opium
Barbiturates	Morphine
Tranquillizers	Heroin

Stimulants	*Hallucinogens*
Amphetamines	LSD
Caffeine	Marijuana
Cocaine	Mescaline
Ecstasy	Psilocybin
Nicotine	

This perspective points out the shopping list of drugs available in the United States and around the world. We should all be aware of the many problems associated with drug use from coverage in newspaper articles and television. To no one's surprise, substance-related abuse can affect all life roles, especially the work role. Although there seems to be an endless number of new drugs that emerge, there is one encouraging statistic: There has been a dramatic decline in drug use by young people since the 1970s, and patterns of substance use vary by age, gender, and race (National Center for Health Statistics, 2003).

It should not be surprising to find that alcohol is the drug of choice among high school seniors. Binge drinking is highest for White male seniors. Cigarettes and marijuana are used more often by all groups than cocaine, inhalants, and Ecstasy (National Center for Health Statistics, 2003). A major concern of substance use among young adults, however, is the tolerance factor: A person can develop a drug tolerance, which requires increasing amounts of the substance to produce the desired results. Drug dependency is often linked to tolerance (Nairne, 2003). At the beginning of this discussion, I pointed out that helpers interested in working as substance abuse counselors will need specialized training and supervision. The following paragraphs summarize the concerns associated with different classes of drugs. Let's begin with depressants.

Depressants

Depressants are a class of drugs that slow or depress activity of the central nervous system. Depressants have many effects on behavior, including relaxation, reduction of anxiety, and decreased attention. When depressants are ingested the sympathetic nervous system slows, and so does reaction time. Behavior can get out of control—a person who is quiet and unassuming can change to one who is loud and boisterous, and an inhibited person can become very provocative. Consequences of overconsumption are many, including impairment of work skills, fatigue, nausea, and depression. One of the most commonly used depressants is alcohol: Researchers estimate that approximately 15 million U.S. adults are alcohol dependent (National Institute of Mental Health, 2003).

Barbiturates and tranquilizers also are classified as depressant drugs. This group of drugs has been used as sedatives for calming, inducing sleep, and reducing anxiety. Unfortunately, barbiturates and tranquillizers have addictive properties that increase their abuse by many adults (Franklin & Frances, 1999). The abuse of these drugs can cause significant maladaptive behavior, such as inappropriate sexual or aggressive behavior and severe mood swings; social and occupational functioning also can be impaired (American Psychiatric Association, 2000).

Stimulants

The class of drugs labeled *stimulants* will increase central nervous system activity and enhance neural transmissions. Stimulants such as caffeine, nicotine, amphetamines, and cocaine are thought to be the most frequently consumed drugs by Americans. Small doses of caffeine as in the morning cup of coffee can improve attention and mood, although health care personnel encourage moderate use of caffeine. The negative effects of nicotine have been well documented with articles appearing regularly in the daily news, especially when tobacco companies are being sued.

Users of amphetamines and cocaine inject, smoke, or snort them to induce feelings of euphoria, vigor, and elation, but only for short periods of time. These drugs are generally fast acting, resulting in a quick high but one that eventually ends up as a sudden crash. What follows is usually a desire for more of what brought on the high and may end up becoming an addiction. Similar results are derived from the designer drug Ecstasy, which has increased in popularity. All of the stimulant drugs obviously can affect social and occupational functioning and are dangerous as well; they can lead to brain damage (Nairne, 2003).

Opiates

Examples of opiates include opium, morphine, and heroin. Opiates are also referred to as *narcotics*. These drugs depress nervous system activity and thus they reduce anxiety, lower sensitivity to pain, and elevate mood. Withdrawal after one has become addicted to this group of drugs is one of the most difficult, and the symptoms can be very debilitating. Withdrawal can last for several days and can include excessive yawning, nausea, and severe chills. Users of opiates are at risk for HIV infection through injection of drugs, and they tend to die at an early age (Nairne, 2003).

Hallucinogens

This class of drugs includes LSD, mescaline, psilocybin, and marijuana. These drugs produce variations in sensations and perception and change the way an individual generally perceives the world. Sounds, sight, smells, and tastes, for example, can be distorted, and one can experience hallucinations. Physical symptoms include pupillary dilation, rapid heartbeat, blurred vision, and excessive sweating (American Psychiatric Association, 2000). Tolerance for some of the hallucinogens increases quickly, causing users to consume larger quantities. Of major concern for helpers is a client's development of an addiction to one or more substances.

In the next section of this chapter, I look at causes of substance abuse, but not before providing a concise explanation of how an addiction can affect the lives of people involved in substance abuse. Wilson (2003), a biological psychologist, summarized the consequences of an addiction as follows:

> When a person begins to use a drug, that drug use is sporadic and voluntary. But after an addiction develops, the addicted individual is compelled to seek out the drug and consume it. This compulsive drug use is the hallmark of addiction. Addicts lose control over their drug intake. They have a difficult time thinking of anything but acquiring the drug, and they will forsake all kinds of social obligations (including family life and work) in order to obtain and use the drug. We still do not know for sure how an addiction develops, but research in this area has given us some clues. (p. 402)

Some Causes of Substance Abuse

One of the reasons for displaying a list of drugs available to users and a brief explanation of their effect on individual lifestyles was to illustrate the complexities of how an addiction develops. Alcohol is very easily available and legal, whereas cocaine is not and is much more expensive; a person is subject to arrest if he or she is found to be in possession of cocaine. This raises the question of whether alcohol is more addictive because it is readily available. Because of these differences of availability and different effects of drugs, researchers have studied substance abuse by specific substances. Kalat (2004), for example, studied the risk factors of alcohol abuse by identifying sons of alcoholic fathers and following their drinking habits and, more important, their reactions to ingesting alcohol. Some sons of alcoholics, for instance, were found to be more sensitive to alcohol and less sensitive to negative consequences after drinking. A follow-up study revealed that men who were sons of alcoholics and did not become intoxicated after moderate amounts of alcohol were more likely to become alcoholics (Schuckit & Smith, 1996). In addition, sons of alcoholics experienced more than average relief from stress after consuming alcohol. Most interestingly, sons of alcoholics were found to have some brain peculiarities, which may be a potential predisposition in alcoholism. Finally, a tendency toward sensation seeking was a good indication of someone whose chances of being a heavy drinker were better than average (Kalat, 2004). These findings suggest that alcoholism and drug abuse in general are composed of a complex interaction of influences, including unspecified genetic factors; people can be genetically vulnerable to substance abuse (Barlow & Durand, 2005).

In the psychological domain researchers have focused on cognitions, that is, beliefs and expectations individuals have about the effects of drugs. The belief and expectation that drinking alcohol will have positive effects can tempt one to drink heavily. Thus, positive reinforcement from drinking leads one to attempt to recapture pleasurable experiences through more consumption of alcohol. Other users drink or use drugs to escape from pain or from unpleasant life experiences, such as stress and anxiety; in this case, the substance is providing *negative reinforcement*. How clients reinforce their substance abuse provides helpers with beliefs and expectations that can be addressed through cognitive restructuring. Other psychological interventions are discussed in the next section of this chapter.

In the social domain, people can be influenced to use alcohol and/or drugs by friends, family members, peer group members, and others in their environment. There is also a significant exposure to the use of alcohol and drugs in the media, such as use by popular musicians and others. Evidence suggests that less supervision by parents who are preoccupied by their own addiction to drugs and/or alcohol can influence their children to experiment with these substances (Barlow & Durand, 2005). Finally, cultural expectations differ when it comes to the use of alcohol and/or other drugs; some cultures expect heavy drinking on certain occasions—it is the norm. Thus, what is considered abnormal behavior in some cultures may not be perceived that way in other cultures (Matsumoto & Juang, 2004).

Effective Interventions

The following examples of interventions to combat substance abuse are divided into three areas: (1) biological, (2) psychological, and (3) social. They are compiled from Barlow and Durand (2005).

Biological Interventions

The biological interventions include agonist substitution, antagonist drugs, and aversive treatments.

Agonist substitution consists of providing a safe drug that produces the same effect as the client's drug of choice. Heroin users have been given methadone with some success, but it was found that methadone can also be addictive. *Antagonist drugs* block the effect of the person's drug of choice with limited success. They are primarily used to help in the withdrawal process. *Aversive treatments* are used to make the drug of choice very unpleasant for the user. Antabuse has been used to combat alcoholism by causing a person who ingests alcohol to become ill and vomit. The disadvantage is that this drug requires close supervision by a professional and it has been found that when Antabuse is discontinued a number of clients return to drinking. In the meantime, research continues to try to find more effective drug treatments.

Psychological Interventions

One well-known method of treating substance abusers has been placement in *inpatient facilities*, where they receive combinations of treatments. Inpatient treatment can be very expensive. Probably one the most popular methods of addressing alcoholism is through programs offered by *Alcoholic Anonymous*. There are examples of success with their step-by-step interventions but, as one would suspect, some people do not respond to their programs. *Aversion therapy* consists of pairing the abused substances with something unpleasant. One example consists of slightly shocking the client when a drink or drug is offered. Likewise, in what is called *covert sensitization* the substance abuser is required to develop unpleasant images, such as vomiting when snorting cocaine or getting up in the morning and not being able to go to work. Negative images, therefore, are thought to be strong enough influences to discourage use of substances. The use of *contingency management* requires clients to select desired behavioral changes and to choose desired reinforcers as rewards when they make gradual improvements and progress in reaching their goal of being drug free. Finally, cognitive–behavioral interventions are used to address beliefs about the positive aspects of drug use.

Social Interventions

Social support is a most important method of assisting individuals in combating addiction to substances. Support from family and friends is most valuable, but support from other members of a community can be very impressive to an individual who is striving to be drug free. The process of withdrawal can be a most trying period in one's life; clients often need all the encouragement they can get and community support can be a valuable tool to combat a relapse.

The Career–Work Connection

Alcoholism and drug abuse in the workplace has been a hot topic over several decades. In the 1980s, it was estimated that about two thirds of the people entering the workplace had used illegal drugs (Tyson & Vaughn, 1987). By the 1990s, four to five million people living in the United States used cocaine monthly, and marijuana use was thought to be much higher (Schwenk, 1999). Today, substance abuse remains a major problem in the workplace. Industrial organizations have invested considerable funds for substance abuse programs specifically designed for their employees.

Of major concern have been the long-term negative relationships to work adjustment. Galaif, Newcomb, and Carmona (2001) found that the use of alcohol, marijuana, and/or cocaine predicted lower job satisfaction in a 4-year follow-up study. In addition, job instability (e.g., being fired) was a predictor of subsequent substance abuse. Of primary concern in the workplace, however, are performance impairment and absenteeism (Muchinsky, 2003).

Other concerns include employee theft to support a drug habit and the potential negative influences alcohol and drug users could have on fellow workers—for example, the temptation to join the group for a few rounds before going home could lead others to seek relief from work stress through substance abuse. It seems quite clear that alcohol and drug abuse can create serious problems for workers that are very inclusive. Solutions should include a recognition of the pervasive nature of substance abuse in which most aspects of life are addressed, including career, work, and mental health; they are indeed intertwined.

Schizophrenia

In the beginning of the 20th century, a German psychiatrist named Emil Kraepelin (1898) used the term *dementia praecox* to label a psychiatric disorder that he thought was caused by the deterioration of the brain. About the same time, another psychiatrist in Switzerland, named Bleuler (1908), who had observed patents with disconnected thoughts, words, and inappropriate emotions, labeled this disorder *schizophrenia*. Bleuler suggested that schizophrenia was a physiological dysfunction in which patients could at times function normally while at other times were completely disorganized and functioned abnormally. Bleuler did not agree with Kraepelin that degeneration of the brain was the primary cause of schizophrenia. Thus began the controversy and mystery that continues to challenge researchers who seek to answer a long-standing question: What are the causes of schizophrenia? The simple answer to that question is that all the causes of schizophrenia are still not known (Kalat, 2004; Nairne, 2003; Wilson, 2003).

Helpers do have criteria for diagnosing schizophrenia; the following symptoms are included: apathy, flat affect, blunted mood, disorganized speech and behavior, delusions, and hallucinations. There are other requirements to be met, including the ruling out of organic causes of psychosis, and the symptoms observed cannot be explained by drug intoxication. One must also rule out medical conditions such as cerebrovascular disease, hepatic encephalopathy, or Huntington's disease (Wilson, 2003).

Because some people with schizophrenia suffer from delusions but with no signs of hallucinations while other people with schizophrenia have both, the logical question is: What, then, is true schizophrenia? In an attempt to solve this problem, researchers have identified subtypes of schizophrenia as including both positive and negative symptoms. *Positive symptoms* are the most obvious signs of psychosis: delusions and hallucinations. *Delusions* are thought content disorders that are misrepresentations of reality, whereas *hallucinations* are perceptual disturbances, such as when a person sees or hears things that are not real or actually present. *Negative symptoms* indicate a diminished capacity to function, including emotional and social withdrawal, flat affect, apathy, inattention, poverty of thought and speech, and poor judgments (Barlow & Durand, 2005).

The numerous symptoms identified with schizophrenia have suggested to some researchers that this disorder is actually a group or class of disorders (Nairne, 2003). To identify a distinctive course and treatment of symptoms, a revised classification system was constructed by the American Psychiatric Association (2000). Diagnostic criteria for subtypes of schizophrenia include the following types: paranoid, disorganized, catatonic, residual, schizophreniform, delusional, and schizoaffective. Each type has specific criteria that dominate the clinical picture; for example, criteria for the catatonic type include motoric immobility as evidenced by catalepsy. These subtypes and the established criteria for each one underscore the many levels of schizophrenia; as Barlow and Durand (2005) pointed out, schizophrenia "defies our desire for simplicity" (p. 467).

Some Causes of Schizophrenia

Causes of schizophrenia have been the major focus of an impressive amount of research that has been well documented by Barlow and Durand (2004), Kalat (2004), and Wilson (2003). Most attention has been directed to the identification of genes involved in the development of schizophrenia, the contributions of brain abnormalities, and drugs that can be used as effective interventions. Research is ongoing and extensive; it is hoped that further findings will enlighten our understanding of the causes and treatment of schizophrenia. In the meantime, there are some answers to the above-mentioned questions regarding genes, brain abnormalities, and the use of drugs for treatment. Concerning genes, there appears to be agreement that there is no single gene but rather multiple genes that contribute to one's vulnerability to being diagnosed with schizophrenia. This conclusion offers some credence to the observation that schizophrenia cannot be narrowed to a unitary cause but has different causes for each subtype (Heinricks, 1993).

Fifty or more studies have been conducted on the abnormally large lateral ventricles in the brain that have been observed in people with schizophrenia. Researchers are quick to point out that ventricle size itself is not the problem. What does appear to happen, however, is that the enlargement of lateral ventricles affects the development of adjacent parts of the brain. It has been observed, for instance, that some areas of the brain near enlarged lateral ventricles have atrophied. Additional findings indicate that the enlargement of lateral ventricles may be inherited, thus increasing the individual's vulnerability to develop schizophrenia (Barlow & Durand, 2005). Brain abnormalities are thought to be a major contributor to the development of schizophrenia. Wilson (2003), a biological psychologist, observes that "Today it is clear that schizophrenia is a disease of the brain, in which certain areas of the brain become damaged early in life, perhaps prenatally in some cases" (p. 456).

Interventions

Some of the early treatments of schizophrenia involve insulin drug therapy, prefrontal lobotomies, and electroconvulsive therapy. Small doses of insulin that are used to treat diabetes have been given to patients with schizophrenia to induce coma. During my personal observations of people who had been given insulin I noticed that some patients were very still and quiet, while others shouted, screamed, and had to be restrained. Nurses were constantly on the move, going from one bed to the next. Eventually, all patients remained quiet as the effects of the drug lessened. This method of treatment has been halted because of illness from side effects. Prefrontal lobotomies were considered to be psychosurgery and a most drastic treatment of schizophrenia. Electroconvulsive therapy has not been considered to be an effective treatment for schizophrenia and has limited current use for treating chronic and severe depression (Barlow & Durand, 2005).

Around the 1950s, drug therapy was used to relieve symptoms of schizophrenia. The group of medications used were known as *neuroleptics* and are often referred to as *antipsychotic drugs*. Although drug therapy was effective for approximately 60% of the patients who used them, some experienced significant side effects, and some patients were not helped (Barlow & Durand, 2005). Eventually, new medications were developed that have proven to very helpful in relieving symptoms and have few side effects. The current problem, however, is that many patients fail to take their medications properly. Thus, helpers must recognize that medications affect people differently; therefore, each client must be approached as a unique individual, and drug therapy should be followed by interventions that are more integrated and inclusive, as discussed in the next paragraph.

Noncompliance with medications is a significant problem. Side effects such as blurred vision and drowsiness have caused users of antipsychotic drugs to view them negatively. Clearly what is needed is an approach that addresses multiple areas of functioning that combine drugs with social support and supportive therapy. To assist people with schizophrenia to improve their quality of life, an integrative approach includes collaborative psychopharmacology, assertive community treatment, family psychoeducation, supportive employment, illness management and recovery, and integrated dual-disorder treatment (Barlow & Durand, 2005). What is stressed here is that multiple needs are to be addressed that can support proper use of medications. People with schizophrenia, for example, need to learn to cope with disruptive symptoms. One goal is to help clients recognize when assistance is needed and how and where it can be obtained. Family members are to be educated regarding the severity and consequences of problems with schizophrenia and how they can manage symptoms as well as methods to reduce their own stress and tensions. Another major goal is to help clients become active participants in their own treatment. Finally, helpers should support clients in their efforts to find meaningful employment and maintain work efficiency (Mueser, Torrey, Lynde, Singer, & Drake, 2003). As the reader may recall, work identity is a most important element in the lives of most people, including people with schizophrenia. Even though the work role may be impaired by relapse, working per se can be very therapeutic in addressing the multiple needs associated with chronic cases of schizophrenia.

At this point in the discussions of the complexity of schizophrenia, one can conclude that the counselor's role is not clearly defined. The purpose of this section, however, is to introduce symptoms of schizophrenia from a biological, psychological, and social/cultural perspective. It should be quite obvious that adults with schizophrenia will have difficulty in maintaining gainful employment. Helpers therefore can refer clients to vocational rehabilitation counselors who have programs for treatment, job placement, and maintenance. In some situations, counselors can play a supportive role as a coach, teacher, and/or mentor to help individual clients meet the challenges of a work role. In the meantime, there is some encouraging research. People with schizophrenia have been able to perform successfully at work with the support of coaches who provide on-the-job training. Other programs that involve social skills training and family interventions also have yielded encouraging results (Barlow & Durand, 2005).

Summary

1. It is well known that mental health concerns can influence one's ability to function in society. Mental health issues that lead to work impairment are identified and addressed. Helpers assist clients in recognizing distorted thinking, disruptive behavior, and consequences of work impairment.

2. Problems in living are associated with fear and apprehension. Fear is considered to be an immediate emotional reaction to a real or perceived danger. Panic attacks include intense fear and extreme apprehension. People with generalized anxiety disorder (GAD) are consumed with worry, have difficulty in concentrating, are very intense, and experience muscle tension. GAD affects all areas of functioning, including the ability to perform at work. People may inherit vulnerabilities associated with being tense and anxious. Lack of self-confidence, low self-esteem, stressful life events, and a general sense that one is not in control can contribute to the development of GAD. Relaxation and cognitive–behavioral techniques are used to counteract anxiety provoking thoughts.

3. Fear of social situations and being around others is another problem of significance. Social phobia can interfere with one's work role and personal relationships. Vulnerability to the development of social phobia can be traced back to early childhood. Children who have learned to fear being evaluated by others may have been influenced by observing their parents' reactions. Early symptoms of social phobia that should be addressed are indecisiveness, inhibitions, and low self-esteem.

4. Fear of serious health problems that are nonexistent is known as hypochondriasis, a somatoform disorder. Hypochondriacs are people who regularly seek medical attention for complaints that are unfounded. They are preoccupied with bodily functions to the point that it interferes with commitment to work and other daily activities. There appears to be agreement

that hypochondriasis is a disorder of cognition and perception. Interventions include cognitive–behavioral techniques and stress management.

5. Substance-related disorders have received a great deal of publicity for a very good reason: They have the potential to become a very serious debilitating problem. Drug addiction can include one or more substances. Drugs have been classified into depressants, stimulants, opiates, and hallucinogens. Drug dependency is often linked to tolerance. People can be genetically vulnerable to substance abuse. Interventions include drug therapy, inpatient treatment, Alcoholics Anonymous, aversion therapy, covert sensitization, contingency management, and cognitive–behavioral therapy.

6. There is a definite career and work connection. Substance abuse continues to be a major problem in the workplace. Long-term negative relationships to work adjustment brought on by drug abuse can be very destructive to workers' career development. Performance impairment and absenteeism are significant workplace problems that are associated with substance abuse.

7. The numerous symptoms of schizophrenia suggest a group or class of disorders. Schizophrenia defies our desire to simplify its causes and treatments. Combinations of drugs, psychological interventions, and social programs have received considerable attention.

8. Schizophrenia may be one of the most misunderstood disorders. All the causes of schizophrenia are currently not known. Positive symptoms include delusions and hallucinations. Negative symptoms include diminished capacity, emotional and social withdrawal, inattention, and poor judgment. Multiple genes can contribute to a person's vulnerability to develop schizophrenia. Interventions include drug therapy combined with supportive therapy, social support, and proper use of medications to combat relapse. State vocational rehabilitation programs for people with schizophrenia are designed for treatment, job placement, and follow-up.

Supplementary Learning Exercises

1. What would you expect to be the underlying causes of dysfunctional behavior that is the result of fear and apprehension? Defend your answer.

2. The fear of social situations could be an inherited predisposition. Describe how the development of this disorder could be interrelated to psychological and social/cultural domains.

3. Describe how the fear of a medical condition that is nonexistent is related to cognitions and perceptions.

4. How would the disorders mentioned in Exercises 1, 2, and 3 affect one's ability to perform at work?

5. Defend or disagree with the position that schizophrenia is a disease of the brain.

8

Cultural Diversity Dimensions

The role of culture in the shaping of mental processes and behavior has been the focus of numerous research projects published in professional journals and textbooks that represent several academic disciplines. Cross-cultural studies have uncovered significant differences and similarities between cultures in attitudes, behaviors, beliefs, norms, and values, among other important factors. Much more remains to be learned, but in the meantime cultural diversity remains a major challenge for helpers. The term *culture* can describe mainstream tendencies that are unique to most of the people in any society. Culture is dynamic in that it is constantly changing. Beliefs, behaviors, and norms that develop from shared cultural values are subjective aspects of culture (Matsumoto & Juang, 2004). The study of culture can greatly contribute to one's understanding of human behavior, including modes of problem solving, attitudes, opinions, motivations, and beliefs that significantly influence choice, work maintenance, and mental health status. Helpers should recognize the importance of culture in relation to identity and self-referent evaluations. Helpers develop a greater understanding of a client's worldview when they examine how that worldview has been shaped by the person's culture; a client's view of the world may be quite different than one's own.

In this chapter, I narrow the focus on differences between cultures in attitudes, behaviors, beliefs, norms, and values. These factors offer an opportunity to examine how differences develop and how they are moderated in the helping process. Be aware that observed differences in some clients should not be considered abnormal but can best be accounted for as part of the norms or practices of a particular culture. Some residents in Central and South America, for instance, have chewed coca leaves for centuries in order to find relief from hunger and fatigue (Musto, 1992). In some cultures, certain religious rituals include practicing voodoo or speaking in tongues, which, for example, can be mistakenly diagnosed as some form of a thinking disorder (Barlow & Durand, 2005). Helpers' sensitivity to cultural practices should significantly reduce misinterpretations of unusual behavior among people who participate in practices unique to their culture. This principle is cited frequently in the pages that follow.

Because the term *culture* is so complex and inclusive, researchers have come forth with numerous definitions over time. The definition chosen for this chapter, however, is from Matsumoto and Juang (2004):

> Culture is a dynamic system of rules, explicit and implicit, established by groups in order to ensure their survival, involving attitudes, values, beliefs, norms, and behaviors, shared by a group but harbored differently by each specific unit within the group, communicated across generations, relatively stable but with the potential to change across time. (p. 10)

What we have here is a dynamic process of socialization and enculturation; culture promotes a general system of rules that includes unique thinking processes and behaviors. Culturally influenced behaviors are learned and shared, and helpers must understand that behavior is best understood and judged only in the cultural context in which it occurs. This does not mean that helpers should condone all cultural practices, but it does suggest that if one is aware of unique cultural traditions and rituals, for example, then one can better understand why people behave the way that they do (Andersen & Taylor, 2006).

In this chapter, I continue to focus on the case for the individual in that I subscribe to the challenge of uncovering unique qualities of each client. Helpers do not stereotype people because of their culture but recognize that each person is biologically, socially, and psychologically unique. The unique qualities of beliefs (cognitions), values, attitudes, and mental health concerns of culturally diverse individuals are discussed in the first section of this chapter. I provide an overview of how uniqueness is shaped and dealt with in the helping process. As in previous chapters, I focus on career, work, and mental health issues, which are intertwined. In the second section of the chapter, I direct attention to culture and mental illness; some psychological, social, and cultural factors involved in diagnoses and interventions are highlighted. Finally, because culture is such an inclusive and complex subject, I limit my discussions of culture in this chapter and provide numerous references for readers who want more information.

Some Perspectives of Culture

The definition of culture given in the preceding section suggests that culture is a learned behavior, but one must also recognize that there are differences of values, attitudes, and behaviors *within* cultural groups as well. Thus, one should not assume that any ethnic group is homogeneous. In helpers' quest to uncover unique qualities of each client, they search for individual perceptions and understandings of the world, that is, each client's *worldview*.

Perception of human nature, the role of families, relationships, locus of control, work values, and core beliefs are examples of what is meant by one's worldview. There are worldviews that are common among members of a specific culture. In many collectivist cultures, such as those in Africa, Asia, and Latin America, the individual focuses on the welfare of the group; family is more important than the individual. In the individualist cultures of Europe and North America, more value is placed on individual accomplishment (Zunker, 2006).

The individualism-versus-collectivism (IC) dimension has received considerable attention from the research community. This dimension presents the researcher with specific information in an attempt to reduce culture from the abstract and allow helpers to more fully understand specific differences that exist between some cultures. Helpers use this information not only to understand differences but also to understand how these differences may become observable in the helping process. Client B, for example, may be less interested in pursuing his individual interests in making a career choice and more interested in involving his family in the choice process. Client C may decline to pursue an opportunity to advance his career that requires a move to a distant city not because he lacks motivation to succeed but because he is more concerned about the effect his move to another city will have on the extended family group. One should also recognize that clients who have been socialized in a culture that endorses individual accomplishment do not necessarily dismiss family matters as not being important. As in all cases in the examples cited, clients weigh advantages and disadvantages of all situations, but cultural influences can make a difference in the outcome.

To reduce culture from the abstract to more specific finite elements, Matsumoto and Juang (2004) suggested that one should focus on *cultural domains* and *dimensions*. *Domains* are opinions, attitudes, values, behaviors, and norms, whereas *dimensions* are general tendencies that can affect behavior, such as individualism versus collectivism (which are discussed in the next paragraphs), power distance, uncertainty avoidance, and masculinity. This scheme was constructed for conducting cross-cultural research but can also serve as a perspective for helpers to use to make more informed decisions about culturally diverse clients. The dimension *power distance*, for example, refers to one's perception of the degree of inequality in power between a less powerful person and a more powerful other (Hofstede, 1984). This term also refers to status differences in cultures (Matsumoto, 1991). *Uncertainty avoidance* is the degree to which cultures develop institutions and rituals to deal with the anxiety associated with uncertainty and ambiguity (Hofstede, 1984; Matsumoto & Juang, 2004). Finally, *masculinity* refers to traditional gender differences among members of a particular culture.

Meaningful dimensions of cultural variability provide a useful means of predicting and interpreting cultural differences. Helpers are particularly interested in how cultural dimensions affect behavior and how cultural domains can provide helpers with a better understanding of culturally different values, opinions, norms, and behaviors. Not surprisingly, the IC dimension has received the greatest attention. Hofstede's (1984) study of employees in international corporations in 50 countries is often quoted. The countries in which people were more individualistic were the United States, Australia, and Great Britain; workers in Venezuela, Colombia, and Pakistan were the most collectivistic. One of the important conclusions involving cultural differences on the IC dimension suggests that collectivistic cultures depend heavily on the effective functioning of groups and are more committed to groups than are individuals from individualistic cultures. These findings illustrate important differences in the perceptions of relationships and in social behavior in general. Triandis (1995) has done considerable work on developing measures of IC to determine an individual's IC tendencies. Researchers are looking at measures of IC as a cultural syndrome that involves beliefs, attitudes, values, and behaviors (Hui, 1988; Matsumoto, Weissman, Preston, Brown, & Kupperbusch; 1997; Triandis, McCusker, & Hui, 1990). Items that have been used as measures of general values are obedience to authority, social responsibility, sacrifice, and loyalty. Each individual's general values are measured by the degree of importance for four social groups (family, friends, colleagues, and strangers) on an assessment instrument entitled the Collectivism Interpersonal Assessment Inventory (Matsumoto et al., 1997).

Helpers should quickly recognize the importance of assessment results that will help uncover the unique values of each client, especially culturally diverse clients. As with all assessment instruments, the results should be conceived as estimates of what is being measured, in this case general tendencies that shape thinking and behavior. The results of such inventories should be used with other data in the helping process. Thus, measures of values should be viewed not as absolutes but as important information that can be used.

Social behavior is influenced by culture in numerous ways. Two methods used to understand self–other relationships have been studied by the use of self–ingroup and self–outgroup classifications. The self–ingroup consists of individuals that one feels close to, is familiar with, and trusts; there are common bonds and friendships. The self–outgroup is just the opposite: It consists of people with whom one is less familiar, and there is little in the way of common bonds. These distinctions are considered dichotomous even though relationships are very complex and that different degrees of familiarity and closeness can exist; therefore, these two classifications are useful, but they do not account for all variables in social relationships. The important point here, however, is that there are distinct differences in self–ingroup and self–outgroup relationships between individualistic and collectivistic cultural groups. In the United States, people can belong to many ingroups, such as music groups, social groups, and sports groups; people are a part of multiple ingroups for periods of time. In other cultures there tend to be fewer ingroups; thus, group members tend to form stronger degrees of commitment to groups, and the groups become an integral part of their identity. Groups become especially important in collectivistic cultures, and a high degree of importance is attached to group membership. In collectivistic cultures, individuals adhere and conform more to group norms than do individuals in individualistic cultures (Matsumoto & Juang, 2004; Triandis, Bontempo, Villareal, Asai, & Lucca, 1988).

Even though the classification system of self–ingroups and self–outgroups has limitations, helpers can grasp a better understanding of how culture can influence behavior in social contexts by using these classifications. As Triandis et al. (1988) pointed out, people in collectivistic cultures have been socialized to believe that survival is clearly dependent on the functioning of groups rather than individuals. The maintenance of harmony and cohesion is of utmost importance, and in collectivistic cultures there is a strong attachment and identity with one's ingroup. In individualistic cultures people tend to make fewer sacrifices of their goals and desires for the sake of harmony (Matsumoto & Juang, 2004). Such differences of thinking found in IC do indeed suggest that worldviews are best understood in their cultural context. Culturally developed attitudes, beliefs, and values that are crystallized into what are referred to as *cognitive schemas* color one's interpretation of life events and experiences.

_____ Culturally Developed Cognitive Schemas

Cognitive schemas are a relevant part of development that begins in early childhood and can change and/or crystallize over the life span. It is a part of the socialization process that is discussed further in Chapter 4. It should be mentioned that the term *enculturation* is also used to identify experiences that encourage children and adolescents to become respected members of a specific culture (Brislin, 2000). The socialization process is greatly influenced by several factors, including class, socioeconomic status, race, gender, and ethnicity. Six theories of socialization, described in Table 8.1, include (1) psychoanalytic (the unconsciousness mind shapes human behavior), (2) object relations (childhood experiences in social relation determine development), (3) social learning (the social context of socialization is emphasized), (4) symbolic interaction (meanings we attribute to social interactions are most influential), (5) functionalism, and (6) conflict theory (power relationships influence social identity; Andersen & Taylor, 2006). Each theory in Table 8.1 is further explained by individual learning processes, the formation of self, and the influence of society. What is so very powerful about the socialization process is that it creates expectations that influence individual attitudes and behaviors and the way different groups are valued and value themselves. People can also experience significant changes in their expectations and beliefs through what is referred to as a *resocialization process* when they adhere to radically altered or replaced social roles (Andersen & Taylor, 2006). Individuals can and do change their beliefs and attitudes.

Table 8.1   Theories of Socialization

How each theory views:	Individual Learning Process	Formation of Self	Influence of Society
Psychoanalytic Theory	The unconscious mind shapes behavior.	Self (ego) emerges from tension between the id and the superego.	Societal expectations are represented by the superego.
Object Relations Theory	Infants identify with the same-sex parent.	The self emerges through separating oneself from the primary caretaker.	A division of labor in the family shapes identity formation.
Social Learning Theory	People respond to social stimuli in their environment.	Identity is created through reinforcement and encouragement.	Young children learn the logical principles that shape the external world.
Symbolic Interaction Theory	Children learn through taking the role of significant others.	Identity emerges as the creative self interacts with the social expectations of others.	Expectations of others form the social context for learning social roles.
Functionalism	Social roles are learned in the family.	People internalize social expectations; thus, the self contributes to the stability of society.	Socialization occurs in social institutions that function to maintain social order.
Conflict Theory	Individuals learn social identities in the context of power relationships.	People's identities and selves reflect the race, class, and gender relations in society, along with other social influences.	The self reflects the needs and interests of the powerful groups in society, although people can also resist these influences.

SOURCE: From *Sociology, Understanding a Diverse Society* (with InfoTrac®) 4th edition by ANDERSON/TAYLOR .2006. Reprinted with permission of Wadsworth, a division of Thomson Learning: www.thomsonrights.com. FAX 800 730-2215.

An important point to be made here is that cognitive development is indeed a social process in which members of each culture provide certain mental tools of thought. Guided learning provided by parents or important others, for instance, shapes the nature of one's thinking process; thus, cognitive development is not solely universal (Sigelman & Rider, 2003). What we have here is the suggestion that culture and social experiences affect *how* we think, not just *what* we think. According to Frawley (1997), children acquire their society's mental tools by interacting with parents, other members of their culture, and by learning the language of a culture. These ideas were primarily derived from the work of Lev Vygotsky, a Russian psychologist who was born in 1896 and died at the age of 38 (Sigelman & Rider, 2003). His work was banned for political reasons but has been studied by a number of scholars (Bodrova & Leong, 1996; Frawley, 1997; Glassman, 1994). Vygotsky, along with Jean Piaget, is considered a major contributor to our understanding of cognitive development (Sigelman & Rider, 2003).

One of the ways cognitive schemas are expressed and developed is through self-talk, or what Vygotsky referred to as *private speech*. Private speech was considered to be a critical step in the development of more mature thought and the beginning of thinking in words, in which adults engage daily. Research has shown that children's private speech is a sign of cognitive maturity and can contribute to effective problem-solving performance (Berk & Landau, 1993; Chiu & Alexander, 2000). Scholars have debated the contributions of Vygotsky's sociocultural view and Piaget's cognitive developmental view over time; a comparison of their views is summarized in Table 8.2. Note that Vygotsky and Piaget share the importance of social context of development but have different views of emphasis (Sigelman & Rider, 2003). Our interest in the cultural development of cognitive schemas suggests that Vygotsky's sociocultural view of development is most instructive—adults influence development by passing on culture's tools of thinking; thus, cognitive development is not the same universally (Sigelman & Rider, 2003). These two principles provide clues to how people learn and think about their world; their important beliefs; and assumptions about people, events, and environment.

The Cultural Self and Its Career Development Implications

Self-concept, self-knowledge, and a sense of self are not strangers to career development theories and strategies or to mental health issues. One's sense of self, or *self-knowledge*, is a most important factor in the career choice process. In a much broader sense, self-concept certainly plays a major role in how one views the world and relates to others, and in one's sense of well-being. *Self* has been described as a cognitive universe (Geertz, 1975) consisting of awareness and emotions that influence interpretations of daily events and experiences. Thus, the individualistic way of thinking that is dominant in American culture has meaning and relevance to one's career choice and development. Likewise, a sense of self that is shaped by other cultural rules and traditions must be recognized as equally relevant, even though thinking and choices are based on connectedness to others and subsequent social behaviors may be different from the dominant culture. In the next paragraphs, cultural differences in self-concept are examined.

Table 8.2   A Comparison of Vygotsky and Piaget

Vygotsky's Sociocultural View	Piaget's Cognitive Developmental View
1. Cognitive development is different in different social and historical contexts.	1. Cognitive development is mostly the same universally.
2. Appropriate unit of analysis is the social, cultural, and historical context in which the individual develops.	2. Appropriate unit of analysis is the individual.
3. Cognitive growth results from social interactions (guided participation in the zone of proximal development).	3. Cognitive growth results from the child's independent explorations of the world.
4. Children and their partners "co-construct" knowledge.	4. Each child constructs knowledge on his/her own.
5. Social processes become individual psychological ones (for example, social speech becomes inner speech).	5. Individual, egocentric processes become more social (for example, egocentric speech becomes social speech).
6. Adults are especially important (because they know the culture's tools of thinking).	6. Peers are especially important (because children must learn to take peers' perspectives into account).
7. Learning precedes development (tools learned with adult help become internalized).	7. Development precedes learning (children cannot master certain things until they have the requisite cognitive structures).

SOURCE: From *Life-Span Human Development, An Integrated Topical/Chronological Approach* 4th Edition by Sigelman/ Rider. 2003. Reprinted with permission of Wadsworth, a division of Thomson Learning: www.thomsonrights.com. Fax 800 730-2215.

One of the methods that cultural differences in perceptions of self have been evaluated is through an independent versus interdependent construal of self. The *independent construal of self* fits well into an individualistic culture's way of thinking; that is, it is a sense of self that focuses on individual goals and achievement. The *interdependent construal of self* is a sense of self "that is based on the principle of fundamental connectedness among people" (Matsumoto & Juang, 2004, p. 337). The rationale in America is that one takes on tasks with a feeling of confidence that is shaped and influenced by one's self-worth and self-esteem. One focuses on individual abilities, goals, and personal attributes that are intrinsic to the self.

In non-Western societies the emphasis is on the importance and connection to others; there is a sense of interdependence of self with others. Self-worth and self-esteem become less individualized and more dependent on relevant ongoing relationships and an interdependent status with other people who have common goals. Many Asian cultures, for example, foster interdependent construals of self, which promotes harmony with others. Be aware, however, that there are variations of independent and interdependent construals of self within cultures; the degree to which one adheres to one or the other differs within cultural groups. Once again, attitudes, beliefs, norms, and customs are greatly influenced by cultural context. Culture is a major part of what makes us unique and individual beings. Culture shapes our cognitive development, self-concept, behaviors, perceptions, and feelings. Perhaps most important, culture influences core aspects of the self and in doing so influences one's worldview and lifestyle.

Interpretations of life events and experiences are formulated by automatic thoughts and reactions that are triggered from cognitive schemas developed in cultural contexts. Helpers should be alert to culturally diverse psychological processes that drive thinking (cognitive schemas) and subsequent behaviors. One must be constantly reminded that the context in which a person is reared can have tremendous influence on the development of life roles, including the work role; contextual experiences influence the development of one's worldview.

Focus on Some Different Worldviews in the Helping Process

In my brief introduction to differences between cultural groups, I provided only a few examples, but helpers must also recognize that there are numerous cultures that have developed unique traditions, rituals, and ways of thinking. Part of being an effective helper is understanding that each client's unique cultural development is a major source in determining the direction the therapeutic process will take. Several dimensions of worldviews that are of major concern for helpers are as follows: meaning of family, cooperation and competition, communication styles, and locus of control (Gelso & Fretz, 2001; Okun, Fried, & Okun, 1999). A brief discussion of these dimensions of worldviews follows.

Family Views

First, helpers should understand that many new immigrants do not have the opportunity to consider job options but are forced to take work opportunities they find for the sake of survival. In these circumstances the family members find sources of income for the welfare of the group, which may include family members living in their native country. The motivating force behind survival of family is a very strong one that reinforces a strong desire for connectedness that has been deeply embedded in each person's core beliefs. In the extended family resources are shared, emotional support is provided, and caregiving for the young members of the family is a high priority. This is not to imply that an American person influenced by individualism does not care about family but, on the contrary, is highly motivated to be successful to enhance the family's resources. The point here is that the connectedness found in collectivistic societies is a pervasive influence that carries over into other relationships in which one concentrates on group cohesion rather than individualistic-oriented behavior. The fact that a person tends to be less confrontational and more cooperative should not be misinterpreted to mean "This client is not assertive enough." A major problem for helpers is that some clients don't want to be judged as being outspoken, especially in the presence of someone they view as having high status. Some culturally diverse clients may defer to status differences that have been internalized from family interactions. Expect clients from collectivistic cultures to have a high degree of respect for parents, teachers, and other authority figures.

Competition Versus Cooperation

In collectivistic societies the extended family usually has significant influence and control over decisions concerning individual opportunities afforded to family members. Consensus of opinions about career choice, for instance, is highly sought after in families in collectivistic societies. The point here is that one does not want to stick out as a "sore thumb"—just the opposite: One seeks approval and family agreement. The Japanese have a folk saying, offered by Okun et al. (1999), that is indicative of the desire for cohesion: "The nail that sticks up gets pounded down" (p. 148). Important to learn from this quote is the message that risk taking without the approval of the family and community is greatly discouraged, whereas in the United States the rugged individualist is judged by his or her aggressiveness and individual achievement. Clients from collectivistic societies are apt to make decisions based on community approval rather than risk being shunned. In high uncertainty avoidance cultures, such as Arab and Muslim cultures, for example, conformity, safe behavior, and avoiding risks are all encouraged; this is a way of life. Some ethnic groups may indeed find it difficult to develop individual goals and behavioral changes; they may view individuals as selfish if they focus on self-determination rather than what is best for the extended family (Gelso & Fretz, 2001; Okun et al., 1999). Helpers should recognize that their clients' philosophical assumptions cannot all be based on self-determination.

Communication Styles

The communication style used with some cultural groups should be carefully chosen and in some cases should be modified or changed from traditional Western methods. Some cultural groups expect the helping process to be highly structured and solution focused; unstructured approaches that require clients to discuss personal problems could be very threatening. Helpers may want to choose more indirect forms of communicating because some clients may be averse to open discussion of personal problems and family matters (Doyle, 1998). Some cultural groups' styles of communicating with another person are also influenced by status differences and fear that they will be judged as outspoken or aggressive; the ideal of cohesion and deference to important others may be misunderstood. The point here is that client intentions can be misinterpreted. Effective communications can indeed be difficult and complicated because of different assumptions among cultural groups about what is appropriate. We have learned that people from some cultures fear being judged as outspoken; therefore, a reluctance to talk about oneself is perfectly acceptable among some cultures. One could also bring dishonor to one's family by revealing weaknesses and personal problems; helpers may view a reluctance to discuss one's personal life as distrust or even paranoia. One can also conclude that some clients may feel very threatened if a helper touts the individualistic spirit so prominent in America.

Nonverbal communication is usually thought to consist of gestures, posture, silence, emotions, eye contact, and personal appearance. Differences in nonverbal communications can be very informative and quite complicated. Some cultures, such as Native Americans, encourage silence and lack of emotion—they may conclude that a person who speaks before thinking is not to be trusted, and they may view emotional responses as a sign of weakness. Other cultural groups can become very emotional and often use gestures to communicate emphasis. The point here is that there are distinct differences between cultures in nonverbal communications and, more important, that these differences can have important meanings that may be completely different than what they generally signify in the dominant culture. The major solution to all forms of communication is knowledge of the client's specific culture and unique characteristics.

Locus of Control

In Chapter 4, locus of control was briefly introduced in a discussion of differences between social classes in relation to career constraints. Internally oriented people were compared with externally oriented people. Internally oriented individuals believe that their future is influenced by their own actions; that is, one can influence one's chances of succeeding by developing a career. Internally oriented people believe that they have a great deal of control of their future through individual efforts. On the other hand, externally oriented people believe that it is fate or luck that decides one's future almost as if it is one's destiny or the will of an almighty. Thus, one's beliefs and expectations are relevant concerning the role of helping and the helper. Is finding a career destiny or a matter of developing self-efficacy? More information on the importance of locus of control in the helping process is provided in Chapter 4.

The four dimensions discussed in this chapter—individualism versus collectivism, power distance, uncertainty avoidance, and masculinity—point out the pervasive nature of culture and subsequently its major importance as a psychological concept in the helping process. What I have emphasized in the preceding paragraphs is that culture is the key to determining attributes of and differences between clients. Clearly, we need to learn more about culture and its consequences, and this is being done: One can now find complete books on the subject of culture and professional journals that are devoted to reporting relevant studies. In my brief discussion in this section, I have reported on some differences between cultures that affect the helping process. Dimensions of culture challenge helpers to be more alert and knowledgeable about different thinking processes, behaviors, and goals of cultural groups. One must be willing to modify some counseling approaches in order to be more effective with some groups; a great amount of information has been made available so that a helper can become a culturally competent counselor. In the next section of this chapter, I focus on some mental health issues with culturally diverse individuals.

Some Mental Health Issues of Cultural Groups

This section of the chapter focuses on understanding psychopathology and the role of culture in diagnosing and treating psychological disorders. I begin with a definition of *psychological disorders* reported in part by Barlow and Durand (2005) from the *Diagnostic and Statistical Manual of Psychological Disorders* (fourth edition, revised; American Psychiatric Association, 2000): Psychological disorders are "behavioral, emotional, or cognitive dysfunctions that are unexpected in their cultural context and associated with personal distress or substantial impairment in functioning as abnormal" (p. 4). Clearly, the use of cultural contexts and their association with dysfunction suggests that mental health counselors have a cultural perspective as a most important dimension in the helping process. In fact, all helpers who work with culturally diverse populations should be aware of cultural perspectives, including culturally developed cognitive schemas that influence a person's beliefs and subsequent behavior. The decision-making process, status differentiation, views of gender relationships, family values, and success orientation, for example, are influenced by cultural contexts. A cultural perspective is most significant in clinical descriptions, causation (etiology), and the treatment and outcome of psychological disorders.

The cultural perspective in the above-mentioned definition of *psychological disorders* is very inclusive, suggesting the following: the cultural identity of the client is essential; cognitive schemas should be addressed from a culture specific perspective; cultural and psychological environments are to be assessed, including sources of stressors and impact of family and community concerns; the rapport between client and helper should be carefully scrutinized; one is to use intervention strategies that are culturally appropriate; and clients should be viewed in their social context (Castillo, 1997). The use of the term *cultural contexts* in the preceding definition is also thought to be very inclusive. One must also realize that there are distinct and vast differences as well as similar behavior patterns embedded in cultural contexts. Box 8.1 presents different behaviors that are culture specific as examples of behavior in different cultures. One does not expect that many helpers will observe the behaviors described in Box 8.1, but the behaviors described drive home the point that in some remote cultures certain behavioral patterns and beliefs have been developed within cultural contexts that may not necessarily be viewed as a psychological disorder in those cultures. Helpers must consider cultural norms, traditions, and rituals in the client's cultural context when they are clarifying the significance of observed behaviors.

Box 8.1   Running Amok With Cultural Maladies

- **Amok:** Men in Malaysia, Laos, the Philippines, and Polynesia who believe they have been insulted are sometimes known to go amok. After a period of brooding, they erupt into an outburst of violent, aggressive, or homicidal behavior randomly directed at people and objects.

- **Ataque de nervios:** Among Latinos from the Caribbean, the symptoms of an ataque de nervios (attack of nerves) include shouting, crying, trembling, aggression, threats of suicide, and seizures or fainting. Ataques de nervios frequently occur after a stressful event, such as the death of a close relative, divorce, or an accident involving a family member.

- **Ghost sickness:** Among many American Indian tribes, people who become preoccupied with death and the deceased are said to suffer from ghost sickness. The symptoms of ghost sickness include bad dreams, weakness, loss of appetite, fainting, dizziness, fear, anxiety, hallucinations, loss of consciousness, confusion, feelings of futility, and a sense of suffocation.

- **Koro:** In southern and eastern Asia, a man may experience sudden and intense anxiety that his penis (or, in females, the vulva and nipples) will recede into the body. In addition to the terror this incites, victims also believe that advanced cases of oro can cause death.

- **Locura:** Latinos in the United States and Latin America use the term locum to refer to people who suffer from chronic psychotic symptoms such as incoherence, agitation, auditory and visual hallucinations, inability to follow social rules, unpredictability, and violence.

- **Zar:** In North African and Middle Eastern societies, zar is said to occur when spirits possess an individual. Zar is marked by shouting, laughing, hitting the head against a wall, singing, or weeping. Victims may become apathetic or withdrawn, and they may refuse to eat or carry out daily tasks.

SOURCE: From *Introduction to Psychology, Gateways to Mind and Behavior* (with InfoTrac) 9th edition by Coon. 2001. Reprinted with permission of Wadsworth, a division of Thomson Learning: www.thomsonrights .com. Fax 800-730-2215.

The behaviors described in Box 8.1 are often referred to as *culture-bound syndromes*: They exist in cultural contexts and are considered to be a part of indigenous meaning systems (Castillo, 1997). We can learn from these behaviors that one's culture can influence how illness associated with psychological disorders is expressed. This important observation suggests that one may be labeled as having a particular disorder or disease because the symptoms are considered to be universal, but the expression of illness may be culture specific. It is the subjective experience of mental illness that is most relevant for building effective interventions (Castillo, 1997). The differences of expression of an illness described in Box 8.1 are quite extreme, but there could also be more subtle expressions of an illness that provide clues to unique core beliefs. Cultural beliefs influence how each of us reacts to stress levels and anxiety, for instance, and they are instrumental in determining the degree to which experiences and events impact mental health. In the next section of this chapter I briefly review some anxiety, mood, personality, schizophrenia, and somatoform disorders from a cultural perspective.

Abnormality: Universal and Culture-Specific Factors _____

In Chapters 6 through 11, some selected mental disorders are defined and discussed; a review of these chapters may be helpful before reading the rest of this chapter.

This section attempts to answer the question of whether mental health disorders meet universal standards of abnormality or whether abnormality varies across cultures. Not surprisingly, a great deal of research has attempted to answer this question. If, for example, it is proven that there are universal standards of abnormality, then helpers all over the world would use universally validated diagnostic and treatment approaches when addressing mental health disorders. If the opposite were true—that is, if abnormality varies across cultures and is culture specific—then the unique aspects of a particular culture would need to be considered in order to understand and identify behavior patterns; helpers would search for unique aspects of culture; this is known as *cultural relativism* (Matsumoto & Juang, 2004). Let us begin our search for answers to these significant questions by reviewing studies of anxiety disorders.

Anxiety Disorders _____

Most discussions of anxiety disorders point out that anxiety is very complex and pervasive in the extreme. Perhaps because anxiety is so emotionally charged it is seen across a full range of psychopathology. Anxiety may often lead to intense fear and panic accompanied by bodily symptoms of physical tension. Anxiety has been identified as a fear of the future and, as such, is often seen in mood and somatoform disorders. Anxiety has considerable overlap of symptomatology with other categories of mental disorders. This observation has been reported by a number of researchers, including Barlow and Durand (2005) and Matsumoto and Juang (2004). Thus anxiety and fear can fuel panic attacks; therefore, studies of panic disorders across cultures have also included generalized anxiety disorder, which was discussed in Chapter 7. Horwath and Weissman (1997) found similar rates of panic disorders among ethnic groups found in the United States, Canada, Puerto Rico, New Zealand, Italy, Korea, and Taiwan. These findings gives some support to the idea of universality of anxiety disorders in that fear and panic are universally observed. The argument for the other side of the coin is the observation that there are differences between cultures in the way in which a person expresses reactions to anxiety disorders. Interestingly, *somatic symptoms* of anxiety are emphasized by people who live in third world cultures (Barlow & Durand, 2005).

Castillo (1997) argued that anxiety is conceptualized as manifestations of emotional distress that are based on culturally developed cognitive schemas. Furthermore, cognitive schemas are manifested in a three-stage process: "(1) initial appraisal, (2) emotional feeling, and (3) cultural-based behavioral program" (Castillo, 1997, p. 172). Castillo suggested that the key to understanding the emotional process of all clients is to focus on the meaning that a person draws from his or her experiences and events. Meaning in this context is derived from unique aspects of a particular culture; thus, the total sociocultural context should be considered.

Barlow and Durand (2005) reported that panic disorders exist worldwide and, most important, they are expressed in a variety of ways. A study of Khmer refugees from Cambodia and Vietnam who had experienced severe panic disorders found that the respondents frequently reported dizziness and a sore neck and what was referred to as "Kyol goeu," or "wind overload" (Hinton et al., 2001). These refugees thought that faulty bodily functions were the major cause of their problems. In this case, vessels that carry blood and air in the neck and legs could be affected by stress and may rupture, causing death. When Khmer refugees experienced feelings of anxiety, they turned to bodily functions and reported feelings of faintness and neck ache (Hinton et al., 2001). This is only one example of many that support the belief that the expression of psychological disorders is influenced by cultural experiences. In sum, there is evidence from research to support the universality of abnormality as well as the finding that abnormality does vary across cultures. It appears that symptoms of anxiety as a disease are similar among cultural groups, but the expression of anxious feelings tends to be culture specific.

Mood Disorders: Depression

Depression is one of the most common mental health disorders. It takes many forms and has many causes. In the United States, more females than males are diagnosed with depression. As the reader will recall from Chapter 6, some common symptoms of depression are sadness, despondency, and feelings of hopelessness. During severe depressive episodes, some people experience very high levels of anxiety, which can lead to panic attacks. Although anxiety also plays a key role in the emotional expressions of depression, not all people who suffer from anxiety have depression (Barlow & Durand, 2005). Greenberg and Beck (1989) concluded that what one is thinking about (cognitive schemas) is usually more negative in depressed individuals. This suggests that culturally developed cognitive schemas are most relevant in diagnosing and treating depression.

The World Health Organization (1983) conducted one of the most thorough studies of depression that has been published. In Canada, India, Iran, Japan, and Switzerland, depressed patients were interviewed to discover their symptoms and subjective experiences of depression. The researchers found constant symptoms across cultures of "sadness, joylessness, anxiety, tension, lack of energy, loss of interest, loss of ability to concentrate, and ideas of insufficiency" (World Health Organization, 1983, p. 61). These symptoms appear to support the notion that the ways people experience depression are culturally constant (Marsella, Sartorius, Jablensky, & Fenton, 1985). Other studies that have compared different cultural groups have supported this conclusion (Matsumoto & Juang, 2004).

Not surprisingly, other researchers have challenged these findings. One of the arguments has focused on how cultures vary in the way they communicate emotional terminology, that is, how they express symptoms of depression. The major point here is some cultural groups simply have only a few words in their language to convey certain emotions. Klienman (1988) argued that the disease of depression may be universal but the expression of the illness of depression is culturally determined. Castillo (1997) made a valid point when he suggested that Westerners tend to use psychological terms to express emotional distress, whereas many non-Westerners tend to describe their anxiety by focusing on bodily functions. Furthermore, the experience of depression itself may not have the same meaning in non-Western societies; the subjective experience of depression may be different in some cultures. In Micronesian society, for instance, the subjective experience of depression is expressed primarily when there is the loss of a personal relationship but the emotions expressed are considered to be normal and not an illness. The subjective emotions expressed by Micronesians mourning the loss of a loved one are viewed not as internal to the individual but as a matter that can be taken care of by finding a replacement for the person being mourned (Castillo, 1997). As with anxiety disorders, there is research that supports the proposition that symptoms of depression are universal, but there also appears to be valid evidence that expression of the illness associated with depression is strongly influenced by unique culturally developed cognitive schemas.

Personality Disorders

Chapter 10's discussion of personality inventories includes reports of an impressive amount of research that supported the idea that some measured personality dimensions were found to be universal. More specifically, similar personality structures were found in German, Portuguese, Hebrew, Chinese, Korean, and Japanese people (McCrae & Costa, 1997). There is ongoing continued support for these conclusions among current researchers (Matsumoto & Juang, 2004). At the same time, there is also growing support for cultural indigenous personality development. As with other psychological factors I have discussed, the argument for culture-specific factors of personality development suggests that all personality dimensions should be a part of diagnostic and treatment considerations for personality disorders. Indigenous personality has been touted as most relevant because it has been developed in a particular culture and is rooted in culture specific experiences. Efforts to validate indigenous personality development have been intense, and in the next two paragraphs I report a few examples of research.

There appears to be no argument that culture influences the development of such psychological dimensions as values, interests, and personality. Researchers are divided, however, over whether personality characteristics and traits can be both universal and culture specific. There is research that supports both positions—universal and indigenous; in addition, there appears to be a growing interest in adopting the position that using both could be productive. According to Matsumoto and Juang (2004), there could be an agreement on this important point. They summarized it as follows:

> The fact that some aspects of personality may be organized universally, however, does not necessarily argue against the possibility that other aspects of personality may be culturally unique. . . . It may be these cultural unique aspects of personality that give personality its own special flavor in each specific cultural milieu (p. 335).

Examples of current indigenous personality descriptions that have been uncovered through research are the Korean concept of *cheong*, which refers to human affection (Choi, Kim, & Choi, 1993); the Mexican concept of *simpatica*, which refers to avoidance of conflict (Triandis, Marin, Lisansky, & Betancourt, 1984); and the Indian concept of *hishkama karma*, which refers to detachment. Matsumoto and Juang (2004) reported many other examples. These examples represent the support of indigenous personality factors that can be used to supplement universal concepts but, more important, they inform us that we must be cautious in assuming that measured universal concepts of personality traits tap the complete repertoire of personality characteristics of every client.

A good example of how indigenous personality factors are developed can be illustrated by the *Swat Pukhtun* society in northern Pakistan (Castillo, 1997). The people in this society have been reared to trust no one; almost everyone carries a gun at all times. They are highly motivated to protect their honor and personal interests, and most of them are extremely vigilant. Women are confined to their homes, because *Pukhtun* men distrust the sexual loyalty of their wives. They are constantly on guard and very suspicious of everyone. Castillo (1997) pointed out that it would not be appropriate to label someone in this society as having a paranoid personality because the symptoms of this personality pattern are consistent with behavioral norms of the *Swat Pukhtun* society. This example is instructive: Helpers should be alert when diagnosing immigrants, who could very well behave according to the norms and customs of their country of origin. Furthermore, they should keep in mind that personality development can include both universal and culture-specific dimensions.

Schizophrenia

Another of the major psychological disorders is schizophrenia, a very inclusive and complex illness that often makes diagnosis and treatment difficult. People with schizophrenia usually have extreme difficulty functioning in society. As discussed in Chapter 7, schizophrenia is generally characterized by withdrawal from social interaction; disorganization of perception, thought, and emotion; and distortions of reality. Schizophrenia is prevalent worldwide and occurs in people from diverse cultures; most racial and cultural groups have been affected (Patel & Andrade, 2003). Ongoing research has led some researchers to suggest that "genetic variants unique to certain racial groups may be contributing to the development of schizophrenia" (Glatt, Tampilic, Christie, Deyoung, & Freimer, 2004; cited in Barlow & Durand, 2005, p. 469).

The World Health Organization (1981) sponsored and supervised research on the prevalence of schizophrenia in Czechoslovakia, Denmark, England, India, the Soviet Union, Taiwan, and the United States. Interviewers were thoroughly trained for diagnosing schizophrenia to ensure reliability of results. Symptoms of schizophrenia identified across all cultures were auditory and verbal hallucinations, lack of insight, and references to the self indicating that is one is viewed as the center of attention (Matsumoto & Juang, 2004). When focusing on cultural differences, the researchers discovered that the course of the illness appeared to be easier and faster for clients in developing countries than clients in highly industrialized countries (Castillo, 1997). Other differences between cultures included lack of insight and hallucinations by Danish and Nigerian patients when compared with patients in the United States. Matsumoto and Juang (2004) suggested that these differences are probably related to values associated with insight and self-awareness that are highly touted in the United States.

Castillo (1997) made a strong case for differences between cultures in the way schizophrenia is viewed. People in the United States tend to view causation of psychotic behavior as an internal problem that may be incurable, whereas in many other cultures the cause of psychotic symptoms is thought to be external to the individual. The meaning system of many cultural groups places the causation on external forces that can be overcome; therefore, the illness is not considered to be necessarily chronic in nature. In many cultures, one believes along with the family that he or she is not responsible for the illness; thus, there is less criticism and hostility directed toward to the one who is ill. In addition, the senses of self and well-being in collectivistic societies tend to be focused on the extended family, which can provide a united and effective social support network. This may be one reason that the course of schizophrenia is significantly shorter in developing countries that value collectivism. I am not suggesting that schizophrenia does not involve internalized problems but that the course of illness may be different among cultural groups. Once again, note that there is support for both universal and culture-specific symptoms of psychological disorders. Schizophrenia is no exception.

Somatoform Disorders

Key factors involved in somatoform disorders are pathological concern with appearance and functions of the body. The focus of this class of disorders is on diagnosing and treating people with imagined illnesses, those who have a long history of excessive complaints, conflicts that are converted into physical symptoms, feigning of physical symptoms, pain due to psychological factors, and preoccupation with imagined defects in appearance. According to Nairne (2003), a true somatoform disorder involves a lengthy preoccupation with bodily symptoms that have no identifiable physical cause. As we learned earlier, anxiety is a significant factor in the development of psychological disorders, and it plays a key role in somatoform disorders. In hypochondriasis, for example, preoccupation with the fear of having a serious disease can lead to significant distress and anxiety. What appears to be a serious disease usually turns out to be a misinterpretation of bodily functions. Some researchers have concluded that the major problem with some somatoform disorders, such as hypochondriasis, is anxiety (Barlow & Durand, 2005; Castillo, 1997).

Barlow and Durand (2005) pointed out that for many years researchers agreed that the expression of somatic complaints was thought to be more common in developing countries than in non-Western countries. Now, however, more current evidence suggests that psychological stress reactions to somatoform disorders are uniform worldwide and do not vary across cultures (Kirkmayer, 2001). A most interesting point of contention concerning somatoform disorders is the belief that some cultures tended to camouflage psychological symptoms more than others by reporting physically related problems. Lee (2001) reported that Chinese psychiatrists dispute the claim of excessive camouflage among Chinese people and pointed out that the Chinese philosophy of holism endorses the coexistence of mind and body problems but does not agree with the mind–body dichotomy practiced in the United States and in other Western countries. Japanese psychiatrists supported the Chinese position and added that psychological distress expressed by complaints of bodily functions is a universal phenomenon that has culture-specific meanings (Matsumoto & Juang, 2004). In short, there was an earlier belief that somatization was driven by culture-specific factors alone, but more recent research has suggested that there is evidence to support the existence of universal symptoms associated with somatoform disorders. There is also support for culture-specific meanings of the illness and the recognition of expression modes used by different cultures (Matsumoto & Juang, 2004).

To conclude this section of the chapter, note that cultural meaning of psychological symptoms is of inestimable value in understanding the meaning and course of psychological problems. One needs to look beyond Western norms and meanings to develop necessary insight into how problems are perceived by people of different cultures. The question of what constitutes abnormal behavior has tremendous consequences. What is considered normal behavior in some cultures might be judged quite differently in Western societies. The question is not only about who is right or wrong but, more important, how culturally developed cognitive schemas can offer plausible explanations of observed behavior patterns. Cultural relativism is in essence an endorsement of unique individuals whose socialization includes sociocultural events and experiences. Each unique interpretation one makes of events and experiences involves beliefs that are derived from culture-specific contexts. How much has been acculturated from one's culture through socialization varies even within a country's dominant cultural groups (Triandis, 1995).

Summary

The study of culture can greatly contribute to the understanding of human behavior. Cognitive schemas are shaped by culture; a client's worldview may be different from the worldviews of clients from the dominant culture. Sensitivity to cultural practices can reduce misinterpretations of unusual behavior. Unique beliefs, values, attitudes, and mental health concerns of culturally diverse individuals suggest that diagnosis and interventions for psychological disorders need to be made from a universal perspective as well as culture specific.

1. Some perspectives of culture include the following:
   - Do not assume that ethnic groups are homogeneous.
   - Individual worldviews of collectivistic societies focus on the welfare of the group.

- In individualistic cultures, such as Europe and North America, more value is placed on individual accomplishment.
- Cultural dimensions include power distance, uncertainty avoidance, and masculinity.
- Countries in which more people were found to have an individualistic orientation were the United States, Australia, and Great Britain.
- Venezuela, Colombia, and Pakistan were found to be more collectivistic.
- Group relationships are more important in collectivistic cultures.
- Cognitive schemas create expectations that influence behavior.
- Culture provides certain mental tools for learning the norms of a given culture that include guided learning by parents, cultural interactions, and language.
- Cognitive development is not the same universally.

2. The cultural self and its implications include the following:
   - Self-concept, self-knowledge, and a sense of self are intertwined with career development and mental health concerns.
   - Interdependent construals of self fit well with individualistic cultures.
   - Interdependent construals of self, a collectivistic view, is a concern of fundamental connectedness among people.
   - One's worldview is shaped by contextual experiences.

3. This chapter's focus on some different worldviews included the dimensions of meaning of family, cooperation versus competition, communication style, and locus of control.

4. Abnormality is considered to include both universal and culture-specific factors. Cultural relativism includes the unique aspects of a given culture. Evaluations of symptoms of anxiety, mood, personality, schizophrenia, and somatoform disorders has provided support for the concept of universal abnormality and that abnormality also varies across cultures.

Supplementary Learning Exercises

1. Explain why the case for the individual is so important when working with culturally different clients.

2. What are the basic differences between the worldview of individualism and collectivism? How do these differences affect the perception of career choice and development and other life roles?

3. How does the cultural self influence one's perception of life roles?

4. Describe how the context in which one is reared will have significant influence on the development of life roles.

5. List some precautions that should be followed in conceptualizing needs of clients from different cultures.

9

Personality Development and Disorders and Their Effect on Career

This chapter focuses on individual differences in behavior, specifically on personality disorders that interfere with career choice and development. This chapter does not attempt to cover the very pervasive nature of personality theories and development. Some individual theories of personality are referenced throughout this chapter for readers who wish to seek more information about them. In most of the paragraphs that follow, groups of theories—for example, social–behavioristic perspectives and clusters of personality disorders—are addressed. The links among personality development, disorders, and career development and mental health are featured.

I will attempt to uncover some of "the dynamic and organized set of characteristics possessed by a person that uniquely influences his or her cognitions, motivations, and behaviors in various situations" (Ryckman, 2004, p. 4). This definition of personality suggests meaningful relationships between personality and career development over the life span. Both personality and career development are pervasive in nature; that is, they greatly influence, and are influenced by, the development of all life roles. Personal problems evolving from personality disorders can disrupt career development. On the other hand, personality traits are very influential in the career choice process and in how well workers function in certain work environments.

The study of personality is ongoing and has a long and interesting history. There have been understandable shifts in emphasis, such as a move away from a more global approach to theory development toward a current trend of more limited personality dimensions. The current emphasis on personality research procedures is more scientifically based and includes diverse populations. There is less emphasis on case studies of emotionally disturbed people and a greater emphasis on differences reflected in age, ethnicity, gender, and cultural heritage, among other variables (Schultz & Schultz, 2005). Major advances in studying personality have occurred in behavior genetics and integrative theories that evaluate relative contributions of both genetic and environmental influences (Ryckman, 2004). The interaction process involving biological, psychological, and social/cultural dimensions has increasingly become the key focus of research.

There is some agreement as well as differences in the way personality theories have been grouped or categorized. Grouping theories into categories provides a convenient way of comparing similarities and differences between groups and among individual theories within groups. The following categories reflect the historical development of personality theories as they usually begin, with psychoanalytic theory, and moving on to perspectives of trait, cognitive, humanistic–existential, social–behavioristic, and contemporary research with a focus on limited domains. Several theories may be listed under each category, with the exception of the cognitive perspective, under which there is only one listed at present. Not all of the "grand theories of personality" are obsolete, however; many are currently being actively tested by researchers (Ryckman, 2004). Each personality theory contributes to our understanding of how personalities are developed and how they influence our daily functioning.

Helpers must recognize the pervasive nature of personality development, especially the potential influence that personality disorders may have on all life roles. It is generally accepted that personality disorders begin in early childhood and are chronic in nature; that is, they continue into adulthood (Barlow & Durand, 2005). The goal of this chapter, however, is not to concentrate wholly on the different perspectives of how personality disorders are developed but to adopt more limited perspectives that are interrelated to career choice and development. To accomplish this goal, we return to the study of personality development per se to gain a fuller understanding of the common ground between personality and career development. In the next section, I discuss some personality factors in perspective: genetic, social–cognitive and learning, social relationships, personal goals, and cultural diversity issues.

Some Personality Factors in Perspective

The first perspective of personality development—inherited genetic predispositions—suggests that inherited traits exert some influence on personality development. This position has been widely accepted, but not all theorists agree on the degree of influence from inherited genetic predispositions. Influences are thought to be generated from an interaction between genetic factors and environmental experiences. Thus, the degree of influence of inherited genetic predispositions is unique for each individual. Some personality theorists, however, are perfectly clear in their beliefs that some temperaments and factors of personality dimensions are influenced by predispositions that were inherited. Examples include the dimensions of psychoticism, neuroticism, and extraversion from Eysenck's (1990) research. The three temperaments of emotionality, activity, and sociability from Buss and Plomin (1984) and Cattell's (1982) 16 personality factors are other examples. The five-factor model of personality development is also considered to be a theory of inherited predispositions, including Neuroticism, Extraversion, Openness to Experience, Agreeableness, and Conscientiousness (McCrae & Costa, 1997). Be aware that not all theorists consider inherited predispositions to be very important to the development of personality. Personality trait studies do demonstrate, however, that inherited predispositions are a vital part of an interactive process that involves a multitude of environmental factors. Both genes and environment drive human experiences, which in turn consolidate human traits; hence, personality development is thought to be a multidimensional, multifaceted process. Following this logic, personality traits uncovered by research are most effectively used as either a typology that classifies people into distinct categories or a trait perspective from which high or low evaluations are given to sets of traits. In career counseling one should use both distinct categories, such as Holland's (1992) typology and traits measured in degree as well as McCrae and Costa's (1997) five-factor model of personality (Bradley, Brief, & George, 2002). Personality traits and inventories are discussed further in later sections of this chapter and in Chapter 10.

Social Learning and Cognitive Perspectives

Most personality theorists recognize the importance of the social environment on personality development. Although some theorists place more emphasis on other factors, such as motivation and emotion, there is general agreement that environmental factors help shape personality development. Bandura's (2001) social–cognitive theory supports the position that all forms of behavior can be learned with or without reinforcement. According to Bandura, people learn through observation and vicarious reinforcement. Observing the behaviors of others, and especially the consequences of their behaviors, cognitively strengthens that behavior. In this approach to learning, the self is considered to be a set of cognitive processes that includes two important concepts: (1) self-reinforcement and (2) self-efficacy (Schultz & Schultz, 2005). Thus, Bandura's theory blends cognitive, self-regulatory, and motivational processes into a lifelong phenomenon.

Observational learning processes are key elements of Bandura's (2001) theory, as summarized in Table 9.1. The learning factor as an important aspect of personality development is also very important in career development theories. In the social–cognitive theory of personality, and in at least three career development theories, learning is considered an important force in shaping every aspect of behavior (Zunker, 2006). Learning is a most important pathway that leads to an individual's feelings of control and predictability as well as a means of moderating negative thinking. In career development, learning is used to expand an individual's perspective of potential work roles that he or she did not seriously consider in the past. In a more global perspective of personality and career development, learning is a key activity in the development of self-efficacy. Self-efficacy is important to many aspects of life and promotes positive self-regard and optimism about current and future events. Learning also plays a key role in intervention strategies that address cognitive restructuring, as discussed in Chapter 12.

Career development theories that have been built from social learning and cognitive perspectives emphasize self-knowledge as the foundation for making career decisions. One major key to the growth of self-knowledge is learning to process information from a wide variety of sources. Learning to assimilate and interpret information is a key skill in the current environment of multiple sources of career information.

Making a career choice is considered to be a problem-solving activity composed of step-by-step procedures, as discussed in Chapter 3. Learning by observation, as presented in Table 9.1, can also be used to observe models of behavior in the workplace. Although different skills are needed for absorbing career information and making observations, both contribute information that is learned to foster self-knowledge. Also learned and fostered is self-efficacy, which is primarily rooted in personal mastery experiences. What is learned and mastered through a variety of learning experiences are most important preparation activities for making career decisions

Table 9.1   Observational learning processes

Attentional processes	Developing our cognitive processes and perceptual skills so that we can pay sufficient attention to a model, and perceiving the model accurately enough, to initiate displayed behavior. Example: Staying awake during driver's education class.
Retention processes	Retaining or remembering the model's behavior so that we can imitate or repeat it at later time; for this, we use our cognitive processes to encode or form mental images and verbal descriptions of the model's behavior. Example: Taking notes on the lecture material or the video of a person driving a car.
Production processes	Translating the mental images or verbal symbolic representations of the model's behavior into our own overt behavior by physically producing the responses and receiving feedback on the accuracy of our continued practice. Example: Getting in a car with an instructor to practice shifting gears and dodging the traffic cones in the school parking lot.
Incentive and motivational processes	Perceiving that the model's behavior leads to a reward and thus expecting that our learning—and successful performance—of the same behavior will lead to similar consequences. Example: Expecting that when we have mastered driving skills, we will pass the state test and receive a driver's license.

SOURCE: From *Theories of Personality* (with InfoTracA®) 8th edition by SCHULTZ/SCHULTZ. 2005. Reprinted with permission of Wadsworth, a division of Thomson Learning: www.thomsonrights.com. Fax 800 730-2215.

over the life span. Finally, faulty career beliefs are also aggressively addressed in career counseling models that are derived from social learning and cognitive theories.

Secure Relationships

Secure relationships in early infancy with parents have been touted as most important by a number of personality theorists. Some interesting positions include the proposition that parental behaviors can influence aspects of personality such as self-efficacy, need to achieve, and optimism. In contrast, uncaring and punitive parents can stifle the development of inherited traits such as openness to experience and sociability, among others (Schultz & Schultz, 2005). The influence of family interactions on career development was the primary focus of Ann Roe's (1956) work. She emphasized that early childhood experiences play an important role in finding satisfaction in one's chosen field. Her research led her to investigate how parental styles affect need hierarchy and the relationships of those needs to later adult lifestyles. Roe hypothesized that individuals who enjoy working with people had been reared by warm and accepting parents, whereas those who avoid contact with others had been reared by cold and rejecting parents. Although this hypothesis was refuted by a number of studies, Roe maintained that the early social orientation of an individual is related to later major decisions but that other variables not accounted for in her theory are also important factors.

Gottfredson (2002), another career theorist, has studied factors that limit career choice. Her theory of circumscription and compromise explores how individuals view career choice. Her position is that career choices are made by a process of eliminating options in order to narrow the choices one has to make. In this process of elimination individuals may compromise their career goals in regard to gender type, prestige, and field of interest. If there are only a moderate number of alternatives, individuals may be required to make greater compromises. On the other hand, if there are a significant number of alternatives, personality and interests may drive the choice process. Finally, if only a small number of alternatives exist, individuals forego their interests and select a career that fits their gender type. What we have here is a choice process that may or may not exclusively include interests and personality factors. Thus, salient messages from social–environmental interactions may be a key factor in career selection. The current generally accepted position is that personality development is continuous and multidimensional and includes numerous influences over the life span. The important point is that personality can be modified in time. There is also evidence, however, that some characteristics of personality established in early childhood remain relatively stable (McCrae & Costa, 1997).

Personal Goals

A current interesting position is the use of personal goals and the study of life tasks as a unifying concept to facilitate understanding personality and career development (Cantor, Cantor, & Langston, 1989; Ryckman, 2004). Both career and personality development contain elements of goal orientation that are primarily used to organize and direct strategies to overcome obstacles faced in the environment. Life tasks and goals provide the direction and purpose that are so important to all life roles. Because we live within complex social systems, helpers should recognize the relationships between career issues and all other life roles so they can best assist clients to discover healthier ways of living. One way to accomplish this goal is to learn more about personality development.

It is interesting that work experiences, especially work that requires goal creation, development, and successful completion of tasks, are considered to be an important factor in personality development. A study was completed in New Zealand of 910 people between the ages of 18 and 26 who made significant gains in positive emotionality (well-being, social closeness, and feelings of achievement) when they successfully satisfied requirements of high-status jobs at age 26 (B. W. Roberts, Caspi, & Moffit, 2003, as cited in Schultz & Schultz, 2005). One of the logical conclusions from this research was that meeting the challenges of life tasks may have the potential of reinforcing positive individual dispositions. This provides an important perspective for enhancing one's work performance. Learning to develop realistic goals and working through the process of achieving those goals promote the development of a positive self, self-efficacy, and optimism.

Of major interest is the individual's motivation for creating and developing strategies for achieving successful completion of goals. One assumption is that goals are based on one's values and are driven by one's need to feel competent and worthwhile (Baumeister, 1989). The important point here is that people who achieve goals begin with a positive view of self that is reinforced by goal completion. Those who set vague goals and fail to complete them reinforce negative thoughts and self-defeating thinking. It is therefore most important for all clients to develop realistic goals that are reasonably within their ability to successfully complete the tasks required. Clients who experience success with real life tasks will be better prepared to take on future tasks. Therapeutic problem solving and cognitive restructuring, introduced in Chapter 7, are recommended for interventions that precede goal development.

Gender and Cultural Diversity Issues

The basic assumption of most personality theories is that all behavior is learned. Environmental experiences and unique genetic heritage influence how each person interprets life events and develops a worldview. Following this logic, cultural contextual experiences influence how each person thinks and behaves. Individuals observe models and behave accordingly. Customs and traditions are ingrained in one's thinking. In some societies, individuals learn that survival of the family is of utmost importance. Each person is expected to contribute to the group's welfare. In other societies, the focus is on the strength and independence of the individual; an individual's ability to successfully compete, be aggressive, and feel self-reliant is admired. These are examples of how thinking and behavior are shaped in different cultural environments. What is considered acceptable behavior in one cultural group may be judged just the opposite in another. Helpers should keep in mind that personality traits of different cultures must be viewed in context; for example, self-criticism may be traditionally used by some cultures as a means of self-improvement. In contrast, self-enhancement in the United States is thought to be an effective method of debunking self-defeating thinking. These examples suggest that helpers need to be aware of the origin of culture-specific traits (see Chapter 8).

Cultural influences on personality development, however, have yet to be fully addressed. There is a definite growing interest in cultural diversity issues, but there is still much to be learned. We can expect a greater recognition on the part of researchers to include people of different backgrounds in future research participant pools (Ryckman, 2004). In the meantime, helpers must be sensitive to the needs of culturally different clients and are ethically obligated to refer them if they do not have the necessary training to adequately address their clients' needs. Misunderstanding the underlying meaning of personality traits can be very harmful and hinder growth.

As discussed in Chapter 8, *individualism* and *collectivism* are concepts often used to explain cultural differences. In the individualistic cultures of Europe and North America, individual accomplishment is highly valued and often glorified. Individualists strive for self-actualization, autonomy, and independence, and they are considered to be empowered to achieve and be responsible. In collectivist cultures, such as in Africa, Asia, and Latin America, the focus is on the welfare of the group for the members' collective survival. Groups take precedence over self-interests. Sharing, cooperation, and social responsibility are emphasized. The different approaches to life roles among individuals from different cultures suggest that research findings would reveal specific as well as more global areas of differences. An interesting study involving personality factors of *self-effacement* (when one is critical of oneself for purposes of improvement) and *self-enhancement* (when one promotes oneself aggressively) supported ethnic differences: Hong Kong Chinese students scored considerably lower on variables of self-enhancement than American college students (Yik, Bond, & Paulhus, 1998, cited in Schultz & Schultz, 2005).

Other studies of Asian cultures also have revealed significantly more self-criticism and less self-enhancement than from studies that included American and Jewish individuals (Heine & Renshaw, 2002; Kurman, 2001).

These differences support the prevailing notion that social orientations in different cultures create different perspectives and worldviews. Furthermore, it is the accepted way of life in collectivist cultures to be less self-centered and to be less likely to focus on personal achievements. Thus, self-criticism is the modus operandi as the less conspicuous self assumes a role secondary to the welfare of the group. This is not meant to be a criticism but, more important, it points out that helpers must not prejudge Asian clients but put more effort in learning to know them. Finally, when comparisons are made between Western and non-Western cultures one can expect to find differences in interests, attitudes, behaviors, and values. This recognition has prompted researchers to increase their focus on cross-cultural perspectives of personality development. It is hoped that research will go beyond our own cultural perspectives.

Studies of the effects of gender on personality development have been significantly increased in the last decade. Some personality-related studies have suggested that there are significant differences between men and women. Standardized assessment results have indicated, for example, that women tend to score lower than men on measures of assertiveness. Clearly this difference can be accounted for by cultural sex role training that promotes the idea that traditional young women should not be assertive. Different rates of diagnosis based on gender suggest that women are more often treated for mood disorders, such as depression and anxiety, than men are. Also observed was that the average course of therapy is usually longer for women. Although we cannot explain these differences with any certainty, there is speculation regarding gender bias and gender stereotyping among therapists. According to Ryckman (2004), between 5% and 12% of male therapists view women as inferior and have had a detrimental effect on their self-esteem. He also made the point that most male professionals do not view women negatively and are indeed sensitive to their needs. Regardless of the reasons for differences found between men and women, they do exist in regard to personality test results, in diagnosis, and in length of treatment (Schultz & Schultz, 2005).

Another, more interesting explanation of gender differences in personality development has been developed by feminist scholars, who point out that personality theories are based on a male perspective of life. Traits associated with the idealized male role are "strong, self-reliant, powerful, determined, independent, rational, logical, unemotional, aggressive, and highly competitive—for the female—warm, dependent, deferent, passive, emotional, sensitive, caring, and nurturant" (Ryckman, 2004, p. 625).

Feminist scholars claim that females are judged by others and judge themselves by standards originating from an individualistic male-dominated society. Therefore, feminist scholars have supported models that are based on feminine values, such as relationships and nurturance, rather than on masculine values. We can expect further research on the imbalance of attention given to men over women in the study of personality development.

Personality Disorders

Personal problems that evolve from personality disorders can greatly influence an individual's career development and mental health. The ability to make optimal decisions and effectively perform in the workplace usually requires rational decision making and ongoing adjustments to work requirements and associates. A whole-person approach clearly suggests that many other life roles and tasks are marginalized by personality disorders. In this section, attention is directed to how personality disorders may interfere with social relations, the ability to assimilate and interpret information, goal creation, and perceptual distortions that influence behavior patterns that are detrimental to career and personal development. These factors are considered to be important in most areas of human functioning and are most important in the development and maintenance of a work role. Because work and other life roles are intertwined, discussions will focus on interrelationships that are relevant concerns for the helper. A greater perspective of helping in which career and personal concerns are addressed provides direction for developing intervention goals that include interrelationships between life roles. In the paragraphs that follow, discussions focus on clusters of personality disorders, behaviors, beliefs, traits, work and other life role impairments, and intervention considerations.

At present, there are 10 personality disorders listed in the current *Diagnostic and Statistical Manual of Mental Disorders* (fourth edition, text revision; American Psychiatric Association, 2000). These disorders are grouped into three categories: Cluster A, Cluster B, and Cluster C.

Cluster A Personality Disorders

Paranoid personality disorder

Schizoid personality disorder

Schizotypal personality disorder

Cluster B Personality Disorders

Antisocial personality disorder

Borderline personality disorder

Histrionic personality disorder

Narcissistic personality disorder

Cluster C Personality Disorders

Avoidant personality disorder

Dependent personality disorder

Obsessive–compulsive personality disorder

Cluster A personality disorders are referred to as the *odd* or *eccentric* disorders; Cluster B as *dramatic, emotional,* and *erratic*; and Cluster C as the *anxious* or *fearful* group (American Psychiatric Association, 2000). There is not full agreement, however, on the classification of personality disorders that are currently in use. One of the major complaints is that there should be a way of designating the *degree* of a disorder instead of the type of disorder only. The rationale behind this debate is that a person may be temporarily experiencing symptoms of a personality disorder, such as being suspicious, but are far from having a full-blown disorder, especially when compared with another individual who has experienced a number of symptoms over a period of time. Thus, the suggestion for change is to use *dimensions* instead of *categories*. It is thought that dimensions can be used to designate extreme versions of normal personality variation in degree, whereas categories can designate the ways of relating personal problems that are different from those of a psychologically healthy person (Barlow & Durand, 2005; P. T. Costa & Widiger, 1994). Furthermore, when categories are used, the person is classified as either having personality disorder or not having the disorder; there is no in-between. Even though categories are a convenient way of classifying people, there is solid agreement that personality disorders represent extremes on personality dimensions. Although changes tend to move slowly in academia, helpers should be alert to possible changes in designating personality disorders in the future. In the meantime, 10 personality disorders are briefly reviewed next.

Cluster A Personality Disorders

Table 9.2 contains three Cluster A personality disorders that are identified by typical behaviors, beliefs, and traits and how disorders could contribute to work impairment as well as other, more general work role observations. The focus of information in Table 9.2 clearly is related to how personality disorders could influence work role performance and interactions within the work environment and how they can carry over to other life roles. A paranoid individual who has serious interpersonal problems that show up in the workplace, for example, may also be suspicious, hostile, and defensive around family members, as well as members of the community. Helpers should remember that problems in one life role can often spill over into other life roles. The assumption that the interaction and interplay of work and life roles can influence an individual's feeling of well-being suggests that helpers must address all life roles.

Table 9.2   Personality Disorders and Work Role Projections

Paranoid Personality Disorder	Clients may have difficulty working with others and relating to authority figures. They are most likely to be suspicious of fellow workers and avoid group activities. They can be hostile, defensive, and reluctant to self-disclose. This behavior is accompanied by a strong need to be self-sufficient; thus, these clients prefer work environments that are highly structured and nonthreatening.
Schizoid Personality Disorder	Clients with this disorder are usually very indecisive, vague about future goals, and often aloof. They prefer solitary activities and may work well in an environment that provides social isolation. They have a tendency to not seek out close relations, because interpersonal relationships can be difficult.
Schizotypal Personality Disorder	Clients with this disorder are usually very suspicious of others, have odd beliefs and appearance, and are often viewed as eccentric. They are likely to be shunned by work associates because of bizarre behavior and dress.

Paranoid Personality Disorder

As the name of this disorder implies, people with a paranoid personality disorder tend to be very mistrustful and greatly suspicious of others, including those in the work environment. Distrust of others can be harmful in many ways, but in the workplace it is especially detrimental, especially when a person views his or her coworkers as people who are out to harm others. Ned, for example, suspects that every action by a work associate is aimed at tricking him in some way that could end up costing him his job. Under these conditions it should be quite obvious that interpersonal relationships are grossly disrupted, especially if an individual comes to the conclusion that everyone in the work environment wants her or him to fail. When one is preoccupied with this kind of thinking, job performance is more than likely threatened. One can also expect that people with a paranoid personality disorder will be suspicious of the motives of family members without justification. Recurring suspicion of both work associates and family members can be expected. The buildup of unjustified doubts promotes the interpretation of even benign remarks as having a hidden harmful meaning (American Psychiatric Association, 2000).

The descriptions of the symptoms of a paranoid personality disorder in the preceding paragraph suggest a pervasive distrust and suspicion of others that more than likely began in early childhood and has persisted into adulthood. Because of this long-standing distrust of others, people with symptoms of a chronic paranoid personality disorder will usually not seek professional help; thus, the helper's role is to provide a counseling atmosphere that is conducive to developing a sense of trust. Be aware that building rapport will be difficult, because paranoid clients have a strong belief that most people cannot be trusted. Cognitive therapy is also recommended as an intervention designed to debunk beliefs that all people are malevolent. Successful treatment of severe chronic paranoid personality disorders, however, has not been very encouraging (Barlow & Durand, 2005). Intervention goals are discussed further in the following paragraphs.

Schizoid Personality Disorder

An individual with a schizoid personality disorder is often generally described as a loner—he or she sits alone, works alone, eats alone, and prefers isolation. Such individuals are detached from social relationships. Their mood is usually described as *flattened*; that is, they show no emotional response to stimuli, and they appear to be aloof or indifferent. Furthermore, they come across as being turned inward and as rejecting the outside world. They lack emotional expressiveness and withdraw into solitary activities. They often do not even respond to praise or criticism and are unable to express emotion. Social relationships are in most cases nonexistent; there is a lack of close friends or confidants (American Psychiatric Association, 2000).

One can expect to find that individuals with symptoms of a schizoid personality disorder have poor rapport with most, if not all, work associates. One also can expect that they will choose solitary activities, if available, and they may work well in an environment that provides social isolation. Interventions may include a variety of social skills training: role playing, cognitive restructuring, identifying a social network, and learning how others think when experiencing emotions (Barlow & Durand, 2005; Beck & Freeman, 1990; Stone, 2001). Finally, helpers should recognize that there are similarities between paranoid and schizoid personality disorders; however, social deficiencies are more extreme in the latter.

Schizotypal Personality Disorder

People with a schizotypal personality disorder are observed as being odd and bizarre; that is, they have odd and bizarre ways of dressing and thinking. Linda, for example, claims that she is clairvoyant or telepathic and engages in magical thinking. In addition, she believes that everyday events are all about her, saying things like "Everybody talks about me in the cafeteria." Like the other two personality disorders in this cluster, people with a schizotypal disorder are suspicious and focus on paranoid ideation, and they have constricted affect and a lack of social relations and close friends. Thus, social and interpersonal deficits are also typical of this disorder. Interpersonal deficits can be more pronounced, however, such as when an individual wears layers of clothing even in the summertime and/or talks aloud to him- or herself (American Psychiatric Association, 2000).

It should come as no surprise to anyone that people with a schizotypal personality disorder have poor relationship skills and relate in odd ways to coworkers. People with a severe disorder might consider working alone or out of one's home as alternatives for employment. The interventions used with the other two personality disorders in this cluster can be used for schizotypal personality disorder as well, with modifications to meet specific client needs. Again, social training is most important, and emphasis should be placed on appropriate dress and interpersonal relationships. Cognitive restructuring should focus on debunking odd and bizarre ideas of reference.

Cluster A Personality Disorders in Perspective

A review of the symptoms found in Cluster A personality disorders suggests that they are indeed very pervasive in nature and have a potentially negative impact on all life roles. Helpers' focus is primarily on the interrelationships of career and personal concerns, that is, symptoms that can affect both. It seems reasonable to suggest that most of the symptoms of the Cluster A personality disorders indeed have the potential of disrupting career development as well as other major roles in life. Individuals who are overly suspicious and distrustful, for instance, will experience difficulties in the workplace as well as with other relationships. People who do not want to form friendly relationships will be denied an important source of support. Likewise, behavior patterns that are considered odd and bizarre by work associates will make it difficult for cohesive work groups to be formed. Social and interpersonal deficits associated with Cluster A personality disorders should be a major focus of intervention strategies.

Possible interventions have been mentioned for each of the Cluster A personality disorders. Reference was also made to the difficulty of helping someone who is very distrustful. People who are inclined to be suspicious of others will rarely volunteer for help. Of most importance, however, is the belief that personality disorders usually develop in early childhood and continue into adulthood; that is, they are chronic in nature. Chronic disorders are difficult to treat, and in fact the research is not encouraging: Current treatment models have not been very effective. There is also a biological component to treating personality disorders that needs to be mentioned. At present, researchers are experimenting with a number of medications that have been used with similar biological dysfunctions related to early learning and early problems with interpersonal relationships (Barlow & Durand, 2005). Helpers should be aware, however, that medications are used in conjunction with counseling.

Cluster B Personality Disorders

The four personality disorders in this cluster are antisocial, borderline, histrionic, and narcissistic. In Table 9.3 they are identified and described in terms of behaviors, beliefs, and traits. In addition, work role projections are highlighted. The diagnostic criteria for each personality are somewhat overstated for sake of clarity.

Table 9.3   Personality Disorders and Work Role Projections

Antisocial Personality Disorder	Clients with this disorder tend to behave inconsistently, especially in the work role. There is typical nonconformity to social norms, poor emotional control, and extreme aggressiveness that may result in truancy, vandalism, and stealing. Clients are likely to have significant difficulty in sustaining productive work.
Borderline Personality Disorder	Expect clients with this disorder to have a poor self-concept and difficulty with career choice, career maintenance, and establishing long-term goals. Impulsive behavior can interfere with work role functioning and other life role commitments. It is not unusual for clients with this disorder to experience significant problems with relationships, including those with work associates.
Narcissistic Personality Disorder	Clients with this disorder will likely attempt to exploit others, expect favorable treatment, and possess excessive feelings of self-importance; there is a constant search for attention. Ironically, they can excel in work role functioning because they are driven by their strong need for success and power. Be aware of the possibility of unrealistic goals and the exploitation of others.
Histrionic Personality Disorder	Clients with this disorder tend to be overly dramatic, very self-centered and impulsive, and they seek excessive attention. They are often described as being overbearing in most relationships. There appears to be a strong need to overdramatize work requirements, but ironically these people are easily influenced by others. Their strong need for reassurance often turns off work associates.

Antisocial Personality Disorder

People with antisocial personality disorder continually fail to conform to social norms and repeatedly perform aggressive acts that are grounds for arrest. "Why should I care about what happens to her? She is the one who has to take on the pain, not me!" replied Julio when he was asked if he was sorry about an assault that sent a young woman to the hospital. This is a typical response from someone who has reckless disregard for the welfare of others. People of this ilk are indifferent and tend to rationalize their way out of feeling remorse; they are typically irresponsible, impulsive, and deceitful, and they have a disregard for the safety of others (American Psychiatric Association, 2000).

To be labeled as having an antisocial personality disorder the individual must be at least be 18 years of age. It seems that one earns his or her way into this diagnosis, because there is usually a long history of delinquency and conduct disorder at younger ages. Thus, current symptoms can be traced back to early childhood. Truancy and running away from home are typical early experiences. Impulsive behavior experienced at a younger age continues with some individuals, and some can become even more deceitful, for example, using aliases to con people. Interestingly, irresponsibility in sustaining consistent work behavior and not honoring financial obligations are used as illustrations for diagnostic criteria (American Psychiatric Association, 2000; Barlow & Durand, 2005).

Recent research indicates a genetic vulnerability to antisocial behaviors. There may very well be a propensity for weak inhibition systems and an overactive reward system. Taking this into account, one has to add environmental, social, cultural, and biological factors as interacting influences that can facilitate the development of antisocial personality disorder in an individual. Because people with this disorder are often past masters of deception, they attempt to manipulate helpers. Thus there is little evidence of therapeutic success with someone who has a history of an antisocial personality disorder. Interventions therefore usually consist of training parents to spot early onset of symptoms. Antisocial personality disorders are more prevalent in men, whereas borderline personality disorders are more prevalent in women (Barlow & Durand, 2005).

Borderline Personality Disorder

Unstable is perhaps the one word that can best describe people with a borderline personality disorder. They tend to have severe mood swings, are very impulsive, and are often involved in intense relationships. Suicidal gestures and ideation are common, along with continual chronic feelings of emptiness. Another characteristic that stands out in the diagnostic criteria for borderline personality disorder is intense feelings of abandonment; people with this disorder who feel they have been abandoned often experience depression associated with feelings of emptiness (American Psychiatric Association, 2000).

A borderline personality disorder is the most common of the personality disorders (Gunderson, 2001). The beliefs, characteristics, and traits of this disorder include the following: unstable characteristics, turbulent relationships, fear of abandonment, and a lack of self-control (Barlow & Durand, 2005). After reviewing cases of people who have been suspected of having a borderline personality disorder, one should not be surprised to find that research about the effectiveness of treating this disorder is still premature; however, there has been an increase in research efforts to find answers. Interventions currently include combinations of medications, with some positive results (Wilson, 2003). Cognitive–behavioral therapy has been directed at regulating emotions and has gained some success (Gunderson & Links, 2001).

Histrionic Personality Disorder

The clinical description of an individual with a histrionic personality disorder usually begins with the inclination to exaggerate emotions in a highly dramatic fashion; that is, the person exaggerates reactions to events in a rather theatrical manner. There is a definite tendency to be self-centered and vain; people with a histrionic personality disorder are unhappy when they are not in the limelight. In addition, people with this disorder are impulsive, and they constantly seek reassurance and approval. As a result, they may call attention to themselves by being very seductive (American Psychiatric Association, 2000). What readers may recognize here is the profile of a Western stereotypical female. For this reason, it is thought that an overdiagnosis among women has occurred. Some evidence exists to support this assumption (Sprock, 2000).

Treatment for a histrionic personality disorder has focused on problematic interpersonal relationships. Satisfying needs through manipulation of others has been addressed, apparently with some success. However, like most other personality disorders, there is little in the way of research that demonstrates successful treatment (Barlow & Durand, 2005; Wilson, 2003). Helpers should make note of the consequences of these characteristic behaviors in the workplace. In the current work environment, the ability to work effectively with others is highly valued. Overly dramatic attention-seeking behavior has the potential to disrupt work performance and break down interpersonal relationships.

Narcissistic Personality Disorder

A grandiose sense of self-importance is a major characteristic of people who have a narcissistic personality disorder. They consider themselves to be ultra-special and extremely unique; thus, they require excessive admiration that is most appreciated when received from a "high-status" individual. Their view of the world includes an arrogant sense of entitlement that is reflected in a desire for favorable treatment and compliance with their expectations. They have little empathy for others and are prone to manipulating others to satisfy their own needs. Ironically, their grandiose feelings are deflated when they do not live up to their expectations, often resulting in depression. Most important to the person with a narcissistic personality disorder is to be the center of attention that will, the person hopes, reinforce his or her feelings of being very special (American Psychiatric Association, 2000).

Cognitive therapy has been used to address problems associated with a narcissistic personality disorder. One focus has been on coping strategies that address acceptance of criticism through relaxation techniques. Cognitive restructuring has focused on noticing the feelings of others and pleasurable activities that could replace the strong need for attention.

Exploiting others in the workplace to call attention to oneself has the potential of being very disruptive. Hence this kind of behavior can be detrimental to the creation of goal development as well as to the process of working together to achieve success. Extreme feelings of self-importance and the subsequent behaviors that support these feelings can destroy any sense of rapport and cohesiveness.

Cluster B Personality Disorders in Perspective

There is little doubt that people who have been diagnosed as having one of the Cluster B personality disorders will present some significant problems and concerns in the workplace. People who are irresponsible, unstable, or deceitful, for example, can disrupt an effective work environment. Turbulent relationships in the workplace can also spill over into family life. Cooperative and collaborative working relationships require a sense of respect of fellow workers that is not likely to be felt by an individual who has a history of reckless regard for others. Instead of cooperation, the person will likely turn to manipulation. Extremely self-centered individuals exploit others for personal gains and self-gratification, which can effectively destroy a cohesive working group. Workers who find themselves in a work environment with unstable and manipulative people will discover that it is difficult to establish and create personal goals as well as group goals. Under these conditions, work satisfaction is usually limited, and severe work stress can begin.

Although many studies have examined the development of Cluster B personality disorders, there is very little information on effective interventions. I noted in the discussion of Cluster B disorders that some forms of cognitive–behavioral interventions show some promise of effectiveness. Wilson (2003) reported that antidepressants and other drugs that increase serotonin levels can be used to negate the impulsive and violent behavior found in people with an antisocial personality disorder. In the case of a borderline personality disorder, drugs that increase serotonin activity can be used to lessen impairments in mood, self-image, and self-control. We can expect more research on the use of a variety of drugs for treating personality disorders, including those in Cluster B.

Cluster C Personality Disorders

Avoidant, dependent, and obsessive–compulsive personality disorders make up the Cluster C group; they are summarized in Table 9.4. Each disorder includes elements of anxiety and fearfulness. People with these disorders typically view themselves as inept and have difficulty with decision making. These characteristics are detrimental both to social interactions and to interpersonal relationships in the workplace.

Table 9.4   Personality Disorders and Work Role Projections

Avoidant Personality Disorder	Clients with this disorder are usually described as being very threatened by others and tend to avoid interpersonal contacts. They appear to be preoccupied with the threat of being criticized and subsequently rejected by others; interpersonal skills are very poor. Work role functioning is limited to environments that require minimum social contacts.
Dependent Personality Disorder	As the name implies, clients with this disorder are overly dependent, fear abandonment, and have extreme difficulty with decision making; thus, one can expect that clients of this ilk will react poorly to criticism of work performance and usually resist work responsibilities. Their need for strong support and their overdependence on work associates makes it difficult to initiate projects independently. They have a better chance of work success under close supervision.
Obsessive-Compulsive Personality Disorder	The avoidance of decision making is often associated with this personality disorder. Clients are often subject to stress because of indecisiveness and a strong need to work within highly structured and organized tasks. Clients with this disorder are preoccupied with trivial details and seek perfection to the point that task completion is constantly delayed. On the other hand, they are able to function in work roles that require highly organized activities.

Avoidant Personality Disorder

Interactions in the workplace are used as an example in diagnosing an avoidant personality disorder; for example, people who have an avoidant personality tend to avoid occupational activities that require interpersonal contact. They avoid social and work situations, especially where negative criticism is possible. They live with the fear of being rejected; they view themselves as being inept and unable to fulfill required tasks. Feelings of inadequacy inhibit people who have this personality disorder from developing close, intimate relationships and participating in social events unless they are certain they will not be subject to criticism. Extremely low self-esteem drives people with an avoidant personality disorder to be very dependent on others with whom they feel comfortable (American Psychiatric Association, 2000).

One's work role can be greatly affected by a lack of interpersonal skills and the inability to take personal risks. People who are viewed with seriously inhibited lower expectations of performance tend to appear to be quite inadequate. The fact is, they probably are unable to function effectively, especially when they view each coworker as a threat. Interestingly, problems experienced by people with an avoidant personality disorder are thought to be similar to those of people who have experienced social phobia. Helpers can use cognitive–behavioral techniques to have clients rehearse or role play their fear of interacting with others in groups (Turk, Heimberg, & Hope, 2001). Systematic desensitization has also been used to effectively reduce fear in anxiety-provoking situations (Barlow & Durand, 2005).

Dependent Personality Disorder

As the name of this disorder implies, people with a dependent personality disorder are overly dependent on others and have an excessive need to be taken care of. Advice is needed to make even insignificant decisions. A person with a dependent personality disorder has little, if any, initiative. As in avoidant personality disorders, there are feelings of inadequacy and a strong need of reassurance. People with dependent personality disorder are preoccupied with obtaining support, and one of their greatest fears is that they will be left alone to fend for themselves. Therefore, they are extremely reluctant to disagree with others for fear of losing their support (American Psychiatric Association, 2000).

In the workplace, overly dependent people generally resist taking on responsibilities. Their strong need for support and feelings of inadequacy drive them to become dependent on coworkers. They will function best in highly structured work situations that are closely supervised by a patient, understanding supervisor. Similar to people with an avoidant personality disorder, these people have poor interpersonal skills and poor reactions to criticism. However, people with a dependent personality are more concerned about losing support and someone to cling to. This kind of clinging behavior can carry over to relationships between client and helper. Helpers, in the course of encouraging independence, must also discourage a client from becoming overly dependent on them (Barlow & Durand, 2005; Wilson, 2003).

Obsessive–Compulsive Personality Disorder

Obsessive–compulsive people are preoccupied with rules and details; they want to get things done just the right way and according to established rules. Because of this preoccupation, however, tasks are usually never completed. Perfectionism interferes; overly strict standards are barriers that block task completion. On the other hand, people with this disorder are excessively devoted to work and devote little time to leisure activities. A significant problem in the work environment, however, is that the obsessive–compulsive individual does not want to delegate tasks to others unless her or his rules are strictly followed. Thus, obsessive–compulsive people are rigid and stubborn and want to control all aspects of a situation. They obviously have difficulty with interpersonal relations. Interventions used with obsessive–compulsive clients focus on fears associated with failing to do the right thing. Relaxation techniques and cognitive restructuring are used to redirect compulsive thoughts (American Psychiatric Association, 2000).

Box 9.1 illustrates some of the symptoms of Bart, an obsessive–compulsive client, in his quest for a new home. One outstanding problem Bart shares with other obsessive–compulsive clients is difficulty in discarding useless items.

Bringing things to closure is difficult for people who have an obsessive–compulsive personality disorder. Almost every action taken must meet a series of strict and rigid rules, which are often unreachable. They fear failure. Obviously, this kind of thinking and behavior would have negative consequences in the work environment. Interpersonal relationships would be difficult or nonexistent. Bart was working alone and isolated in his home for very good reasons. He was able to organize and structure his work environment as he wished, without interference or threat. His time commitment was not overly restrictive; that is, he could obsess over a task for considerable periods of time. Not all workers with an obsessive–compulsive personality disorder require the isolation that Bart needed; in fact, some are able to be productive workers, especially when their tasks require highly organized and structured assignments. Obsessive traits may actually be beneficial in some work environments.

Cluster C Personality Disorders in Perspective

Fear is one of the characteristics associated with the three Cluster C personality disorders. People who have an avoidant personality disorder fear being ridiculed and rejected. Those who have a dependent personality disorder fear

Box 9.1   Bart's New Home

Bart is a 47-year-old bookkeeper who works in his home. He has lived alone since his parents' death. He never married, because he couldn't find "just the right kind of girl." Ten years ago, he inherited a small parcel of land and immediately started planning for a new home; he claimed his current residence was simply too crowded.

Bart characterized his current residence as entirely too small. He described how he walked through narrow aisles between boxes in each room in the house. He explained that the boxes, full of "things" he had saved, were stacked halfway to the ceilings in most rooms. After inheriting the land, he began to carefully and meticulously draw up plans and sketches as to how every item was to be stored in his new house. The first storage area, in the northwest corner of Room A, for example, would contain his magazine collection. Each box was to be labeled with publication dates and major stories of interest, but he just had not gotten around to it. If an edition of a magazine were lost, he explained, a yellow-and-blue marker would indicate that on the box, and an orange-colored page would be inserted in its place in the stack. Newspapers, collected for several years, would be stored in a similar manner in Room B. Another room, which was to be one of the largest, would contain mixed items, such as an old hand-pushed lawn mower, some broken pottery he had hoped to repair, clothing and shoes, and other miscellaneous items. Currently, Bart was trying to decide which color of bricks to use as well as the type and kind of windows to install. Even after talking to several builders, he couldn't decide. Bart was no closer to building a home than he had been 10 years ago.

abandonment. Obsessive–compulsive clients fear failure of meeting strict and rigid standards. Being fearful suggests that one is also anxious; thus, the combination of fear and anxiety is thought to be a major identifying characteristic of Cluster C personality disorders.

Negative self-referent beliefs also appear to make their way through all of the Cluster C personality disorders. Poor self-esteem and self-efficacy suggest that one is inept, needs to be taken care of, and avoids being exposed to the possibility of failure. Feelings of inadequacy, sensitivity to criticism, and fear of failure also appear to be underlying influences associated with people who have a Cluster C personality disorder. Cognitive–behavioral techniques designed to debunk negative self-referent beliefs and feelings of anxiety could be among the helping interventions that improve an individual's ability to meet the requirements of a job. Desensitization, social skills training, and cognitive restructuring are also important interventions that can address some needs of individuals with Cluster C personality disorders (see Chapter 12).

_____ An Overview of Personality Disorders

People are diagnosed with a personality disorder when they present symptoms that are consistent with a particular disorder and have experienced abnormal patterns of behavior over a long period (Wilson, 2003). Most important, however, is that a true personality disorder consists of symptoms that are severe. Thus, the severity of the symptoms, and the length of time one has experienced abnormal behavior patterns, are major criteria used to distinguish between clients who present some symptoms of one or more personality disorders with no previous history of abnormal behavior. The point is that a healthy, functional individual may be somewhat dependent, suspicious of others, and/or lack self-esteem.

Helpers should also be aware that it is not uncommon for someone with a personality disorder to also experience an accompanying psychological disorder. An individual who has been diagnosed as having an antisocial personality disorder, for example, may also be experiencing a specific phobia. A study of 291 people diagnosed with a personality disorder revealed that those people may also have been experiencing symptoms of another personality disorder (Morey, 1988). The addition of a second psychological disorder suggests that there may be an overlap of different disorders, underscoring the severity of problems.

Thus far, I have introduced the kinds and consequences of personality disorders. The discussions have focused on the assumption that an individual who has been diagnosed with a personality disorder is experiencing severe reactions as described by symptoms. The degree and severity of symptoms, however, need to be determined for appropriate intervention strategies. It stands to reason, for instance, that someone who has a tendency to be suspicious of others but is able to function in a work environment is not as paranoid as someone who is dysfunctional in all life roles and has little or no contact with others.

In some cases, a personality disorder does not prohibit one from having an active lifestyle. A good example involves a person who has been diagnosed as having a obsessive–compulsive personality disorder. Although this person is not able to discard worthless items and lives in a house full of them, this does not necessarily mean that the person is not able to function effectively on a job or to create goals and complete them. Obsessive–compulsive thinking and subsequent actions may actually help some people achieve their goals (Barlow & Durand, 2005). Again, it is a case of degree and inclusiveness that in turn underscores the rationale for addressing the person as a unique individual.

It may be discouraging to some helpers to learn that follow-up studies conducted over time suggest that treatment for some personality disorders has not been effective. The future of helping, however, is encouraging. More effective techniques and procedures may emerge from combinations of interventions that address biological, psychological, and social influences as important factors in the development of behaviors. Chapter 10 focuses on dimensions of personality as measured by some selected inventories.

Summary

1. The study of personality has an extensive and interesting history. The trend today is to move away from global approaches to personality traits and toward limited dimensions. Categories of personality theories include psychoanalytic, trait, cognitive, humanistic–existential, and social–behaviorist.

2. Personality theorists generally take the position that inherited predispositions influence personality development. Both genes and environment drive human experiences, which in turn contribute to human traits. Traits are often used to describe personality dimensions.

3. One's personality is thought to have a major influence on career choice. A social learning and cognitive career development theory, for instance, takes the position that people learn by observation and vicarious reinforcement. Learning can expand an individual's perspective of potential work roles. Self-knowledge is considered to be the foundation for making career decisions, and faulty career beliefs should be aggressively addressed by learning the difference between rational and irrational thinking. Other career development beliefs suggest that a secure relationship with parents in early infancy influences not only personality development but also career choice factors. Still other career development theories suggest that social environmental interactions are key factors in one's orientation to the world and work role.

4. Personal goals and life tasks are viewed as a unifying concept of understanding personality and career development. People who experience success with real life tasks are better prepared to meet the challenges of future tasks; work experiences can contribute to personality development.

5. Gender and cultural diversity also play an important role in personality development. Cultural contextual experiences influence the way one interprets life events. People observe models and behave accordingly (Bandura, 1986). In individualistic societies, individual accomplishments are highly valued. Members of collectivist cultures focus on the welfare of the group and are less self-centered. Social orientations in different cultures create different perspectives and worldviews. One can expect to find significant differences between Western and non-Western cultures. Studies in personality development have found significant differences between men and women. Feminist scholars support the feminist values of relationships and nurturance rather than masculine values as key factors in personality development of women.

6. Ten personality disorders are grouped into three categories, labeled *Cluster A*, *Cluster B*, and *Cluster C*. Cluster A personality disorders are referred to as the *odd* or *eccentric* group: paranoid, schizoid, and schizotypal. Cluster B personality disorders are viewed as the *dramatic*, *erratic*, and *emotional* ones: antisocial, borderline, histrionic, and narcissistic. Cluster C personality disorders are thought of as the *anxious* and *fearful* group: avoidant, dependent, and obsessive–compulsive. The severity of symptoms in each personality disorder and the length of time one has experienced abnormal behavior patterns are the major criteria for identifying a true personality disorder.

Supplementary Learning Exercises

1. What is the significance of the position that some factors of personality are inherited predispositions? Describe the interactive process involved in the development of personality.

2. Give examples of how self-efficacy can influence personality development.

3. Develop a list of how Cluster A personality disorders could contribute to work impairment.

4. A sense of respect for fellow workers is thought to be imperative for a functional work environment. Which of the personality disorders (list three) would you select as offering the greatest challenge to maintaining a functional work environment?

5. Describe the advantages and disadvantages of using *categories* of personality disorders.

Assessing Personality Development Through Personality Inventories

10

The previous chapter focused on symptoms of personality disorders and the pervasive nature of their influence on a person's life. A personality disorder is a *kind* of disorder, for example, paranoid or antisocial. Readers should recall that a true personality disorder consists of severe symptoms and abnormal behavior patterns that extend over a period of time. Helpers can, however, also focus on personality factors that are derived from personality inventories. There are some distinct advantages of using personality inventories in the helping process. Informative personality profiles are straightforward and report score results by personality factors that have been established by empirical support of their validity. Each factor is identified and assigned a score that designates its location on a profile, and a brief explanation of what each score means is provided.

The opportunity to observe dimensions of personality has some distinct advantages in the helping process. Standardized personality inventories are important tools that illuminate how personality dispositions can positively and/or negatively have an impact on all life roles.

One major objective of this chapter is to demonstrate how personality factors can provide a greater understanding of how mental health and work over a lifetime are interconnected. We learned in Chapter 9 that a severe personality disorder can have a negative impact on how one behaves at home, in the community, and in the workplace. Personality factors that are derived from personality inventories, however, provide helpers with both positive and negative dispositions of personality. Personality factors such as sociability, agreeableness, trustfulness, and understanding can promote feelings of well-being that are associated with good mental health. On the other hand, personality factors such as suspicious, withdrawn, apprehensive, and fretful can negatively affect one's feelings of well-being. Personality factors are thought to be rather permanent reaction tendencies that can predict how a person will behave in a given situation (Schultz & Schultz, 2005). Using these perspectives, helpers can assist clients in taking advantage of their positive attributes and target negative dispositions that can be moderated. In this chapter, I discuss personality factors derived from the Sixteen Personality Factor Questionnaire (16PF; Cattell, Cattell, & Cattell, 1993) and the NEO Personality Inventory—Revised (NEO-PI–R), also referred to as the *Big Five Personality Inventory* (P. T. Costa & McCrae, 1992).

Personality Factors From the Sixteen Personality Factor Questionnaire

Personality factors are very often referred to as *personality traits*, that is, traits that were derived from the study of responses on personality inventories by a very complicated statistical procedure known as *factor analysis*. A good example of the use of factor analysis is the 16PF. Source traits, or primary factors, are displayed as the basic elements of personality in Table 10.1. The 16PF is now in its fifth edition and was designed for adults. There are extensions of the original version for high school children ages 12 to 18, a children's version for ages 8 through 12, and a preschool version for children ages 4 through 6 (Whiston, 2000). The meaning or interpretation of both low and high scores or somewhere in between are given for each one of the 16 factors for adults that are thought to control behavior. These 16 factors focus on normal personality; however, extreme scores could indicate the possibility of personality maladjustment (Osborn & Zunker, 2006; Ryckman, 2004; Schultz & Schultz, 2005). A brief summary for each factor is presented in Table 10.1.

Factor A: Warmth. Low scores on this factor may indicate that one is uncomfortable when involved in extensive social interactions. There is a preference for working in solitary environments that provide the opportunity to work alone, such as a mechanic, writer, or artist. High scores suggest that one welcomes interactions with people in work and in social settings. People with high scores on this factor more than likely prefer the rapport and social support they find when interacting with groups of people.

Factor B: Reasoning. This factor is thought to represent an estimate of intellectual ability. In theory, low scorers have less of an ability to solve verbal and numerical problems, whereas high scorers have a higher intellectual ability. This factor may be used as an overall estimate as to one's ability to successfully complete academically oriented training.

Factor C: Emotional Stability. Scores from this factor have many implications for work as well as for personal interactions. A temperamental person who is easily upset and very reactive may be easily frustrated in a number of given situations, especially in the work environment. Therefore, individuals

Table 10.1   Cattell's Source Traits (Factors) of Personality

Factor	Low Scorers	High Scorers
A	Reserved, aloof, detached	Outgoing, warmhearted, easygoing
B	Low in intelligence	High in intelligence
C	Low ego strength, easily upset, less emotionally stable	High ego strength, calm, emotionally stable
E	Submissive, obedient, docile, unsure, meek	Dominant, assertive, forceful
F	Serious, sober, depressed, worrying	Happy-go-lucky, enthusiastic, cheerful
G	Expedient, low in superego	Conscientious, high in superego
H	Timid, shy, aloof, restrained	Bold, adventurous
I	Tough-minded, self-reliant, demanding	Tender-minded, sensitive, dependent
L	Trusting, understanding, accepting	Suspicious, jealous, withdrawn
M	Practical, down-to-earth, concerned with detail	Imaginative, absentminded
N	Forthright, naive, unpretentious	Shrewd, worldly, insightful
0	Self-assured, secure, complacent	Apprehensive, insecure, self-reproaching
Q1	Conservative, holds traditional values, dislikes change	Radical, liberal, experimenting, embraces change
Q2	Group-dependent, prefers to join and follow others	Self-sufficient, resourceful, independent
Q3	Uncontrolled, lax, impulsive	Controlled, compulsive, exacting
Q4	Relaxed, tranquil, composed	Tense, driven, fretful

SOURCE: From *Theories of Personality* (with InfoTracA®) 8th edition by SCHULTZ/SCHULTZ. 2005. Reprinted with permission of Wadsworth, a division of Thomson Learning: www.thomsonrights.com. Fax 800 730-2215.

with low scores should be carefully monitored in any decision-making process involving job change or job selection. On the other hand, mature, stable, and unruffled people (i.e., those with high scores on this factor) are prime candidates for work that may be highly competitive and requires the ability to be productive under stressful conditions.

Factor E: Dominance. Low scores on this factor suggest that one will cooperate and agree to abide by the wishes of the majority. There is a tendency to set aside personal desires in favor of the desires of others. High scorers are, of course, just the opposite. They are very assertive and vocal about their own wishes. High scorers are probably most effective in highly competitive work environments.

Factor F: Liveliness. People who score low on this factor are usually very serious and reflective. They may lack spontaneity, however, and will approach most situations with caution and reserve. High scorers are thought to be lively, the life of the party in social situations, but extremely high scorers may be impulsive, unreliable, and immature. They are far less serious and reflective than low scorers.

Factor G: Role Consciousness. High scores on this factor are desirable when one is searching for individuals who will usually conform to cultural mores of a work environment. They have a strong need to be dutiful. Low scorers tend to be unconventional and may disregard established rules and regulations and/or customs in social and work situations. They may be judged by their peers as nonconforming.

Factor H: Social Boldness. People who score low on this factor will likely avoid being the center of attention in most social situations or in group discussions in the work environment. They will more than likely be unassertive and defer to others. An individual who initiates social contacts and boldly expresses an opinion is likely to score high on this factor. This factor is likely to distinguish between people who are bold and adventurous and those who are not.

Factor I: Sensitivity. Low scorers in this factor are characterized as being tough minded and rather unconcerned about the feelings of others; they may be completely unaware of conflicting viewpoints and opinions. Not surprisingly, people who score extremely low on this factor will more than likely have difficulty working in teams. High scorers may fit well into teamwork because they tend to be attuned to the welfare of groups. They are generally empathic and intuitive; at times, they may be overly sentimental and in the process ignore more practical goals.

Factor L: Vigilance. People who score low on this factor may be overly trusting to the point that they can be taken advantage of in any given situation; they may need to wise up! On the other hand, low scorers tend to have positive expectations that they will be treated fairly, as opposed to high scorers, who are suspicious and distrustful. People who are perceived as being sincere and trusting (low scorers) are usually more acceptable to others than someone who is viewed as suspicious and distrustful (high scorers).

Factor M: Abstractedness. People who score low on this factor tend to think more concretely and focus on specific highly structured tasks. They are practically oriented in their approach to life and work tasks. They may overlook abstract meanings of fulfilling a major task. *Creativity* and *imagination* are key terms to describe people who score high on this factor. They tend to become fully absorbed in thought to the point that they can be impractical.

Factor N: Privateness. Low scorers have no problem with talking about themselves. They are willing to freely share their life stories. They tend to be forthright and unguarded. High scorers tend to maintain their privacy and may discourage the formation of friendships by being overly guarded. People who score high on this factor tend to study the motives of others and are most tactful and diplomatic when interacting with individuals and groups.

Factor O: Apprehension. A person who is self-assured and complacent is expected to score low on this factor. Low scorers tend to be very self-confident and untroubled. They may view most life situations with confidence that they are capable of meeting the necessary challenges each situation presents. High scorers, on the other hand, tend to be self-doubting and apprehensive about what the future may hold in store for them. Because of the very negative nature of the way they interpret life events, they may have few, if any, friends.

Factor Q1: Openness to Change. People who score low on this factor are prone to upholding traditions and the familiar. They are more comfortable when they have a sense of being able to predict and control future events. They strongly resist change. High scorers tend to be very open to change and in fact encourage the change process. There is a definite feeling of wanting to challenge authority and to experiment with something viewed as new or different. Extremely high scorers may have the tendency to be preoccupied with changing the status quo.

Factor Q2: Self-Reliance. Low scorers much prefer to work in groups; they are people oriented. They have a strong need to be affiliated with a desirable organization or a particular social group. They desire to follow others. High scorers are very individualistic and consider themselves to be self-reliant. They much prefer to remain solitary in pursuing their interests. They tend to feel very resourceful, self-sufficient, and independent.

Factor Q3: Perfectionism. People who score low on this factor tend to act out with little concern for the consequences of their actions. They may be quite impulsive, uncontrolled, and undisciplined; they tolerate disorder. *Perfectionist* is the term used to describe high scorers. They tend to be very exacting and compulsive. They strive for complete control of life activities and are most comfortable in highly structured situations.

Factor Q4: Tension. Those who score low on this factor are usually laid back, relaxed, and tranquil. Extremely low scores suggest that the respondent may not be motivated to do much of anything. Jobs that require high levels of commitment and speed of response would not be a good fit for low scorers. High scorers tend to be driven and can be highly impatient. It is not uncommon for high scorers to be tense and fretful.

Global or Second-Order Factors

An overview of an individual's score results on the 16PF is provided by five major global factors, or what Cattell referred to as *second-order factors*. These factors are used to provide preliminary information about a client's responses before the 16 source traits are observed. A bipolar profile consisting of both high scores and low scores and those in between includes information about the meaning of each score. The following very brief explanation of each factor is paraphrased from Ryckman (2004):

Introversion/Extraversion: Low scorers usually enjoy solitude in both work activities and in social situations, whereas high scorers are happier when involved with groups of people at work and in social gatherings.

Low Anxiety/High Anxiety: Low scorers are not easily upset by unpleasant situations and events, whereas high scorers become perturbed very easily.

Receptivity/Tough-Mindedness: Low scorers are generally open to new ideas, people, and events, whereas high scorers stick with the familiar and prefer concrete tasks.

Accommodation/Independence: Low scorers tend to go along with the wishes of others, whereas high scorers aggressively assert themselves and want to take over.

Restraint/Self-Control: Low scorers are likely to have difficulty in controlling their actions and thus impulsively react to situations, whereas high scorers are well controlled and disciplined.

These second-order factor scores are used as a backdrop for evaluating 16PF source traits. As the name implies, global factors are broad in scope and present more general behavioral tendencies; they provide an overview of personality factors in five dimensions. Source traits in 16 dimensions provide the uniqueness of an individual's personality.

The 16PF has been used extensively in career counseling (Osborn & Zunker, 2006). A personal career development profile utilizes global factor patterns, a 16PF factor profile, response style indices, broad patterns, leadership subordinate role patterns, career activity and career field interest scores, occupational interest scores, and item responses (Walter, 2000). Client scores are compared with the personality profiles of people who are working and performing well in a variety of occupations. Clients can then evaluate occupations in which people with similar personality patterns are successfully content and comfortable. Personality appears to be linked to many aspects of career and work per se, including vocational interests, career progression, job performance, and work behavior (Tokar, Fisher, & Subich, 1998). Currently, the 16PF is primarily used to assess personality for research, clinical diagnosis, and predicting occupational success. It has been translated into 40 different languages (Schultz & Schultz, 2005).

An Integrative Perspective

It should be quite clear that one of the great advantages of using a personality inventory is the inclusive nature of data available to the helper. A second advantage is that the data are considered to be objective, especially when compared with subjective interpretations of projective assessment instruments such as the Rorschach inkblot test. Some researchers have complained, however, that in the process of labeling factors subjective interpretations are made of the meaning of each factor. Nevertheless, the 16PF underwent decades of research that included data from thousands of people. Although some people have questioned the statistical techniques Cattell used, he was honored by the American Psychological Association with the Gold Medal Award for Life Achievement in the Science of Psychology shortly before his death in 1998 (Ryckman, 2004).

The major source traits, or the primary factors, on the 16PF provide a wealth of information for identifying specific areas of personality that are well defined. The bipolar profile has the advantage of identifying the strength and meaning of low and high scores. Most important, however, the underlying position of the 16PF is that source traits can predict how each person will behave in a given situation (Schultz & Schultz, 2005). It seems clear that Cattell recognized the complexity of personality development, hence his theory for measuring personality traits was very comprehensive and inclusive. "His theory addresses a wide range of diverse phenomena, both normal and abnormal, and seeks to account for both biological and sociocultural factors" (Ryckman, 2004, p. 329).

At this point in the discussion, let us pause to review some general guidelines for selecting and effectively communicating assessment results. The use of any standardized test is established well before it is given. I now turn to a conceptual model for using assessment results involving the following four steps: (1) analyzing the needs, (2) establishing the purpose, (3) determining instruments, and (4) utilizing results.

The needs analyses can come from various sources, including the interview. Helper and client spend the time necessary to collaboratively establish significant concerns and needs. It is important to point out to the client that assessment is only one important part of the counseling process. Hence, in the next step helper and client establish the purpose of using a specific assessment instrument. The client should be made aware of how assessment results are used in conjunction with other data in the helping process. Personality inventories, for instance, are used to provide clues to individual traits that influence behavior. Determining the most appropriate instrument suggests that helpers are familiar with basic standards of test reliability and validity. The evaluation of any instrument also includes test purpose, instrument development, appropriate selection of the norm group or criterion, bias, interpretation materials, and user qualifications (Whiston, 2000). The final step, utilizing the results, should be enhanced by previous steps, and the client should be involved in the selection process. In general, clients learn to use assessment results to view themselves from a whole-person perspective. Keep in mind that communicating test results is an extremely important part of the helping process (Osborn & Zunker, 2006).

Personality inventories that are designed to measure factors of personality present results that often need further delineation. Consider, for example, a male client who has scored high on Factor M of the 16PF, indicating that he is apprehensive, self-doubting, and guilt prone, and scored low on Factor Q2, suggesting that he is group oriented, affiliative, and group dependent. These factors indicate dispositions and tendencies that need further evaluation. The astute helper will want more specific information before conceptualizing this client's concerns, even though the client's presenting problems may be related to the measured source traits. Some examples of pertinent questions are as follows:

Under what conditions do you feel most apprehensive? (With whom and where?)

Could you give me an example of when and where it is you feel less self-assured?

What kind of conditions are most upsetting to you?

Could you give me examples of when you feel comfortable at work and when you don't? (also in social situations)

Under what job conditions have you been most successful?

Severe self-doubts presented by a client may exist temporarily. Some clients, for example, may interpret the actions of others at work to be very threatening or may feel very uncertain of their ability to fulfill the requirements of a job. The point is that clients who have a predisposition toward self-doubt may react to current threatening situations that should be specifically identified. Helpers can begin their inquiry by asking their clients to identify situations and conditions that have been pleasurable and fulfilling before probing the unpleasant or threatening. When the helper has identified the situations, or the individual, or both, that are threatening to this client, then more appropriate interventions to moderate the client's apprehension can be made. Interventions for the embedded predisposition of self-doubt will likely require a combination of proven techniques and follow-up. Helpers should attempt to specify threatening situations, conditions, and people in order to address cognitive and behavioral problems. The purpose is to improve the client's mental health, that is, her or his feelings of well-being; the goal is to keep clients functional in both work and social settings. Instead of emphasizing only the relevance of past experiences, helpers should focus on the here and now in an effort to help clients reduce feelings of apprehension. Suggested intervention techniques include desensitization, role rehearsal, and cognitive restructuring, which are illustrated in Chapter 8; however, there is always the possibility that a change of job or working environment may be warranted.

Personality factors derived from questionnaires such as the 16PF provide important information for the helping process. Following the logic presented earlier, and methods employed in the case of a client who is experiencing self-doubt, helpers should fully evaluate the meaning of a score on a questionnaire that indicates, for example, that the respondent is distrustful and suspicious. How severe these feelings are, and in what circumstances they are heightened, are two relevant questions a helper must ask. The helper may find, for example, that feelings of distrust are very pervasive, that is, that the client has difficulty with personal relationships in most situations and conditions in daily life. On the other hand, helpers may find that feelings of distrust are related to an even more severe problem of a paranoid personality disorder. By exploring the underlying meanings of personality factors, helpers uncover the information necessary to determine effective intervention strategies.

Feelings of well-being, which are so important to mental health, clearly can be negatively affected by a personality disposition of suspicion and distrust. Severe suspicion and distrust can make it extremely difficult for a person to feel comfortable in any and all group activities. Preoccupation with distrustful thoughts can lead to serious stress reactivity. The potential problems evolving from a severe personality disposition of suspicion and distrust are indeed numerous, including disruptions in the family, loss of job, and violent behavior, among other serious potential problems. A whole-person perspective of mental health suggests to helpers that personality dispositions can influence cognitive and behavioral domains. Some personality predispositions are very positive ones and should be encouraging to clients, but negative thinking and subsequent behavior is indiscriminate: All life roles are affected. In the next section, I review the use of another well-known personality inventory, the NEO-PI–R.

The NEO Personality Inventory—Revised

The NEO-PI–R is also known as the *Big Five Personality Inventory*. After gathering multiple descriptors of personality, several researchers used factor analysis to develop a comprehensive five-factor model of personality structure. The publication of this research gained considerable attention from the academic community when it was proposed that personality can be described by five factors (Digman, 1990; Goldberg, 1992; McCrae & John, 1992). The original five factors were named as follows:

Factor I: Surgency or Extraversion

Factor II: Agreeableness

Factor III: Conscientiousness

Factor IV: Emotional Stability or Neuroticism

Factor V: Intellect or Openness to Experience

An impressive number of research projects have concurred with the position that only five factors are required to describe personality. There also is significant evidence to support the position that these factors are universal in that similar structures of personality factors were found among Germans, Portuguese, Hebrew, Chinese, Korean, and Japanese (McCrae & Costa, 1997). These findings also supported the position that this instrument can be used across cultures. The substantial research supporting the five-factor model of personality and its possible use with diverse populations created a growing interest in its commercial value. Additional information on cross-cultural studies of personality is presented in Chapter 12.

P. T. Costa and McCrae (1992) developed the revised version of the NEO-PI and an abridged version the NEO-Five Factor Inventory. The latest publication, NEO-4 (Costa & McCrae, 1997), is a short version of the original inventory that measures four key constructs: (1) Extraversion, (2) Openness to Experience, (3) Agreeableness, and (4) Conscientiousness. The focus in this chapter, however, is on the NEO-PI–R and the numerous research projects that present some interesting findings about the five-factor model. Personality testing used in industry for personnel selection, for example, has been significantly increased in the last decade (Muchinsky, 2003). The five-factor model of personality has received significant attention from a wide range of potential users in industry and from researchers in career counseling.

The original five factors listed earlier created some controversy concerning the name used to label them (Goldberg, 1992; Widiger, 1992). That debate continues; however, some changes in naming the original five structures of personality are used in the NEO-PI–R inventories as follows: (1) Neuroticism, (2) Extraversion, (3) Openness, (4) Agreeableness, and (5) Conscientiousness. These five factors of personality structure have encouraged considerable interest in the use of personality inventories for research, selection of employees, and career decision making and maintenance. Empirically validated personality factors have also captured the interests of helpers who work primarily with personal concerns. Thus, the five-factor personality constructs were among the most researched personality constructs in the 1990s (Whiston, 2000). In the following paragraphs, each of the five factors is briefly reviewed, with information compiled from the following sources: Muchinsky (2003), Ryckman (2004), Trull (2005), and Whiston (2000).

Neuroticism is considered to be a measure of a person's level of emotional stability versus instability. Characteristic traits associated with people who score high on this factor are anxiety, angry hostility, depression, impulsiveness, self-consciousness, and vulnerability. High scorers tend to experience negative feelings and the tendency to cope poorly with stress. Low scorers have the tendency to be less excitable, and unemotional.

Extraversion is a measure of the tendency to be sociable, assertive, active, talkative, and outgoing. Characteristics traits associated with people who score high on this factor are warmth, gregariousness, active, excitement seeking, and positive emotions. Low scorers tend to be shy, introverted, and unhappy.

Openness is a measure of one's tendency to be willing to take part in a variety of experiences. Low scorers would tend to stick with the familiar and are rather unreflective. Characteristic traits associated with high scorers are insightful, perceptive, artistic, creative, imaginative, and introspective.

Agreeableness is a measure of the disposition to be cooperative and helpful. People who score high on this factor are usually easy to get along with and desire to help others. Characteristic traits associated with this factor are trust, straightforwardness, altruism, compliance, modesty, and toughmindedness. Extremely high scorers may be subject to dependency problems. Low scorers may tend to be suspicious of others, antisocial, and manipulative.

Conscientiousness is associated with the traits of self-control and being well organized. Characteristics associated with people who score high on this factor are competence, order, dutifulness, achievement striving, self-discipline, and deliberation. High scores suggest that one has sufficient self-control. Extremely high scores suggest that one may be compulsive and a workaholic. Low scorers tend to be laid back and pursue goals in a lackadaisical manner; they could be undependable and erratic.

Some Big Five Factor Research Results

As mentioned earlier, the results of cross-cultural validation studies were impressive in that the Big Five factors and their traits appear to transcend cultural differences. The same factors were found to be common in many other cultures; however, there are differences between cultures in the relative importance of some factors. Australians, for example, consider Agreeableness and Extraversion to be the most desirable traits. In Japan, Conscientiousness is given the most importance. In Hong Kong and India, Agreeableness was most important. In Singapore, emotional stability was most important, and in Venezuela, Extraversion was most important (Schultz & Schultz, 2005).

The stability of personality factors has significant consequences for helpers. Schultz and Schultz (2005) reported an impressive list of studies on the stability of factors. P. T. Costa and McCrae (1988) found high stability in all five traits in the same participants over a 6-year period. A high degree of stability for Extraversion and Neuroticism was found for both men and women in Finland in a study of 15,000 twins ages 18 to 59 (Viken, Rose, Kaprio, & Koskenvuo, 1994). Extraversion, Agreeableness, and Conscientiousness remained stable over a 4-year period in a study that included 2,000 Americans and 789 Belgian adolescents (McCrae et al., 2002). These examples indicate that there is evidence that the Big Five factors tend to remain fairly stable over time (Schultz & Schultz, 2005).

Measures of emotional well-being were also a part of a larger study of the Big Five factors of personality structure. Extraversion appears to be related to emotional well-being, whereas Neuroticism is negatively related to it (P. T. Costa & McCrae, 1984). Thus, clients who score high on Extraversion and low on Neuroticism are likely to be predisposed to emotional stability. Extraverts, for example, tend to be more able to cope with the give and take of everyday life and find social support to be helpful when faced with stressful conditions (Amirkhan, Risinger, & Swickert, 1995). Among college students, extraverts experienced a greater number of positive events, including good grades and pay raises in later work. Students who were more predisposed to negative events (illness, weight gains, rejection from graduate schools) scored high on Neuroticism (Schultz & Schultz, 2005).

In related findings, people who scored high on Agreeableness and Conscientiousness tended to experience more emotional well-being than those who scored low on these factors (McCrae & Costa, 1991). Among 48 healthy male adults it was found that those who scored high on Neuroticism experienced more distressing daily problems that those who scored low (Suls, Green, & Hillis, 1998). The Openness factor appears to be related to a wide range of intellectual interests: People who score high on Openness may change jobs frequently and try different careers and seek variety in life experiences more so than those who score low (McCrae & Costa, 1985). A 25-year study of 194 residents in Finland who were high on Agreeableness at age 8 earned better grades and had fewer behavior problems than those who scored low on this factor. A follow-up of these student 25 years later revealed that high-Agreeable types had lower levels of depression, were less prone to alcoholism, and had greater career stability than those who scored low on Agreeableness (Laursen, Pulkkinen, & Adams, 2002). These studies and others suggest that the five factors of personality measured by the NEO-PI–R have high predictive value. As one would suspect, high- and low-level scores have higher predictive validities (Schultz & Schultz, 2005).

Ryckman (2004) reported that Agreeableness has been found to be a good predictor of adjustment and performance in schools. People who score high on the Agreeableness dimension tend to get along well with others and learn to control negative emotions. Another interesting point Ryckman made is that personality traits "might be modified by the demands of a given situation" (p. 645). An individual, for example, may not behave in an overly aggressive manner in all situations. Perhaps a person may behave aggressively when confronted by a fellow student over the use of a handball court. That same person may behave quite differently when there is a dispute in a different setting, such as a church or at a formal reception. The point is that we can better understand personality functioning by focusing on the demands of a given situation. In the next section, a case example is used to illustrate the use of NEO-PI–R scores.

Implications for Interventions From the NEO Personality Inventory—Revised Domains and Facets

In Table 10.2, five personality domains, and six facets for each domain as measured by the NEO-PI-R, are displayed. The information in this table is used to illustrate the position that the structure of one's personality consists of five major domains and is further delineated by six facets of personality for each of the five domains as discussed earlier. Be aware, however, that the NEO-PI–R profile of scores is presented by five factors rather than domains, and by six subscales rather than facets for each of the five factors. Thus, a typical profile report focuses on the Big Five factors and subscales of these factors. An individual, for example, may have a high score on the Neuroticism factor that is accompanied by a range of subscale scores from very high to average. Subscales as measured by this instrument, such as anxiety, hostility, depression, self-conscious, impulsiveness, and vulnerability, provide additional specific information regarding one's characteristics and traits that are associated with the factor of Neuroticism. Helpers should be alert to extremely high and low scores on all factors as well as subscale scores. The case of Lee is presented next as a brief example of how the NEO-PI–R can be used as a counseling instrument.

Let us begin by observing factor and subscale scores reported for the personality domains of Neuroticism and Conscientiousness. A client named Lee had score elevations on Neuroticism and all the subscale scores for this factor. The score results also indicated that Lee had scored high on the Conscientiousness factor and had elevated scores on the competence and achievement striving subscales of this factor. Lee's high Neuroticism score suggests to the helper that she is predisposed to instability and impulsiveness. Conversely, high scores on the subscales of competence and achievement striving, associated with the Conscientiousness factor, suggest that Lee may

Table 10.2   Domains and Facets of Personality Measured by the NEO Personality Inventory—Revised

Domain	Facets
Neuroticism	Anxiety, hostility, depression, self-consciousness, impulsiveness, vulnerability
Extraversion	Warmth, gregariousness, assertiveness, activity, excitement seeking, positive emotions
Openness to Experience	Fantasy, aesthetics, feelings, actions, ideas, values
Agreeableness	Trust, straightforwardness, altruism, compliance, modesty
Conscientiousness	Competence, order, dutifulness, achievement striving, self-discipline, deliberation

SOURCE: Adapted from *Clinical Psychology* (with info Trac®) 7th edition by Trull, 2005. Reprinted with permission of Wadsworth Learning, a division of Thomson Learning: www.thomsonrights,com. Fax 800 730-2215.

see herself as competent and as somewhat of a perfectionist. This pattern of scores points out the possibility of internal conflicts that could be contributing to Lee's reported feelings of indecision about the future. These tendencies can be impacted by depression, anxiety, and self-blame. People who have elevations on the Neuroticism factor can be generally prone to illness and impulsive behavior, which can be most troublesome in a work environment and in other life roles.

The helper also noticed several low scores on Extraversion and Agreeableness. Low scores on Agreeableness can be associated with antisocial and paranoid behavior; therefore, the helper would be alerted to identifying any indications of distrust of others or the tendency to be oppositional rather than cooperative. Maintaining good relationships with other workers may be difficult for Lee. In addition, low scores on most subscales of Extraversion suggested that Lee may find it difficult to build relationships. In general, one could tentatively conclude that Lee's low scores on Agreeableness and Extraversion support a concern for poor interpersonal relationships as well as poor emotional stability.

On the positive side of Lee's score report, an elevated score on the Conscientiousness factor and high scores on two subscales suggests that Lee is able to control impulses. Troubling, however, are indications of instability, as indicated by a high elevation on the Neuroticism factor. These mixed messages suggest that Lee may indeed have the self-discipline to profit from cognitive restructuring, in which negative self-defeating thoughts are debunked and self-enhancing thoughts are encouraged. It is also encouraging to observe Lee's elevated scores on the subscale achievement striving and high sores on the Openness factor. Elevated scores of achievement striving and Openness suggest that Lee's efforts to counteract negative cognitions can be successively reinforced by positive personal experiences.

In the case of Lee, examples of implications that might indicate certain predispositions or reactions to events, circumstances, and relationships are identified. A person who is considered impulsive as measured by this instrument may be viewed as erratic or unpredictable. One who has high scores on Conscientiousness, for example, may indeed be very dependable and could be somewhat of a perfectionist. A person who has elevated scores on the Openness factor should be willing to take part in a variety of experiences. All of these examples of score results from the NEO-PI–R provide meaningful information for addressing personal and career concerns. Tentative conclusions reached from the results of personality inventories, however, are to be used with other information uncovered in the intake interview as well as with other tests and inventories. Personality inventories are an important part of the counseling process when determining appropriate and effective interventions. Helpers who are interested in using the NEO-PI–R will need to complete creditable and recognized programs of professional training and supervision.

Helpers are given relevant information from personality inventories that may need further clarification. In what places and conditions do disruptive thoughts and behaviors happen most often? Situational context can give meaning to the expression of behaviors. Personality inventory scores should be considered one source of information that is to be used with other data to confirm or to question the meaning of responses on a profile. Astute helpers withhold final judgment until all data and information have been collected and reviewed. Nevertheless, personality inventory results provide a wealth of information for the counseling process. Both negative and positive results provide opportunities for in-depth discussions and further evaluation. The predictability and stability of NEO-PI–R score results have been widely researched and confirmed. There are, however, continuing suggestions from some researchers that more than five personality structures are needed to identify all personality factors. Helpers must remain alert to future research in the area of personality structures.

Personality–Outcome Relationships

In this chapter, the major focus has been on personality–outcome relationships. The discussions have primarily been concerned with how measured personality traits and facets of traits are related to career choice and development and mental health; thus, references were consistently made to how personality predispositions can affect work roles and general feelings of well-being; the whole-person approach is a priority. Current research on the stability of personality traits and their predictive validity suggests that personality traits remain stable over the life span. Stability of personality appears to be the position advocated by most of the researchers referenced in this chapter. Personality development is considered to be multidimensional, but personality types and traits are determined primarily by heredity, although researchers did not rule out the influence of the environment (Eysenck, 1990). What is suggested here, for example, is that an introverted child will likely remain introverted as an adult. The connection between genetics and personality has received increased acceptance among researchers (Schultz & Schultz, 2005).

In the meantime, there has been considerable interest in the importance of personality facets or variables of the Big Five factors of personality. The rationale is that each of the five factors is a collection of many variables that have something in common; however, each variable or subcomponent may be just as distinct as the broad factor (Paunonen & Ashton, 2001, cited in Bradley, Brief, & George, 2002). Achievement striving, for instance, may be more related to upward mobility than to the broad factor of Conscientiousness. Some facets of the Big Five factors are indeed hierarchical in nature. Thus, specific trait descriptors of personality measures would be very helpful in integrative counseling; trait factors provide information that needs more in debt specification. It is quite likely that further research of personality traits will yield more distinct factors (Bradley et al., 2002).

Finally, there is a growing interest in cognitive personality approaches as a supplement to personality traits and types. Cantor and Langston (1989) suggested that one's life tasks and personal projects are quite informative about self-perceptions involved in accomplishing tasks and how these perceptions influence behavior. Obviously, there are individual differences in the way people view life tasks and the methods they use to accomplish those tasks. Second, individuals must prioritize competing life tasks by rating their importance, enjoyment, difficulty, and control. As they pursue goals, some tasks may be hindered and others facilitated. Thus, life task selection and fulfillment provide opportunities to observe individual differences. Furthermore, the underlying motives for choosing life tasks may provide a unifying concept in understanding personality over time.

The role of organizing and directing one's life gives important meaning to how each individual creates personal goals. The cognitive process employed in selecting personal goals is thought to reflect values and motives as well as personality dispositions (Ryckman, 2004). Accurate self-knowledge, as well as planning ability, suggests emotional stability and a maturity similar to what Super (1955) labeled *career maturity*. Career decision making requires an extensive evaluation of self and the ability to project the self into work environments. This is considered to be a major personal goal. Thus, research reported earlier suggesting that vocational interests, job performance, work behavior, and career progression are related to personality variables (Tokar et al., 1998) supports the relevance of cognitive personality approaches. What one chooses for a career and other personal goals reflects unique personality dispositions as well as how one goes about fulfilling a goal. On the other hand, the selection of personal goals suggests that one is relatively free to choose, that is, there are no restraints on choice. Limitations and restraints that affect freedom of choice were discussed in Chapters 4 and 5.

Summary

This chapter focuses on the use of personality inventories in the helping process. Informative personality profiles report results by personality factors that are established by empirical support.

1. Personality factors are thought to be personal traits derived from factor analysis. The 16 Personality Factor Questionnaire (16PF) is an example of personality traits derived from factor analysis. 16PF results are given for each of the 16 factors and for 5 global factors. Personality appears to be related to vocational interests, career progression, job performance, and work behavior. The 16 source traits measured by the 16PF are thought to predict how each person will behave in a given situation. 16PF results present personality disposition and tendencies that require further delineation. General guidelines for using personality results include analyzing the needs, establishing the purpose, determining the instruments, and utilizing the results.

2. The NEO Personality Inventory—Revised (NEO-PI-R) is also known as the *Big Five Personality Inventory*. The five factors derived from factor analysis describe personality. The NEO-PI-R is a measure of Neuroticism, Extraversion, Openness, Agreeableness, and Conscientiousness. This instrument can be used across cultures. Stability of the NEO-PI-R personality factors has been validated by numerous research projects in the United States and many other countries. Measures of well-being are also supported by combinations of factor scores. Individual profiles suggest positive and negative client predispositions to emotional stability, impulse control, and interpersonal relationships.

3. Personality–outcome relationship studies have revealed some interesting conclusions. First, personality factors that affect mental health also are related to career choice, career progression, and work behavior. Also, research conducted over several decades suggests that personality traits are determined by heredity and remain stable.

Some facets or subcomponents of the Big Five factors are hierarchical in nature. Life tasks and personal goals are thought to be a unifying concept of personality. There is a growing interest in cognitive personality as an alternative to personality traits and types.

Supplementary Learning Exercises

1. List five reasons for using a personality inventory in career and personal counseling.

2. What are the advantages of a bipolar profile used in personality assessment?

3. Explain why it is most important to identify specific activities, conditions, and people that are threatening to individuals. Give examples of interrelationships that could be addressed.

4. Which of the Big Five factors of personality are related to measures of emotional well-being? How would you use these factors to predict adjustment and performance in school?

5. Defend or disagree with the following statement: An introverted child will likely remain introverted as an adult.

11

Work Stress

Work stress has been the topic of numerous research projects over several decades. The concerns surrounding work stress appear to be well founded. In 1999, for instance, it was estimated that 550 million working days were lost annually in U.S. industries because of stress-related absenteeism (Danna & Griffin, 1999). The pervasive nature of work-related stress may also be responsible for negative reactions to the workplace and/or to other employees and supervisors, and it has been known to promote poor job performance (Sulsky & Smith, 2005). In addition, health concerns such as gastrointestinal problems and cardiovascular disease have been associated with work stress, particularly shift work (G. Costa, 1996). Serious concerns over the health of the workforce have become a significant issue of the 21st century. In 1991, for example, almost 72% of workers in a national survey reported that they had experienced frequent stress-related problems (Muchinsky, 2003).

Like the previous chapter, this chapter focuses on developing an understanding of the interplay of influences that leads to symptoms of work stress. In the process of discovery helpers must recognize that many events in life can be stress related: First day in school, meeting new friends, prepping for an exam, and starting a new job are examples of stress-related events. The point here is that people face stress-related activities in almost all dimensions of their lifestyle; therefore, stress in the workplace consists of stressors that originate from multiple sources of experiences. Understanding the whole person as a member of a complex social system is a challenge for all helpers. In the pages that follow, however, the focus is on the work role, which for most individuals is a pervasive part of human existence. A person's work role is often at the center of his or her life story. It offers the individual a career identity, a way of life, friends and important associates, and a means of personal satisfaction, as well as needed financial resources. Work role problems occur at all levels of employment, including top-level managers, workers who are free agents (i.e., workers who contract with organizations), and workers who are self-employed, as well as those in blue collar jobs. A multitude of concerns, therefore, can develop from reactions to workplace stressors, including disrupted relationships, physical health problems, maladaptive behavior, and work–family conflicts.

In this chapter, work stress symptoms are addressed from an interactionist's view of the stress process. The following topics are discussed: Type A behavior, job stressors, dimensions of psychological feelings of well-being, guidelines for perspectives of mental health, work–family conflict, coping strategies to reduce effects of stress, cognitive schemas, self-enhancing thoughts, and culturally diverse issues.

The pervasive nature of the psychological symptoms or outcomes of work stress, developed by Rice (1999), are as follows:

Anxiety, tension, confusion, and irritability

Feelings of frustration, anger, and resentment

Emotional hypersensitivity and hyperactivity

Suppression of feelings, withdrawal, and depression

Reduced effectiveness in communication

Feelings of isolation and alienation

Boredom and job dissatisfaction

Mental fatigue, lower intellectual functioning, and loss of concentration

Loss of spontaneity and creativity

Lowered self-esteem

These psychological symptoms of work stress suggest to helpers that carefully selected interventions are needed for adults in the workplace who experience this stress. Also suggested is a convincing case for helpers who fuse career and personal concerns. Almost every symptom listed has the potential of being a very pervasive negative influence on all life roles and one's feelings of well-being in general. The potential interplay of personal and career concerns is illuminated by such symptoms as withdrawal, depression, lowered self-esteem, boredom, and job dissatisfaction. The major point here is that reactions to concerns associated with work stressors are expressed in both personal and work-related activities. Sets of concerns that are interrelated are a major focus of this chapter.

Several models of stress exist, and a number of definitions of stress have been developed. Therefore, when one discusses the subject of stress it is important to specify the type of stress and the model of stress being addressed. One could discuss biological stress theories, for instance, or, in another situation, one could discuss the psychological and/or the social stress theories. One should identify independent variables in discussions, for instance, biomedical versus psychosocial stimuli. Other distinctions can be made for clarity when discussing behavioral, emotive, cognitive, and physical symptoms. Work-related stress, however, is the primary focus for investigating its impact on career development and other life roles. In sum, stress is viewed as an interactive process that can affect physiological, psychological, and behavioral domains, as illustrated in the interactionist viewpoint of the stress process depicted in Figure 11.1.

_____ Stress Process From an Interactionist Viewpoint

The stress process depicted in Figure 11.1 suggests that a *stressor* is an environmental event that is perceived as threatening and is appraised by the individual through a variety of coping responses (physiological, emotional,

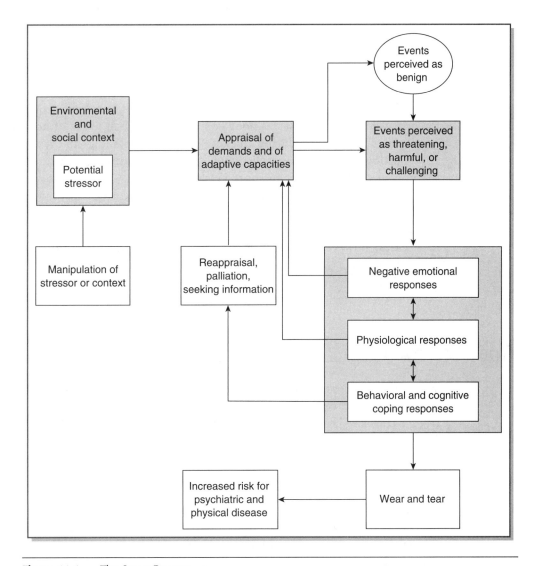

Figure 11.1   The Stress Process

SOURCE: From *Health Psychology* (with InfoTrac) 1st edition by Rice. 1998. Reprinted with permission of Wadsworth, a division of Thomson Learning: www.thomsonrights.com. Fax 800 730-2215.

cognitive, and behavioral) that lead to changes in how the stressor is perceived through re-evaluations (Rice, 1998). This schema is clearly an interactionist viewpoint that depicts stress as a dynamic process involving the total experience of the individual; the stressor is processed by several interactive coping responses. Furthermore, stressors place demands on the whole person that can lead to physiological, psychological, and behavioral outcomes (Sulsky & Smith, 2005). An individual, for instance, who learns that his job is to be outsourced could experience a significant increase in blood pressure, extreme mood changes, and begin to drink excessive amounts of alcohol. These physiological, psychological, and behavioral problems may end up being short-term problems, especially if the threat of job loss ends. On the other hand, this individual could experience long-term effects by developing a serious physical problem (gastrointestinal), depression, or maladaptive behavior. Thus, the individual's reactions to stress should be not considered one dimensional but, more important, as integrated, interactive influences that are indeed multidimensional.

In the workplace, it is important to point out that the same or similar stressors frequently occur. It is the frequency of stressors that may account for increased stress reactivity among some workers. High levels of noise or extreme temperatures during working hours, for instance, can eventually contribute to stress reactivity. On the other hand, the individual's reaction to shift work may be more gradual in nature. Adjustments that are necessary with a changed work schedule may eventually affect family members as well; for example, the stressors associated with shift work may affect relationships to the point that there is work–family conflict. In both cases, however, helpers address physiological, psychological, and social domains.

A well-known example of behavior that can lead to severe stress is known as *Type A behavior.*

Type A Behavior

We cannot overlook the profiles of some individuals that closely resemble clusters of Type A behavior, which is known to put a person at considerable risk for coronary heart disease. Such an individual is described in Box 11.1. The well-known Type A behavior pattern has long been associated with cardiovascular concerns among individuals overcommitted to work. Type A individuals have an intense drive to achieve and develop feelings of guilt when relaxing; they tend to be impatient, competitive, and restless, and they are overly involved in multiple functions. Type B persons are just the opposite. Interestingly, the Type A behavior pattern is widely accepted in the hard-driving, goal-oriented culture of the United States (Barlow & Durand, 2005).

The lesson here is that a worker's core beliefs influence behavior patterns at work and in other life roles. A typical Type A individual can be described

> ## Box 11.1 Rapid Roger
>
> Roger is a successful business executive who owns and operates his own company. He is known as a highly effective salesperson with a lot of energy, and he covers a vast territory. He seems to never take a break; even after a very successful sale, he catches the next plane in pursuit of yet another conquest. Typically, he moves in, talks fast, is very convincing, and just as quickly is on his way to another meeting. Roger is usually viewed by his peers as being preoccupied and always in a hurry. He is described as someone who seems to have a very urgent mission, is always focused on getting ahead, doesn't have time for small talk, and is very impatient. This is how Roger got his nickname, "Rapid Roger."
>
> To no one's surprise, Roger has high blood pressure and has been taking medications to lower it for several years. His doctor has reminded him that his father had died of a heart attack and that he should exercise, lose weight, and slow down. Roger sees things differently. He ignores good health practices and continues to smoke more than a package of cigarettes a day. Roger spends very little time with his family and even skips vacations. He often works on sale proposals at home. His social life is practically nonexistent. He usually has lunch alone and, while eating, makes phone calls, reads memos, and writes proposals. He is not liked by his business associates, and his employees find him to be very demanding, distant, overbearing, sometimes hostile, and supercritical.

as achievement oriented, hard working, and reluctant to ask for help. As a Type A individual's coping methods falter, he or she may experience muscle pain and/or headaches, mood swings, and an overly aggressive lifestyle that turns off work associates and family members. Type A behavior frequently triggers stress or illness that can be debilitating; the individual may be unable to function in a job (Sharpe, 1997).

The generally accepted position of health psychology is that psychological and social factors influence biology. Another way of stating this is that psychological and behavioral factors are major contributors to illness and even death. The significance of this position points out the relevant issues surrounding the study of work stress. There appears to be valid evidence that stress, anxiety, and depression can weaken the immune system and thus compromise the nervous system, leading to severe illness as well as maladaptive behavior. It is most important to understand that no one influence—biological, behavioral, cognitive, emotional, or social—occurs in isolation (Barlow & Durand, 2005). The essence of this statement is that both normal and abnormal behavior are the product of interaction among psychological, biological, and social influences. Some stressors, such as the job stressors described in the next section, are more specific in nature.

Job Stressors

Job stress has been defined by several experts who have studied its potential harm to individual workers, the employer, and the worker's family. Most of the definitions suggest that there are dimensions of job stress that lower a worker's performance and disrupt normal operations in the workplace and, in the process, increase the worker's physical health problems, psychological distress, and behavioral problems. Thus, specific job features can pose a threat to the worker. Edwards (1992) suggested that job stress involves interactions of work conditions with worker traits that change normal psychological and/or physiological functions. The distinction between *work stress* and *job stress* is simply that job stress involves features of a job that exceed the worker's coping ability, whereas work stress is a broader concept that includes, for instance, the worker's core beliefs about work per se. In other words, stress related to job conditions can be one factor among others that leads to work stress.

Major job stressors are reported by contributing factors and possible consequences in Table 11.1. Helpers are given a substantial overview of potential contributing factors that can affect a worker's feelings of well-being as well as his or her general health, job satisfaction, and fit. The sources of stress as outlined in Table 11.1 suggest windows of opportunity to help clients identify specific areas of concern, such as work overload, technostress, role ambiguity, under- and overpromotion, spillover, and electronic performance monitoring (EPM; Rice, 1999; Sulsky & Smith, 2005).

Work Overload

Several types of work overload can be found among professionals or white collar employees as well as assembly plant line workers. Although stress across levels of the workforce may be derived from different sources, the reaction to work overload also has broader consequences. Work overload is viewed as a compromise between quantity and quality of performance. Teachers, social workers, and health care workers, for example, typically describe their work demands as excessive. Responses by the individual worker to the work role, such as reactions to work overload, are key factors in developing interventions. Keep in mind that in all cases there are interacting influences.

Role Ambiguity

Role ambiguity occurs when workers are not certain as to what management expects them to accomplish. Workers can also experience conflicting demands, especially in large organizations. There is some evidence from results of research to suggest that women experience more role ambiguity than men do (French, Capland, & Van Harrison, 1982). Role ambiguity especially affects job performance; for example, high levels of anxiety and tension can result in the desire to change jobs.

Table 11.1   Summary of major job stressors

Job Stressors	Contributing Factors	Possible Consequences
Job conditions	Quantitative work overload Qualitative work overload Assembly-line hysteria People decisions Physical dangers Shift work Technostress	Physical and/or mental fatigue job burnout Increased irritability and tension
Role stress	Role ambiguity Sex bias and sex-role stereotypes Sexual harassment	Increased anxiety and tension Lowered job performance
Interpersonal factors	Poor work and social support systems Political rivalry, jealousy, or anger Lack of management concern for worker	Increased tension Elevated blood pressure Job dissatisfaction
Career development	Underpromotion Overpromotion Job security Frustrated ambitions	Lowered productivity Loss of self-esteem Increased irritability and anger Job dissatisfaction
Organizational structure	Rigid and impersonal structure Political battles Inadequate supervision or training Nonparticipative decision making	Lowered motivation and productivity Job dissatisfaction
Home-work interface	Spillover Lack of support from spouse Marital conflict Dual-career stress	Increased mental conflict and fatigue Lowered motivation and productivity Increased marital conflict

SOURCE: From Rice, P. L. (1999). *Stress and Health* (3rd ed.), p. 199, Copyright 1999 Brooks/Cole, a division of Thomson Learning, Inc. Reprinted with permission of the author.

Technostress

Technostress, as the name implies, involves changing technology in the workplace, that is, stress that is the result of technological advances and changes that require workers to learn new skills. There is no doubt that changes in work procedures can be threatening to workers who have been comfortable with work procedures that they have mastered as a result of several years of experience. The requirement that one must learn a new skill to keep his or her job can lower self-esteem and increase feelings of job insecurity and, subsequently, diminish feelings of well-being. Individual responses to technostress are keys to determining appropriate interventions.

Under- and Overpromotion

Underpromotion is most difficult for many workers, who may feel that their abilities are not appreciated by supervisors. They may perceive their work environment as having little in the way of prospects for promotion to a higher level job. The feeling that one is being passed over or not noticed has a devastating effect on one's work role. Overpromotion, on the other hand, suggests that a person is not capable of fulfilling the job requirements of the position to which he or she was promoted. This perception on the part of the worker is also devastating to one's work role. In both cases, loss of self-esteem, lowered productivity, and increased job dissatisfaction are probable.

Spillover

According to Zedeck (1992), the *spillover model* asserts that there is similarity between what occurs in the work environment and what occurs in the family environment. This definition is in agreement with Super's (1980) concept of *life roles*, that is, events and experiences in one life role can affect other life roles. Work–family conflict is a good example of how difficulties in one life role are likely to lead to difficulties in another. There appears to be general agreement that when workers experience positive relationships at work it usually enhances family life; that is, there is a spillover effect.

Electronic Performance Monitoring

A recent innovation in contemporary workplaces is EPM. Management can use EPM to access computer terminals throughout the workplace to check the accuracy and pace of employees while they are working online. Clerical workers who perform repetitive office work have been the main targets of monitoring; however, there are indications that other employees (i.e., those in the upper echelons) are also being monitored. It should not be surprising to learn that a growing amount of data indicate that EPM is associated with stress at work (Sulsky & Smith, 2005).

The solution to EPM and stress in the workplace is currently being debated. Some people have suggested that such monitoring creates adversarial worker–management relationships. EPM systems, however, are on the increase. Organizations use data found from EPM studies to structure and integrate new and emerging technology. It appears that as more systems are being introduced researchers will be in a better position to evaluate how they affect employee attitudes and stress (Sulsky & Smith, 2005). Next, I briefly review the potential of stressors in specific occupations.

_____ Work Stressors in Specific Occupations

Sources of work stress also evolve from specific occupations and physical work environments. Some occupations that are known to be very stressful include the following:

Police and firefighters

Social workers and teachers

Health care workers

Air traffic controllers

Office and managerial workers

There are, of course, many other occupations that are associated with stressful work conditions; however, the preceding list of specific jobs provides examples of jobs that require work quantity or overload accompanied by high levels of quality. The qualitative overload of work typically is reported by managers, but other workers experience stress daily. Police and firefighters, for instance, are called on to make life-saving decisions. Teachers and social workers make responsible decisions that are most important for the future of children. These examples point out the relationship between quantitative and qualitative overload found in some work roles.

Examples of work stressors found in the physical work environments include noise, temperature, lighting, assembly line work, physical danger (e.g., bridge worker), hazardous work (e.g., chemical plants), and sweatshops that are very crowded. Methods of production and construction have been a part of the workplace for several decades. A growing and increasingly technological sophistication has created constant changes in the physical work environment. Thus, there are sources of stress that evolve from the nature of some jobs and interact with sources of stressors that are found in the physical work environment. Finally, stress in the workplace can come from numerous sources and affect individuals in different ways. Hence, stress is believed to be primarily responsible for some physical illnesses suffered by workers as well as major concerns involving one's career and personal life. The next paragraphs focus on workers' feelings of well-being and mental health.

Dimensions of Psychological
Well-Being and Good Mental Health

In the previous paragraphs, discussions of work and job stress have primarily dealt with sources of stress from one's work and work environment. Attention is now focused on how work stressors can affect feelings of well-being. One way to answer this question is to review determinants in the work environment that enhance a worker's feelings of well-being. It is important to keep in mind that the way workers interpret events and situations in the work environment is also a major determinant of one's feelings of well-being and fit. At this time, nine determinants that contribute to an individual worker's well-being in the work environment are presented in an abridged format (Warr, 1987):

1. *Opportunity for control.* Work environments that promote opportunities for control enhance mental health and feelings of well-being. This logical conclusion suggests that when individuals are able to make decisions concerning their work procedures they are in a better position to predict the consequences of their actions.

2. *Opportunity for skill use.* What is promoted here is the idea that each worker is able to utilize and develop skills. The inability to make use of one's skill is very frustrating and does not provide opportunities for growth; the lack of opportunities for advancement can be a very frustrating experience.

3. *Externally generated goals.* An individual who is not challenged and encouraged in the work environment lacks the opportunity for experiencing a positive impact on mental health. Individuals should be given opportunities to successfully complete difficult tasks and experience the rewards of a job well done. Some workers, however, experience little in the way of feedback from supervisors.

4. *Environmental variety.* Work tasks that are repetitive and invariant provide little in the way of intrinsically rewarding experiences. This is a major problem for workers who hold jobs on assembly lines or in meat packing plants, as well as other jobs in which repetitive tasks are required.

5. *Environmental clarity.* Clarity of role assignments, explicit standards, and feedback about the consequences of actions are major determinants of feelings of well-being. Some beginning workers express the desire for more explicit directions from supervisors.

6. *Availability of money.* The lack of adequate pay for work creates numerous problems, including reduced opportunity for control of one's life. The ability to earn adequate levels of compensation can enhance one's self-esteem.

7. *Physical security.* This dimension refers to the need of a physically secure living environment that is reasonably permanent. The provision of adequate living quarters for oneself and/or one's family is a valuable and pervasive means of reinforcement for working.

8. *Opportunity for interpersonal contact.* Interpersonal contact provides the opportunity for social support and reduces feeling of loneliness. Goals that are achieved through interdependent efforts of several people working together provide contact needs and the potential for forming friendships.

9. *Valued social position.* A person's work is a major part of his or her life story. Role membership with an organization or with a certain job provides public evidence of personal achievement.

Environmental influences on mental health suggested by Warr can serve as a guide for workers to determine whether their current work environment is sufficient and/or what one should look for in a future work environment. A most important point for helpers is that environmental influences in the workplace are very pervasive. Work provides the opportunity to fulfill some important personal goals. Most people seek security, interpersonal contact, and a valued social position in society but, perhaps more important, they also search for opportunities to enrich their lives and enhance their feelings of well-being. Warr also provided guidelines for perspectives of mental health in the form of five major components that signify good mental health:

1. *Affective well-being.* This component signifies mood and arousal level of the individual; for example, feelings of well-being are illustrated by workers who are happy, excited, and full of energy. On the opposite end of the spectrum are those workers who present depression. Individuals can also fluctuate between being happy and sad; the highest levels of affective well-being are associated with those individuals who may be judged as happy the majority of the time.

2. *Competence.* This component has received more attention as a factor that drives some clients to change careers. In this case, however, it is used as a broader representation of competence that includes interpersonal relationships, problem solving, and other spheres of activity. Successful responses to pressure in the workplace, for example, reinforce feelings of competence.

3. *Autonomy.* A fundamental characteristic of a mentally healthy person is that he or she strives for independence and self-regulation. Autonomy is considered to be more important in Western cultures than in Eastern cultures. In Western cultures, an autonomous person is viewed as having the self-confidence to act independently.

4. *Aspiration.* The basic assumption of this component of mental health is that a person who aspires to reach new opportunities is usually

highly motivated. They have a commitment to meet new challenges head on. A person who faces stressful conditions successfully is considered to be one who engages with the environment. All these traits are considered to be related to good mental health.

5. *Integrated functioning.* This component refers to the person as a whole. A person exhibiting good mental health displays a healthy balance, harmony, and inner relatedness. Thus, one is able to deal with stress and strain at work and find time for relaxation (Muchinsky, 2003).

It should surprise no one that there appears to be a solid case that work stress can negatively affect a person's feelings of well-being (Muchinsky, 2003; Rice, 1999; Sulsky & Smith, 2005). As a result, researchers have focused on the causes of stress reactivity and its affect on job performance, motivation, and career progression as well as lifestyle and family relationships. Stated another way, the pervasive nature of work stress reactivity suggests that feelings of well-being are important not only at work but also in the give-and-take of everyday life. The human problems associated with work stress, therefore, are thought to be very inclusive. Work stress can take place at any time during one's career, but beginning workers are especially vulnerable to stress at work.

A newly hired worker, for instance, expresses feelings of insecurity and isolation. Another worker who contracts with companies for services rendered expresses similar feelings when entering a new work environment. Yet another worker who has been on the same job site for several months expresses similar reactions. In the case of the first two workers, a new work environment understandably can present situations that challenge individuals to adapt both to a new group of associates and work environment. In the last case, however, the individual has been in the same work environment long enough to make adjustments but has obviously failed. In all three of the cases, interacting influences that lead to sources of stress should be identified for the purpose of building effective interventions. Because stress is viewed as multidimensional, it is more than likely that a helper would find individual sets of concerns for each client. In all of these three cases, however, stress reactivity may be moderated by psychological benefits associated with an individual's sense of predictability and controllability (Kemeny, 2003; Sapolsky & Ray, 1989). In the case of a new work environment, the new employee usually has little in the way of predicting his or her ability to be accepted as a contributing member of the work environment. Certainly there is no or little sense of control, that is, the ability to exert some influence over one's circumstances.

Two keys to reducing stress in one's early career are regular and frequent supervision and consultation that focuses on (1) specific expectations required of the worker's role or job and (2) how the new employee can specifically contribute to the goals of the workforce. When an employee has a sense of predicting his or her chances of being successful and in a sense can exert influence over the process of his or her work procedures, feelings of well-being should be improved. Be aware that failure to perform well on a job assignment in one's early career can have long-term effects on future work roles. In the following section, I briefly discuss work–family stress.

Work–Family Stress

There is a growing interest concerning the interplay of work and family conflict among employers. Research on work–family stress has been on the increase in the last two decades. Competing role demands have become more obvious as organizations require more production from employees as a result of downsizing, merging, or restructuring. Work–family conflict has been recognized as a potential source of stressors that can destroy a worker's ability to meet work requirements (Duxbury & Higgins, 1991). The marked increase in work–family stress has led to research projects aimed at determinants or sources of stress. Current restructured work environments have been closely examined. Workers, for instance, are required to work longer hours, some work in their home, and some work on evenings and weekends. It is not surprising that such work requirements interfere with normal family functions.

Most research studies, however, target three areas: (1) the effect of work on the family, (2) the effect of family on work, and (3) the family–work interaction (Zedeck, 1992). Kossek and Ozeki (1998) conducted a meta-analysis of several research studies to determine the effects of work–family conflict on both work and life in general. They determined, as expected, that family role demands negatively influenced work role, and work role demands negatively influenced the family role. Of the two roles studied, the negative relationship was stronger for work role demands influencing family role demands.

In the early 1990s, Williams and Alliger (1994) studied the effects of work–family conflict on individual family members. Not surprisingly, they found that work–family conflict adversely affects mood.

Another study, by Allen, Herst, Bruck, and Sutton (2000), focused on several relationships between work–family conflict, such as work-related outcomes (job satisfaction), nonwork outcomes (life and family satisfaction), and stress-related outcomes (depression and burnout). The strongest relationship was found to be between work–family conflict and stress-related outcomes. Sulsky and Smith (2005) concluded that the results of these examples of research suggest that family interferences brought on by work demands can be very devastating and pervasive. One way to balance effects of stress is through the development of coping strategies.

Coping Strategies to Reduce the Effects of Stress _____

Although the meaning of a *coping strategy* on the surface appears to be straightforward, there are some problems with terminology. *Coping* can be simply referred to as the worker's way of softening the impact of demands in the workplace, but when one speaks of *coping strategies* is one referring to the *process* of coping or the *outcome* of coping? Thus, it is clearer to use *coping response* to represent a deliberate action, *coping goal* as the objective of the action, and *coping outcome* as the consequence of coping (Rice, 1999). Researchers and helpers are in a better position to study effective coping strategy when the terminology is clear. Helpers also communicate more effectively when there is specificity of terms used. In the following paragraphs, coping responses, actions, and outcomes are discussed. I begin with the pervasive nature of self-efficacy.

Self-Efficacy

There are individual coping resources that are considered assets and offer support to reduce the effects of stress. Personal resources, for instance, are considered to be very important traits of self-efficacy, such as an attitude of optimism, the perception of controllability, and a strong sense of self-esteem. *Self-efficacy* is thought to be the individual's perception of capability, or a self-referent belief that one has the skills and performance ability to be successful in given situations (Bandura, 1997). Bandura also made the important point that successfully coping with past situations increases one's feelings of self-efficacy. The positive responses we receive for our efforts in a work environment, for example, reinforce our beliefs that we can also conquer other challenges in the workplace and in other life roles. Thus, self-efficacy influences feelings of optimism. If one believes just the opposite, for instance, that one's skills are very poor, then logically one would view a new task as unmanageable, and this conclusion could lead to stress reactivity. Be also aware that some workers can make faulty self-appraisals and, when confronted with their failure, are also subject to stress reactions. Finally, strong feelings of self-efficacy will foster good health; research suggests that the immune system functions are enhanced by self-efficacy (Wiedenfeld et al., 1990). As with most personal traits, self-efficacy is not considered to be permanent, that is, there can be can changes over time with new and different experiences. In career development, self-efficacy has an important function in career choice and development.

Self-efficacy is a key theoretical construct in *social cognitive career theory* (Lent, Brown, & Hackett, 2002). It is considered part of a triadic causal system that determines the course of career and its outcome. Self-efficacy is viewed not as a unitary or fixed trait but rather as a set of beliefs about a specific performance domain. Self-efficacy is developed through four types of learning experiences: "(1) personal performance accomplishments, (2) vicarious learning, (3) social persuasion, and (4) physiological states and reactions" (Lent et al., 2002, p. 380). Self-efficacy is strengthened when success is experienced within performance domains, whereas it is weakened when there are repeated failures.

Self-Esteem

Self-esteem, another important personal resource to combat stress, is a significant part of one's self-concept. It implies that one has feelings of high regard and the very important trait of *self-acceptance*. Rice (1999) suggested that individuals who cope well when encountering stress are found to have high self-esteem and feelings of self-worth, especially when compared with individuals with low self-esteem. Efforts to improve self-efficacy and self-esteem can be very productive and worthwhile objectives in terms of self-empowerment to reduce reactions to stressors in the workplace.

In career construction theory, self-concept dimensions are thought to direct the content of alternative choices, whereas the meta-dimensions of self-esteem, realism, and clarity direct the process of making a choice. Thus, an individual may project the vocational self-concept into a certain work environment of interest but withdraw from it because of poor self-esteem (Savickas, 2002). People with low self-esteem have higher levels of fear and perceive themselves as being inadequate; they believe they cannot cope (Rice, 1999). Clients with low self-esteem may have difficulty in developing personal relationships, making career decisions, and have difficulty in coping with stress.

Social Support

Another coping strategy is *social support*, which acts as a buffer or shield from the effects of stress. Family, friends, and coworkers are examples of an informal structure of social support. Workers who have good rapport with coworkers, for example, increase their chances of building positive coping mechanisms. Keep in mind that some coworkers may be completely negative concerning the workplace and their work role and thereby can have an adverse effect on another worker's positive coping. Helpers often assist clients in sorting out the most effective coping support from individuals and/or groups. Evidence from research suggests that religious groups can offer strong support, and one should be aware that social support is most effective when it is used in conjunction with other coping techniques (Cohen & Wills, 1985; Rice, 1999).

Cultural Diversity Issues

The study of stress and its effects on multicultural groups is in its infancy. The position that stress is a dynamic, ongoing process suggests that individuals who are members of ethnic minority groups may perceive and respond to stress differently than the White majority. There is, of course, general agreement that members of ethnic minority groups may have different life experiences and social influences that are unique to their culture (Sulsky & Smith, 2005). Focusing on unique stressors that affect minority groups, Bartoldus, Gillery, and Sturges (1989) found that minority home-care workers experienced racist attitudes while on the job. One would suspect that minority workers in other work environments have experienced similar attitudes and reactions. Clearly, minority workers have the added burden of racist attitudes and stereotypes that expose them to additional stress. For a fuller understanding of cultural stress-related dimensions, let us examine a multicultural model of stress.

The multicultural model of stress depicted in Box 11.2 is from Rice (1999), who incorporated models of stress from Lazarus and Launier (1978) and from Slavin, Rainer, McCreary, and Gowda (1991). The Lazarus research team incorporated transactional–relational themes, whereas the Slavin group based their model on what they viewed as culturally relevant dimensions. These approaches suggest that culturally relevant experiences include thoughts, beliefs, and behaviors of particular cultural groups as they respond to their unique history and ecological experiences, including those in social and religious organizations. This is one view of observing how cultural diversity exposes individuals to additional stressors in society. This model also calls attention to significant events that are related to minority status, such as acts of discrimination and racism that occur with great regularity. Low socioeconomic status can expose cultural groups to strong stressors that have a spillover effect on family life. Finally, unique cultural customs of a group make them vulnerable for additional stressors (Rice, 1999).

Box 11.2   The Case of Coping Skills for Culturally Diverse Individuals

Jose was asked by his supervisor at work to seek out a counselor at a local mental health facility because he had verbally attacked a customer who had ordered a sandwich. The customer had questioned Jose's ability to make a proper sandwich and followed this with a racial slur. Jose described his reaction to the customer's comments as follows: "I just lost it! This guy doesn't want a Black man fixing him a sandwich." Jose stated that he was very anxious since taking on two different jobs and as a result has difficulty in controlling his emotions. Jose continued by expressing hostility and identity confusion, and he complained about being depressed. He ended his dialogue by stating he feels lost and confused: "I don't know which way to turn!"

Jose was born in Arizona and has four siblings. His parents grew up in Central America and became farm laborers when they moved to Arizona. The primary language spoken in the home is Spanish. Jose stated that his grandfather was an African American and "that's where my dark skin comes from." Jose self-identifies as an American but also embraces traditional Hispanic social customs and values. He currently resides in a section of the city that is primarily occupied by Hispanics. Jose dropped out of school at age 16 in order to work. His work experience includes janitor, yard work and maintenance, construction work, and working for a landscaper. He is currently employed in a fast food establishment that specializes in freshly made sandwiches. Jose also has a second job as busboy in a local restaurant. He works in the sandwich shop from 9:00 A.M. until 4:00 P.M. and then begins his second job at 6:00 P.M. and works until 12:00 A.M. He wants to contribute to the family's welfare, especially because his mother is unable to do part-time work.

During the course of the intake interview it became obvious to the counselor that Jose was reacting to numerous sources of stress with which he was unable to cope. The counselor was sympathetic for Jose's situation and was aware of potential sources of stress for someone who holds down two jobs, has difficulty finding time to sleep, and has lost hope for gaining a sense of control over his lifestyle. Jose has the added burden of discrimination that he experiences almost daily at work.

What is most important for counselors to recognize is how being a member of a cultural group that is subject to discrimination can affect the way an individual such as Jose makes primary and secondary appraisals of an event. Jose may no doubt come to the conclusion that his problem is one of skin color and racial harassment; he may be convinced that all members of the majority group think the same way. The chances are good that such a conclusion can increase the intensity level of all stressful events and can create an oversensitivity to even benign events. It is not surprising that when people feel marginalized and are harassed by the majority society they are likely to experience high levels of stress.

Helping Jose build coping skills to counter the effects of stressors was the immediate counseling goal. The counselor was concerned that, without immediate assistance, Jose could easily develop full-blown depression. A sense of control and the ability to cope with anxiety primarily brought on by stress suggested that Jose could be helped to gain self-confidence by addressing self-efficacy and self-esteem. The counselor's major focus will be on cognitive–behavioral approaches that enhance a client's understanding of how events influence one's thinking process and subsequently influence behavioral reactions. The counselor will begin, however, with muscle relaxation through systematic desensitization. Jose's future workplace will be addressed by introducing him to occupations he can observe and that provide him with the opportunity to participate in work activities in which he can achieve success. The counselor will also solicit the help of a fellow counselor whose ethnic background is similar to Jose's. The rationale here is that Jose may be more comfortable with someone he believes has had similar experiences to his own.

This case is used to illustrate that minority groups do indeed face multiple stressors that include discrimination and problems related to socioeconomic status. In addition, one may experience a complete lack of understanding and disapproval of unique cultural customs. The important point is that the oppressed and ethically different experience stressors on a regular basis. An individual's coping skills tend to break down as he or she regularly experiences increased levels of stressors, as in the case of Jose. Other cultural groups experience similar stressors, but counselors should be reminded that individuals within groups can interpret stressful situations differently. Effective interventions should be tailored to meet each client's unique needs. What should be taken from this case is that there appears to be general agreement that some cultural groups are generally subjected to multiple stressors that include racial discrimination (Coon, 2001; Rice, 1999; Slavin et al., 1991); counselors should be prepared to address numerous sources of stress.

It is clear that culturally different individuals can experience multiple sources of stress in the workplace. Many sources of stress evolve from coping with social change, such as modified beliefs about work as well as lifestyle. Although sources of stress can be identified, the process of social change and adjustment to new traditions and lifestyle is an individualized matter that is both continuous and time consuming. A significant element in social change, however, is that it is constant. Individuals living in a new world of customs, traditions, and language can be overwhelmed with constant stressors. Helpers can support clients' progress by emphasizing that learning to cope with a new way of life and work in a different culture can foster personal adjustments that moderate the stressors that are encountered. Helpers have a number of tools that have proven effective for culturally diverse clients. The paragraphs that follow suggest culturally appropriate techniques to combat the effects of multiple stressors. The major focus will be on cognitive restructuring.

Cognitive and behavioral techniques are considered to have distinct advantages for culturally diverse clients. It is important, however, that helpers understand the core values of their clients (Corey, 2005). This is a very relevant beginning suggestion. What is emphasized here is that helpers should have an understanding of the client's conflicting thoughts and beliefs in order to help him or her moderate the effects of stressors.

Hays (1995) agreed that cognitive and behavioral techniques can be effective with culturally diverse clients, provided some modifications are made in terms of cultural adaptations of interventions. Helpers must be cautious, for example, to not overemphasize self-control as a primary coping technique. Personal autonomy and empowerment are European American values that can be misinterpreted and confusing for clients who have been reared in collectivist-oriented societies. Personal autonomy may also suggest to some clients that they should challenge their beliefs and thoughts that contradict well-engrained traditions of avoiding conflict that are contrary to their cultural norms (Cormier & Nurius, 2003).

In spite of the cautions, cognitive and behavioral techniques are more acceptable to culturally diverse clients in several ways. One distinct advantage is that helpers and clients collaborate on structuring interventions. Helpers function as teachers, advisors, or advocates, and they encourage learning skills. Specific goals of learning skills for living and working in a new environment are more acceptable than vague concepts of insight, for example. Cognitive and behavioral techniques that are culturally appropriate counteract the stigma of mental illness that cultural groups associate with counseling (Sharf, 2004).

Some suggestions for using cognitive restructuring with culturally diverse clients are as follows:

1. Stress that cognitive restructuring is specific and direct. Point out that it focuses on alternative actions rather than emotional states.

2. Carefully choose expressions and/or psychological terms when describing an example of a thinking process. Use straightforward sentences that describe conditions that are culturally sensitive. Terms such as *irrational*, *maladaptive*, *distorted*, and *dysfunctional* could be confusing and threatening.

3. Stress that cognitive restructuring is educationally oriented. Explain that homework assignments will be required to emphasize learning objectives and activities.

4. As you would in any other helping situation, make sure to adapt your choice of words to the educational and language level of clients. Avoid clichés and slang.

5. Recruit helpers who are culturally similar to clients. They can be used as consultants as well as peer helpers who address client concerns (Cormier & Nurius, 2003; Hays, 1995). Cognitive–behavioral techniques are discussed further in Chapter 12.

_____ **Summary**

1. Work stress can be responsible for health problems of workers and for negative reactions to work, other employees, and absenteeism, as well as poor work performance. Negative reactions to stressors usually will spill over into other life roles. Psychological symptoms of stress are very pervasive, suggesting that helpers should help clients fuse career and personal concerns.

2. Stressors frequently occur in the workplace. One key method of observing the outcomes of stress is through an interactivist's viewpoint in which physiological, psychological, and behavioral reactions are observed. Type A behavior has long been associated with work stress.

3. Job stress involves features of a job that exceed the individual's coping ability. Specific job stressors include work overload, technostress, role ambiguity, under- and overpromotion, spillover, and electronic performance monitoring.

4. Warr's (1987) nine determinants in the work environment that contribute to mental health are opportunity for control, opportunity for using skills, externally generated goals, environmental variety, environment clarity, availability of money, physical security, opportunity for interpersonal contact, and social position. Five components of good mental health are effective well-being, competence, autonomy, inspiration, and integrated functioning.

5. There is a growing interest among employers concerning harmful effects of work–family stress; work–family conflicts are thought to interfere

with work performance. A major concern is that work role demands can interfere with family role demands and vice versa.

6. Helpers encourage clients to develop coping strategies to reduce effects of stress. Effective strategies include cognitive–behavioral techniques illustrated in Chapter 12.

7. Clients who are members of ethnic minority groups may respond to stress differently than the White majority. Minority workers have the added burden of racists' attitudes and stereotypes. Low socioeconomic status can expose cultural groups to strong stressors.

Supplementary Learning Exercises

1. Describe the interactionist's viewpoint of the stress process. Why is this viewpoint of significance to the helper?

2. Identify needs of the Type A individual described in Box 11.1. Describe and defend the interventions you would recommend.

3. Rank order (1 being most important) Warr's (1987) nine determinants that contribute to good mental health in the work environment.

4. What advice would you give to newly hired workers in a large organization concerning stress reactions?

5. Describe why self-efficacy is most important in coping with stress reactions.

12

Interventions and Case Studies

Helpers who offer career counseling are challenged to find effective interventions for both career concerns and a host of personal concerns. As one would expect, most of the career counseling models developed during the latter part of the 20th century were focused on career decision making. In a review of five counseling models, I (Zunker, 2006) reported similarities and distinct differences in conceptualizing the needs and concerns of clients. What was most revealing, however, was the diagnostic process drawn from the five models reviewed:

> Identifying client problems is a major focus of the diagnostic parameter— not only for providing a client label but, more important, as a starting point from which goals can be set to resolve client problems. . . . The diagnostic parameter is also used to identify client mental health problems that require further psychological evaluation of treatment. (Zunker, 2006, p. 128)

In addition, diagnosis was focused on irrational or dysfunctional thinking that could interfere with processing information for career decision making and/or lead to behavioral problems. The overarching goals of these five counseling models were directed toward helping each client make an optimal career decision and to use the skills developed in this process to make other important decisions in the future.

In the last three decades, there has been a gradual but growing shift to develop career counseling programs for adults, especially for those who are in career transitions. Chapter 5 provides some information on the changing nature of work and subsequent problems adults face in the workplace as well as the need (or desire) to make career transitions. Intervention counseling programs for adults have been developed that usually include experience, interest, and skills identification, and values clarification; in the process, clients are provided information about educational and occupational planning and a review of career decision-making skills with an emphasis on developing a life-learning plan. The interventions contained in this chapter, however, focus on cognitive–behavioral techniques that are more therapeutic in nature.

The goals of interventions that follow are *concern specific*; that is, they can be used to address the interrelationships of personal and career concerns. Faulty beliefs and "emotional concerns," for example, can be addressed effectively with cognitive–behavioral interventions. More specifically, mood disorders, such as depression, and work stress concerns, which were covered in Chapters 6 and 11, are used to illustrate the use of some of the following interventions: problem solving, assertiveness training and behavioral rehearsal, systematic desensitization, cognitive restructuring, role of cognitive schemas, Ellis's A-B-C theory of personality, self-enhancing thoughts, homework assignments, Meichenbaum's behavioral change, and stress inoculation training.

Cognitive–Behavioral Techniques

The rationale for cognitive–behavioral approaches suggests that behavior is driven by cognitions. Internal anxiety felt in response to interpersonal interactions with an authority figure (boss) is a good example of a conditioned reaction to a feared situation. Although the reasons why clients fear interpersonal interaction with others would be of interest, the major focus of cognitive–behavioral approaches is on presenting concerns and symptoms that involve cognitive schemas that influence behavior. One of the basic assumptions of cognitive–behavioral approaches is that behavior that has been learned can be unlearned and relearned. By focusing on the client's concerns and symptoms, the helper can establish clear and specific goals (Gelso & Fretz, 2001).

Problem Solving

Problem solving is an important skill that provides clients with methods of finding solutions to personal conflicts in the workplace and in other important situations and places. It is a method that promotes self-agency. Helpers focus on how to help clients identify a means of coping with problems on a daily basis (D'Zurilla & Nezu, 1999). What is suggested in this context is that problem solving is more that just a step-by-step exercise—it should also involve a therapeutic relationship in which helper and client individually and together search for methods of coping with stress in the give-and-take of daily living. Helpers, for instance, assist clients in recognizing irrational thinking and distorted cognitions. During the process of identifying problems, the helper and client develop strategies for implementing approaches to solving them.

In a more structured approach to problem-solving, D'Zurilla and Nezu (1999) and Cormier and Nurius (2003) have suggested the following steps:

1. *Rationale.* This involves the discussion of goals and a format of client training. Next, client concerns are identified and are followed by a discussion of potential strategies to address identified concerns. Clients are informed that effective problem-solving skills are essential for developing effective coping methods.

2. *Problem orientation*. Clients are asked to describe how problems have been solved in the past. Helpers point out any maladaptive coping styles they have observed in the client, such as the client completely depending on others to solve his or her current problems. Helpers identify other faulty client problem-solving styles and inform clients how their cognitions and emotions, for instance, affect their ability to solve problems. There is a very thorough constructive process of identifying faulty problem-solving techniques followed by the rationale for change and the learning of effective techniques.

3. *Problem definition and formulation*. Clients are required to carefully and thoroughly state an important problem to be solved. They should mention obstacles to solving the problem; conditions, situations, and locations involved with problem; plus any unresolved issues that are a part of the problem. Clients should also define goals and desired outcomes.

4. *Generation of alternative solutions*. Helpers and clients create a variety of solutions that could be effectively used. Each solution is discussed and evaluated. The therapeutic process is highlighted as client and helper discuss and identify solutions.

5. *Decision making*. Clients and helper discuss anticipated outcomes before a "best" solution is selected from alternatives. Clients are to leave the decision making process with a positive perspective of how problems can be solved.

6. *Solution implementation*. Clients may want to cycle through several solutions to determine the best course for implementation. Clients may also be encouraged to recycle through the problem-solving strategies.

Helpers are to follow up solution implementation to assist clients in determining whether the problem-solving goals have been met. Helpers concentrate on the effectiveness of the coping skills that have been learned, and they help clients develop self-evaluations to determine the effectiveness of each problem solution employed. Clients must determine whether the solution meets the expected criteria of success or whether some troubled areas need to be readdressed. Finally, helpers should evaluate the effectiveness of each client's problem-solving skills. More in-depth individualized problem-solving training designed to address specific concerns is used to enhance each client's ability to solve problems. A therapeutic relationship of problem-solving training suggests that constant scrutiny should be maintained during the entire process.

_____ Assertiveness Training and Behavioral Rehearsal

Assertiveness training, which may include behavioral rehearsal, addresses anxieties that stem from timid modes of coping with given situations, especially with stressful ones. *Behavioral rehearsal*, also known as *psychodrama*, is suggested for expanding a client's repertoire of coping behaviors. Keep in mind that the goals for assertiveness training may vary according to nature of the client's concerns. The major goal of behavioral rehearsal or role playing for improving coping techniques is to alter the client's cognitive structure (Trull, 2005). Goldfried and Davidson (1994) developed a four-stage behavioral rehearsal intervention that includes the following steps, in paraphrased format:

1. *Preparation.* The client is given a careful explanation of the process and reasons for acquiring new behaviors, such as being assertive but not aggressive. The client is informed of the potential benefits of role playing as a means to acquire new behaviors.

2. *Selection of target situations.* A hierarchy of role playing is related to specific situations. A hierarchy of concerns is developed in the interview. Some examples include communicating effectively with a supervisor or work associates.

3. *Actual behavioral rehearsal.* The client assumes assigned appropriate roles, and the helper provides both coaching and feedback. Clients may participate in several roles, such as supervisor, a work associate, or a customer.

4. In vivo *experiences.* The client engages individuals with newly learned assertive skills. (The client is exposed to actual feared conditions.) Client and helper discuss real life experiences and consequences of actual interactions with others.

One of the benefits of role playing is the development of insight into a stressful relationship as well as an opportunity to express feelings and practice in using targeted skills. Role playing with groups of real people provides an opportunity for reality testing (Sharf, 2004). Role playing, sometimes (like behavioral rehearsal) referred to as *psychodrama*, has long been considered an effective tool for assertiveness training, especially for individuals who have a behavioral deficit regarding how to behave assertively (Kipper & Ritchie, 2003).

Meichenbaum (1977) made a very strong case for modifying a client's cognitive position through role playing and imagery. In the process of modifying cognitions, clients evaluate their anxiety level, learn to become aware of anxiety-provoking situations, examine and re-evaluate their self-statements, and make note of changes in their level of anxiety (Corey, 2005). Research has demonstrated success in lowering levels of anxiety through the application of coping skills that address individual reactions to stressors (Meichenbaum, 1985, 1993).

Systematic Desensitization

Systematic desensitization, a progressive muscle relaxation, has been around since the 1950s. It was developed by Joseph Wolpe (1958) as a method for reducing anxiety through muscle relaxation while visualizing anxiety-pro-voking situations and events. *Reciprocal inhibition*, a term coined by Wolpe, suggests that one's emotional state is used to block another emotional state (Coon, 2001). Thus, a relaxed state of mind inhibits the severity of stress. The major goal was, and has been, to have clients replace anxious feelings with relaxation. Systematic desensitization has effectively been used to help clients deal with specific phobias. The focus in this chapter is on its use as a method to compete with and replace anxiety in the work environment. The components of a desensitization procedure developed by Cormier and Nurius (2003) comprise a model as follows:

Rationale

Identification of emotion-provoking situations

Hierarchy construction

Selection and training of counter conditioning or coping responses

Imagery assessment

Scene presentation

Homework and follow-up (p. 550)

The rationale for using desensitization to help one relax is explained to the client in detail. The helper makes the point that feelings of anxiety have been learned, and that therefore the overarching goal is to unlearn anxiety-provoking situations so they will no longer be stressful. Thus, one precedes relaxation with a very careful analysis of the sources of anxiety through an initial interview, client self-monitoring, and self-report questionnaires (Cormier & Nurius, 2003).

An *eventual desensitization hierarchy* is constructed, usually during the first two relaxation training sessions. Anxiety-provoking situations are ranked from least to most intense. One can construct a hierarchy by simply making a list of situations that cause anxiety. From this list, clients develop a hierarchy, starting with the least disturbing situation to the most disturbing. An example of a hierarchy used for work environment desensitization follows:

1. Take the bus to work

2. Log in

3. Change clothes in the locker room

4. Discuss work situations with associates

5. Review notes from previous meetings

6. Decide on recommendations

7. Enter the meeting room

8. Obtain prepared list of topics to be covered

9. Review list

10. Leader enters room and calls meeting to order

11. Presentation and discussions of recommendations from all members of group

Coon (2001), among others, suggested that the key to desensitization is relaxation. A very brief description of the relaxation process is as follows:

> Tense the muscles in your right arm until they tremble. Hold them tight for about 5 seconds and then let go. Allow your hand and arm to go limp and to relax completely. Repeat the procedure. Releasing tension two or three times will allow you to feel whether or not your arm muscles have relaxed. Repeat the tension-release procedure with your left arm. Compare it with your right arm. Repeat until the left arm is equally relaxed. Apply the tension-release technique to your right leg; to your left leg; neck and throat. Wrinkle and release your forehead and scalp. Tighten and release your mouth and face muscles. As a last step, curl your toes and tense your feet. Then release. (pp. 624–625)

After the client has mastered the relaxation exercises, the previously completed hierarchy list is used. Clients are to vividly picture and imagine that they are currently in the first situation at least twice, without increase in muscle tension. As clients slowly progress through each situation in the hierarchy they are instructed to stop when they are unable to visualize a situation without becoming tense. They may be required to recycle through the relaxation process until they are able to move forward without becoming tense. Clients continue to work through the list until the last situation on the list is experienced without tension. Homework assignments may include practicing muscle relaxation techniques. Variations of systematic desensitization can be found in Cormier and Nurius (2003).

Cognitive Restructuring

Cognitive restructuring is a key method used in cognitive–behavioral approaches. It is an engaging intervention component that is used to attack and replace faulty cognitions, including irrational thoughts or beliefs, with rational ones. It addresses distorted or invalid references, such as "There is only one job for me" or "Choosing a career is a one-time act," and other schemas that reflect errors in reasoning. The following examples of other irrational ideas that one internalizes is from Corey (2005):

> "I must have love or approval from all significant people in my life."

> "I must perform important tasks competently and perfectly well."

> "If I don't get what I want, it's terrible, and I can't stand it." (p. 274)

Cognitive distortions often surface as irrational behavior, such as disruptive actions in the workplace, worker absenteeism, and psychological distress. In cognitive restructuring, helpers do not focus completely on events themselves, but rather on the underlying causes, such as how clients interpret and react to real events in the workplace and in daily living (Meichenbaum, 1985). Cognitive restructuring is one of the most important tools that has been developed to combat work stress and its effect on feelings of well-being in all life roles. The bottom line here is that irrational ideas and beliefs that one internalizes and takes to the workplace must be addressed to avoid stress reactivity, which can lead to physical problems as well as significant individual problems that surface in the work environment and spill over to other life roles.

To develop a fuller understanding of cognitive–behavioral counseling, it is helpful to examine the nine basic assumptions of cognitive–behavioral approaches put forth by Gelso and Fretz (2001). These assumptions are essential guidelines for every helper. Gelso and Fretz suggested that not all helpers uniformly agree with these nine assumptions because of the great diversity among behavioral approaches. Therefore, one should be cognizant of the fact that there are differences of opinion between what is a behavioral or a cognitive approach to counseling as well as differences of opinion between psychoanalytic and humanistic approaches when compared with cognitive–behavioral ones. The nine assumptions are as follows:

1. When interviewing, it is best to attend to overt behavior or at least processes close to overt behavior.

2. Behavior is learned and thus can be unlearned and relearned.

3. The most effective treatment integrates cognitive and behavioral approaches.

4. Although the past is important in shaping behavior, it is most effective to focus on the present when attempting to change behavior.

5. The client's presenting problems and systems should be the focus.

6. Counseling should proceed when clear and specific goals have been established for the treatment.

7. The cognitive–behavioral counselor must frequently and effectively work in an active, directive, and prescriptive manner.

8. The client–counselor relationship is important in cognitive–behavioral counseling, but it is not sufficient for constructive change.

9. The cognitive–behavioral counselor is an applied behavioral scientist who stays abreast of and applies research findings to practice. (Gelso & Fretz, 2001, p. 336)

In the first assumption, the helper focuses on the client's overt behavior. The second assumption underscores the need to recognize overt behavior that will become the focus of restructuring or change. In the third assumption, the connection between cognitive and behavioral is made to solidify the position that cognitions must be evaluated to gain a fuller understanding of what drives behavior. The fourth through the ninth assumptions are straightforward; however, it should be clear that the counseling focus is on presenting problems and symptoms that lend themselves to clear and specific objectives for direct and prescriptive action. Although the relationship between the client and helper is most important, the major focus of counseling is on constructive change. Finally, it is recommended that helpers are to be vigilant regarding applied counseling research findings.

Gelso and Fretz's (2001) nine assumptions make it clear that the helper's role in cognitive–behavioral counseling is relatively well defined in terms of objectives, procedures, and goals. Helpers should concentrate on locating problems and symptoms that exist in the present but place little emphasis on past experiences. Ellis, Gordon, Neenan, and Palmer (1997) made the point that past experiences may be of interest but that it is irrational and distorted thinking in the present that cognitive–behavioral restructuring addresses. Clear and specific objectives that provide prescriptive actions are time efficient and provide pathways to research for determining their effectiveness.

Cormier and Nurius (2003) delineated six components of cognitive restructuring procedures, which are listed at the end of this paragraph. This outline illustrates an excellent conception of cognitive restructuring; readers should turn to the original source for details of all the procedures. I do, however, discuss parts of this outline along with other suggestions for cognitive restructuring in the paragraphs that follow.

1. Rationale: purpose and overview of the procedure

2. Identification of client thoughts and schemas during problem situations

3. Introduction and practice of coping thoughts

4. Shifting from self-defeating to coping thoughts

5. Introduction and practice of positive or reinforcing self-statements

6. Homework and follow-up (Cormier & Nurius, 2003, p. 441)

Helpers should carefully explain to the client the rationale and overview of cognitive restructuring.

Rationale: Include the suggestion that goals are designed to help clients become aware of their thoughts and self-talk when they experience anxiety while at work. After they identify thoughts, clients are helped to change or replace them. Stress the point that negative thoughts about work requirements can contribute to anxiety. Anxious thoughts are most likely to be the product of performance requirements, worker associates in the workplace, and/or the feelings one has about the work environment. Regardless of source, potential stress reactivity can trigger physiological responses that could lead to physical illness, and one's work performance can also be negatively affected by irrational beliefs that trigger faulty thinking. Thus, the first goal is to identify automatic thoughts that disrupt performance (Cormier & Nurius, 2003).

Overview: Awareness of automatic thoughts related to certain situations is a major objective of cognitive restructuring. Equally important is the identification of self-talk that is triggered by thoughts or by certain situations. The helper and client's mutual goal is to discover when automatic thoughts occur and uncover the meaning of self-talk. This is the first step necessary in the process of decreasing anxiety associated with working and the workplace. Eventually, clients learn to shift self-talk that is self-defeating to self-enhancing statements and thoughts that can improve work performance and extinguish self-defeating anxiety. Self-enhancing thoughts can also reduce negative physiological and emotional responses. The outcome of these efforts will aid in the shift to using self-enhancing statements before performing on the job, while the client is in the act of performing, and after he or she performs (Cormier & Nurius, 2003).

Clients should identify their cognitive schemas during problem situations. The first step involves the recognition of differences between self-defeating and self-enhancing thoughts. Examples of thinking that can disrupt or color performance are "I'm just not smart enough to learn this new computer program"; "I can't give a report in front of all those people"; "Those people I have to work with will probably not like me." This self-defeating thinking obviously reflects the thoughts of an individual who has little self-confidence and has the propensity to approach most challenges with negative thoughts. Interestingly, these thoughts may be representations of past experiences from which they were reinforced. Thus, a client may have developed a schema of thinking that he or she is inferior, has been a failure, and is rejected by others. Such clients will resort to thinking in these terms in the workplace when they are faced with job requirements, or simply by being a part of the work environment. To restructure and replace such a schema of thinking, the helper encourages the client to come to terms with a thinking process that needs to be changed to more self-enhancing thoughts. To accomplish this goal, they address cognitive schemas as a prevailing influence that colors one's interpretation of life events.

Cognitive Schemas

In the previous sections of this chapter, discussions have emphasized the importance of helping individuals learn how they think about their place in the world as well as their beliefs about important others, situations, and their environment. Helpers address how cognitive schemas are developed from early childhood experiences and how they change and/or crystallize during critical events over a life span. The activation of schemas suggest that one has developed basic and conditional beliefs that activate automatic thoughts involving emotions, behaviors, and physiological responses (Liese, 1994). Schemas can be positively or negatively oriented. A negative schema is associated with cognitive vulnerability that can lead to feelings of distress. A predisposition toward psychological distress is evident in the following evaluations of self: "I can't do anything right" and "I'll never make it in this job." Obviously, these examples of thinking are viewed as distorted, negative schemas.

Helpers must assist clients in understanding how a person integrates data and acts in accordance with his or her unique interpretations; for example, a worker who is threatened by a work assignment may be reacting to a false sense of his abilities to appropriately respond to the necessary work tasks. The unfortunate worker has a distorted view or negative schema of what he is capable of accomplishing. The negative consequences of distorted schemas can be illustrated with an example of individuals who have little self-confidence in their ability to perform at work and for those who simply feel threatened by interactions with others in the work environment. The ability to change or restructure the thinking process, however, is much more complicated. One method of attacking distorted thinking is through the use of Ellis's *A-B-C theory of personality* (Ellis, 1994; Ellis et al., 1997).

Ellis's A-B-C Theory of Personality

The A-B-C theory of personality is a part of REBT theory developed earlier by Ellis. Helpers should inform clients of the meaning of each variable in Ellis's model. In brief, A (an activating event) is not responsible for causing C (emotional reactions); it is B (beliefs) that causes C. Then, Ellis suggests that D (a disputing intervention that addresses irrational beliefs) will lead to E (effect) in which the individual sees the cause as being faulty beliefs and, finally, one experiences F (a new feeling) (Corey, 2005).

Component A is the activating event and/or an important event in the client's life. It is very important to understand that it is *B*—one's belief—not *A*—the activating event—that causes emotional and behavioral consequences (C). To illustrate the interaction of the components of this model, consider the case of an individual who has recently been fired from his job and is experiencing depression. Ellis would suggest that it is not the job loss but rather the individual's beliefs that she or he is a failure, that is, has failed in a major life role, that is causing the depressive reaction. Thus, according to Ellis, the helper must focus on the feelings of failure and rejection that have caused depression rather than the loss of job. This position suggests that it is not necessarily the event, but instead the individual's belief system, that causes stress reactivity. This position also suggests that each person is responsible for creating feelings that are harmful and disruptive (Ellis et al., 1997).

The interaction of self-talk that is self-defeating often drives the emotional and behavioral consequences. "I was too stupid to keep my job," "What a failure I have turned out to be," and "I've totally messed up my family" are examples of self-defeating self-talk. These are in fact irrational ideas that have been created by the individual's self-defeating belief system (Sharf, 2004).

Components D (disputing) and E (effect) were added to the model to better communicate the consequences of change. The term *disputing* (D) implies that this component is the client's challenge of her or his irrational belief. It has three parts: (1) detecting, (2) debating, and (3) discriminating. This process suggests that clients learn to detect faulty cognitions or irrational beliefs, debate these beliefs internally with logical questions, and convince themselves to stop believing them. The highest achievement in D is when the client is able to discriminate self-defeating beliefs from self-helping ones. At this point, clients find a pathway to develop an effective philosophy (E) that helps them replace irrational thoughts with rational ones. The successful completion of E leads to F, new feelings, suggesting that unhealthy thoughts have been replaced with healthy ones (Corey, 2005). In the case of the fired worker, the termination of a job turned out to be a matter of outsourcing and not his failure to perform. Career counseling can take place when the worker has reached Component F in Ellis's paradigm. In the next section, I present other methods to help clients restructure their thinking process.

Self-Enhancing Thoughts

Let's return to Cormier and Nurius's (2003) model of cognitive restructuring and discuss their examples of helping clients generate self-enhancing thoughts. They suggested that clients be given examples of both enhancing self-talk and of negative, defeating self-talk to help them observe the differences in content and meaning. The following scenario includes negative self-defeating thoughts and self-enhancing thoughts of a worker during three periods of a work day: (1) before-work thoughts, (2) during-work thoughts, and (3) after-work thoughts. First is negative self-defeating talk:

Before work

I don't believe that the people I work with like me.

I really don't have much to contribute.

In the work group sessions I have always had difficulty with expressing myself.

During work

I should have known that I couldn't do this well.

Everyone thinks that I don't contribute much.

Everyone will reach their goals except me.

After meeting

I'm just a failure again!

They all must think that I'm Miss Dumb Dumb.

I can't seem to get along with anyone!

Before work

I am well organized and prepared to make a contribution.

I will not pretend to be something I am not—I think they will like me.

I have new concepts to talk about that should be of interest to all.

During work

I know my business and they are buying it.

The opportunity to work with others is challenging.

I have made my share of meaningful contributions to our goals.

After work

This day was successful; I felt at ease once I got started.

I was able to communicate effectively to my fellow workers.

This day was a great productive experience and I expect to do better tomorrow.

SOURCE: Adapted from Cormier & Nurius, 2003, pp. 441–442.

The value of this exercise should be obvious to most clients as helper and client discuss significant differences in thinking and their implications. Counselors should challenge their clients to develop more self-enhancing thoughts that may involve different life roles. Effective homework assignments using a similar format should encourage clients to build a better understanding of the differences between negative, self-defeating thoughts and self-enhancing ones. The significant consequences of adopting a self-enhancing approach to daily living should evolve as clients learn to maintain rational thinking.

The therapeutic relationship should also include other methods in the cognitive–behavioral playbook. One might suspect that some adult clients have been stressed by negative self-defeating thoughts for significant periods of time. Their lifestyles may have been overwhelmed by irrational believes and negative schemas. Obviously, these clients will need in-depth assistance and follow-up care. Clients who have frequently changed jobs and/or have a history of disruptive behavior in the workplace are critically in need of help. Absenteeism from work, excessive illness, family–work conflicts, and difficulty with interpersonal relationships all suggest that a wide range of behaviors need to be addressed. Many client concerns regarding work and the workplace can be resolved through cognitive restructuring, which was discussed earlier in this chapter.

Homework Assignments

Ideally, helpers should give clients homework assignments that should be completed between counseling sessions. Completed homework assignments, as well as new ones that are given, should be discussed in counseling sessions. The following are examples of such assignments.

Ask the client to daily record as many of his or her negative thoughts as possible, not only those related to work but also those related to other life roles. Then discuss with the client the interrelationships of life roles.

Ask the client to record advantages and disadvantages of his or her beliefs. If the client responds, for example, with the following belief, "I must be promoted to a higher level job," then use this statement to steer the client away from an all-or-nothing approach (Sharf, 2004).

Ask the client to relax in the privacy of his or her home by relaxing muscle groups one at a time, as in desensitization. Then evaluate with the client the effectiveness of this self-induced relaxation.

Ask the client to make a list of his or her problems and describe how he or she would dispute his or her negative beliefs.

Helpers can also develop exercises to assist clients with specific thinking problems. Sharf (2004) developed a good example:

Often it is helpful for the therapist to question or challenge an absolute statement so that a client can present it more accurately, as in the following example:

Client: Everyone is smarter than me.

Helper: Everyone? Every single person at work is smarter than you?

Client: Well maybe not. There are a lot of people at work I don't know well at all. But my boss seems smarter; she seems to really know what's going on.

Helper: Notice that we went from everyone being smarter than you to just your boss.

Client: I guess it is just my boss. She's had a lot of experience in my field and seems to know just what to do. (p. 374)

What is suggested here is a collaborative working relationship between the helper and the client. The helper provides methods and material that promote the client's ability to overcome irrational thinking. Together, they establish goals and select material and procedures to accomplish them. As mentioned earlier, the process of restructuring the thinking process requires complete dedication on the part of the client. Meichenbaum (1977) suggested that behavior changes take place through an interactive process involving inner speech, cognitive structure, and behaviors, as follows:

1. *Self-observation.* Clients learn how to observe their own behavior. They increasingly become aware of negative, defeating thoughts and their consequences. They develop a sense of evaluating their inner thoughts and the meaning of their self-talk.

2. *Starting a new internal dialogue.* Clients' new inner dialogue of self-talk becomes a guide to new behavior. Conflicts and/or disputes are modified with the new inner dialogue.

3. *Learning new skills.* Clients learn more effective coping skills. It is a modification process, such as learning to cope with failure, for example. Instead of retreating into self-defeating thinking, clients are able to change their negative views to positive ones. Clients continually learn to modify their self-talk and are willing to engage in daily activities involving the give-and-take of life.

Learning new skills that lead to self-enhancing thoughts and self-talk are keys to restructuring the thinking process. The helper's role is to assist clients in understanding the pervasive consequences of irrational beliefs, self-defeating self-talk, and negative schemas. The ways one interprets many events in life, for instance, are colored by the negative consequences of irrational beliefs. Irrational beliefs should be aggressively attacked through learning exercises, discussion, and homework assignments that are carefully monitored. Follow-up of clients' continued progress toward building new feelings and healthy thoughts is essential. Some clients may need to periodically recycle through the modification process. Next, I briefly examine a stress inoculation training program developed by Meichenbaum (1993).

Stress Inoculation Training

As the name of this program implies, stress inoculation training (SIT; Meichenbaum, 1985) is perceived as a means to help clients combat the effects of stress-related stimuli. It is a proactive program that is designed to help clients increase their coping ability so they can deal with increasing levels of stress that they may experience in the future. In essence, clients prepare for stress-related activities in the future by gradual exposure to stressful conditions with suggestions for building coping mechanisms to offset the consequences of negative thinking and self-talk. The helper's role includes providing methods and procedures of cognitive restructuring, problem solving, relaxation training, role playing, and other techniques from cognitive and behavioral approaches. There are three phases to SIT:

1. *The conceptual phase.* The thrust of this phase focuses on the client's perception and understanding of cognitive and behavioral interactions and, more important, how and why people responds to events and situations as they do. How to think about problems in the workplace is a good example of how to begin the conceptual phase. A client informs the helper about the concerns caused by stress. The helper suggests to the client that it is not the events that are causing stressful reactions but that the client's thinking process and self-defeating self-talk have created the framework for increasing the effects of stress. This logic turns attention to self-talk and its consequences. Keep in mind, however, that the focus throughout this process is on changing behavior. Helpers use exercises mentioned in the preceding paragraphs, including having clients record self-talk that is used in the therapeutic process.

2. *Skill acquisition.* Meichenbaum suggested that helpers use a variety of cognitive and behavioral techniques to inoculate themselves from the affects of stress reactivity: cognitive restructuring, relaxation techniques, problem-solving approaches, enhancing self-efficacy, and others. Combinations of techniques are also suggested. An example of combining techniques, such as relaxation exercises and imagery, to cope with stressful work experiences focuses on changing self-defeating self-talk to positive, self-enhancing talk and thoughts. Other combinations of coping skills incorporate effective moderators to combat stress-related situations.

3. *Application.* This third phase requires that clients put what they have learned into practice. Clients may use the format described earlier when using "before work," "during work," and "after work" as preparatory phases for an actual situation. Mental rehearsals are practiced daily until the client has more confidence in coping with targeted workplace problems. Clients should focus on moderating the effects of stress specific situations. Follow-up, during which the helper may suggest that clients recycle through specific intervention components, is an important part of the therapeutic relationship. Helpers assist clients in moderating the effects of stress-specific situations.

Before ending this discussion of SIT, it should be made clear that coping is not a simple, one-shot event but a dynamic, ongoing process. Each stressful event an individual faces requires the mustering of coping techniques that have been learned from SIT and from other life experiences. A repertoire of acquired skills helps each individual cope with current situations and lays the foundation for coping with new situations that may require different and new methods of support. A client may also discover that using a combination of coping techniques learned through SIT is sufficient to combat stressors involving a new challenge in the workplace. Social support, for example, combined with role rehearsal may provide the combination of coping strategies to moderate a new and different situation of stress. Thus, what is acquired as coping skills in the initial phases of SIT is significantly relevant for coping with future life stressors (Fink, 2000; Rice, 1999). In the next section, three case studies are offered as examples of interventions that address interrelationships of client concerns.

Three Case Studies

This section emphasizes the practical application of the whole-person approach to helping. My goal from the very beginning of this book has been to provide practical applications of concepts and other information presented in the preceding chapters. I of course cannot integrate all the material covered in this text in three case studies, but these case studies underscore the need to recognize that career, work, and mental health are indeed intertwined. Helping as a counselor is a most challenging undertaking; the whole-person approach to counseling enhances the helper's role when addressing the interrelationships of concerns clients bring to counseling. The first case, of John, illustrates how high levels of anxiety, apprehension, and fear can disrupt a person's ability to work. The second case, of Corrina, presents an example of how hypochondriasis can overwhelm one's ability to think rationally and fulfill a work role. In the case of Yolanda, emotional instability and inconsistent behavior associated with a borderline personality disorder have interfered with her ability to function in all life roles.

High Levels of Anxiety: The Case of John

The mental health counselor had difficulty hearing why John came for help. John spoke very softly, almost in a whisper. He was sweating profusely and mentioned that he was worried about a future work role. The counselor encouraged John to continue to express his feelings, and he replied, "I'm ready to give up searching for another job." He explained that his parents thought he was a failure because he had never been very successful in meeting the requirements of several jobs. Before the counselor could respond, John quickly changed the subject to his health problems and complained of headaches and a nervous stomach. He was concerned about the prospect of becoming ill. At this point, John practically erupted into a litany of worried thoughts about future events centered around concerns of relationships, health, religious faith, and general difficulties "controlling his life." John's counselor was aware that many of her clients worried about the future, but in John's case there was excessive anxiety and difficulties in controlling his behavior. John viewed almost every life event as an impending catastrophe. Almost every action or statement he made suggested a high level of anxiety. He was very fearful of what the future might hold in store for him.

The counselor was not surprised to learn that John's work experiences included numerous jobs for short periods of time. After graduating from high school, John briefly attended a tech prep program in a local community college and started a business class, but he dropped out before finishing. The counselor also was not surprised to learn that John felt ostracized by other family members. As he put it, "They try to ignore me!" John was now 28 years old, had never married, and was living with his parents.

At this point, the counselor felt that John's high level of anxiety and his obvious lack of self-confidence and low self-esteem would need to be addressed before other data, such as aptitudes and interests, could be accurately measured. The counselor realized that there was much more to learn about John but opted to make a tentative conceptualization of his problems, mainly because he needed immediate attention. The counselor made the following tentative conclusions in four domains:

Career: John has little in the way of a work identity. He is very indecisive and is experiencing stress reactivity from numerous sources in his environment, including family, friends, and work associates. He simply is not ready to begin a career counseling program. It is suggested that assessment of traits should be delayed until his level of anxiety has been moderated.

Affective: John is subject to panic attacks, feelings of inferiority, and poor self-confidence, and he is emotionally unstable. He will act out without giving much thought to consequences of his actions. His emotional instability appears to have disrupted all life roles.

Cognitive–behavioral: John has a tendency to overgeneralize negative thoughts and experiences, resulting in cognitive distortions associated with anxiety. His feeling of anxiety associated with fear of the future will make rational decision making difficult. His self-talk is very demeaning and exacerbates his inability to function in all life roles. The consequences of his negative cognitions should receive immediate attention.

Culture: John was born into a White working-class home. His observed anxiety suggests that he feels unable to meet the expectations of individual accomplishment so strongly stressed by the White cultural majority. John states that he cannot live up to his parents' expectations. Failure to meet his parents' approval appears to be one of the causal factors of his negative thinking process and subsequent emotional instability. In John's case, readiness for career counseling will have to be determined in the future.

Career counselors are well in tune with the concept of readiness for career counseling thanks to the early studies conducted by Super (1984) on what he referred to as *career maturity*. Readiness for career counseling is evaluated in many ways, including the ability to read, think rationally, use planning skills, develop effective decision-making skills, and ability to accurately assess one's abilities and limitations. One essential skill is the ability to process career information. In case of John, there are numerous obstacles that should be removed or moderated in order for him to begin the career decision-making process; intense levels of anxiety about the future can be very domineering. John's case is a good example of how excessive anxiety can create tension, confusion, and instability. John's lack of self-confidence and low self-esteem, as well as his inability to cope with daily events, will also need to be aggressively addressed.

John's counselor decided to begin interventions that ask him to identify what is actually threatening. After John was able to vocalize threatening situations (where, how, and with whom), relaxation techniques were used to combat tension. John was also asked to practice relaxation techniques as a homework assignment. Faulty thinking was addressed through cognitive restructuring. The focus was on negative work-related perceptions. Another technique was to have John imagine threatening conditions or images and devise ways of coping with them. Drug therapy is also a consideration. The counselor will make periodic appraisals to determine when John is ready to begin career counseling. She projects that effective career planning can be very therapeutic for John. In the meantime, she will use examples of anxiety-provoking thoughts that can originate in the workplace as a precursor to introducing programs that provide skills in establishing and building relationships. Interventions will focus on the interrelationships of concerns, that is, how anxiety can interfere with all life roles.

John's anxiety is most likely the result of numerous sources of events and situations over a period of several years. Anxiety is usually accompanied by extreme fear and negative affect; somatic symptoms of tension; and an obsession about future events, especially the feeling that one cannot predict or control events in the future (Barlow & Durand, 2005). The impact of these symptoms on career choice and career development can be devastating. The inability to concentrate and to think rationally will obviously deter career planning and the ability to evaluate career opportunities. One can also expect to find job impairment to the point that one is not able to meet job requirements or the ability to function with other workers. Step-by-step interventions designed to help John will take considerable time before he is prepared to make a choice and go back to work full time, although job shadowing may help him to return sooner. In the meantime, discussions with John concerning anxiety and subsequent behavior can focus on the workplace and relationship issues with work associates. When John is able to return to work, his progress will be carefully monitored, and follow-up counseling will be available.

The Case of Corrina, a Hypochondriac

Corrina is a 32-year-old divorced African American woman who is caring for two children. Her chief complaint was that she can't hold a job because she is often sick and cannot go to work. She reports that her husband deserted her over 2 years ago, and she has not been able to locate him. She has supported her children by working for short periods of time on several jobs, including waitress, maid, and dishwasher, and she has worked in a meat packing plant. She wants to get a steady job that will pay well.

Corrina grew up in a neighborhood in which there was violence, drug abuse, and high unemployment. She experienced racial discrimination and oppression almost daily. She did graduate from high school and stated that most of her teachers encouraged her to attend college. Corrina had a very good grade point average in high school, was in the upper 5% of her class, and scored well on a college entrance examination. At that time, she wanted to be a teacher and had planned to go to college through a scholarship program—until she got pregnant. She married the father of her children, and for several years she and her husband made ends meet from his salary as a maintenance specialist in a shopping mall. As she put it, things started going downhill when her husband started drinking heavily. He would often arrive at home drunk and turn violent. Corrina eventually moved in with her parents.

Corrina stated that she became ill shortly after her husband abandoned her and their children. She explained her sickness as an infection somewhere in her body, but several doctors have not been able to locate the infection or its cause. She has been told that nothing is wrong and in fact she is in good health. Corrina insists, however, that she is sick and is going to get worse. She explains her illness as devastating; she feels sick all over, with headaches, nausea, twitching muscles, and other bodily sensations. She expects to come down with a serious illness at any time and fears the future. When the illness gets "real bad" and Corrina is convinced that it is spreading, she gives up trying to go to work and eventually loses her job. She informed her counselor, a clinical social worker, that she is now ready to try working again. The following conceptualization of Corrina's concerns was developed from several interviews:

Career: Corrina's faulty cognitions are focused on negative thoughts about her health, and she is not able to accurately process career information. She is an indecisive individual because of a confused thought process, she has attention deficits, and she engages in excessive demeaning self-talk. Her ability to process the information necessary in career decision making is limited. In short, there are deficiencies in occupational knowledge as well as self-knowledge.

Affective: There are strong indications of emotional instability subject to apprehension and anxiety. Corrina is also preoccupied with bodily sensations that could indicate a serious illness. She tends to lose control of her emotions when she reacts to illness cues.

Cognitive–behavioral: Corrina's thoughts are focused on perceived threats. She misinterprets ambiguous stimuli that are most threatening to her feelings of well-being. Corrina believes that she will soon become gravely ill; there is perceptual sensitivity to illness cues.

Culture: Corrina has been subjected to racial discrimination and oppression of career goals. She may have been conditioned to consider only jobs that she perceives are available to African Americans. Environmental influences may have conditioned her to believe the only chance one has is getting a low-level job. Her recent experiences with struggling to support her family may have influenced her to take any job that puts food on the table rather than seek her work of choice.

Recognizing that there are indeed severe personal and work-related problems, the counselor decided that it may be most effective to focus on the interrelationships of problems; thus, she will begin career and personal problem counseling simultaneously. The rationale here is to help Corrina realize the spillover effect of her perceived illness on all life roles, especially the work role. Second, Corrina has a good educational background and may have the skills to qualify for a beginning job in a local industry. The major concern, however, is to address symptoms that strongly indicate she is a hypochondriac. Convincing Corrina that she does not have a serious illness will be difficult and will probably require long-term therapy and continuous follow-up. The counselor visualizes, however, that the career counseling process can also be therapeutic, as could the benefits of eventual placement in a job that enhances her self-efficacy. A strong positive is that Corrina does have good basic skills that can open the door to a broad range of job opportunities.

The counselor decided that she would use cognitive–behavioral therapy accompanied by reassurance and support. The cognitive–behavioral interventions would focus on identifying misinterpretation of bodily functions and challenging all misinterpretations. Certain body areas indicated by Corrina as troublesome will be focal points. Corrina will be asked if she could create symptoms that have caused her to feel ill. The rationale of this exercise is to convince Corrina that she could indeed control symptoms that could lead to illness (Barlow & Durand, 2005; Warwick, Clark, Cobb, & Sailovskis, 1996).

In addition, the counselor will offer reassurance and support on a regular basis. Studies conducted by Haenem, de Jong, Schmidt, Stevens, and Visser (2000), cited in Barlow and Durand (2005), indicate that reassurance by a mental health professional can be very effective in some cases of hypochondriasis. Reassurance and support should be offered regularly in both personal and career counseling. Social support from members of Corrina's family, church, and community members will provide additional encouragement.

For consistency of interventions, the counselor chose a social learning and cognitive career theory of career development. The rationale here was to also focus on faulty cognitions and negative self-talk that could hamper the career decision-making process. When clients recognize the relevance of addressing the interrelationships of concerns, they should be in a better position to appreciate the benefits of balanced life roles and subsequent lifestyle. Box 12.1 contains some guidelines for the prevention of attrition with African American clients. These guidelines offer some very important and relevant advice for counselors who offer their services to African Americans.

Box 12.1   Guidelines for the Prevention of Attrition With African American Clients

1. Discuss racial differences with the client.

2. Avoid linking the client's mental problems with his or her parents' behaviors; the client probably believes that such problems result from environmental conflicts in society.

3. Do not try to gather information about the client's family secrets by questioning the client directly regarding those secrets.

4. Assure the client that members of his or her church can be included in the client's assessment and treatment.

5. Do not recommend medication as the first treatment choice; this is an *impersonal* treatment, and the client may get the impression that you do not want to work with him or her.

6. Avoid giving the impression that you consider yourself to be a "protector of the race" when discussing racial issues.

7. Be aware that the client may view referrals made by the schools or social welfare agencies as a threat to his or her autonomy and an indication of the possibility that family secrets will be made public. Discuss this feeling with the client.

SOURCE: Paniagua, F. A. (2005). *Assessing and Treating Culturally Diverse Clients* (3rd ed.) (p.111). Copyright 2005 Sage Publications, Inc. Reprinted with permission.

Symptoms of Borderline Personality Disorder: The Case of Yolanda

Yolanda, a 40-year-old Hispanic woman, has a history of moving from one job to another. She claims that she is frustrated with having to work and also manage a family. She has been divorced for several years and is the mother of three children, ages 20, 17, and 15. She finished high school and attended a community college for one semester. She is currently employed in an assisted living home for the elderly. She stated that she enjoys her current work but has not always been pleased with other work situations. She has had numerous jobs, ranging from teacher's aide, to cook, to maid, and working in a laundry. Yolanda claims she is searching for something she can't identify and shifts from one job to another. "I have lost confidence in myself and fear failing again if I try something new and different" is an example of her concerns about the future.

Yolanda clearly is currently experiencing depressive feelings, and she often expresses anger and hostile thoughts. She feels helpless and trapped, with no way out. She explained that her moods can go from happy to sad in a blink of the eye in that sometimes she feels very happy and enthusiastic, like she is on the top of the world, while at other times she is very depressed and "angry at everyone and everything." When she is angry and depressed she has difficulty interacting with people and at times is unable to do even simple tasks. Yolanda reports that she went to a mental health facility some years ago and was told that she has symptoms of borderline personality disorder. Yolanda is asking for help to find a way to earn more money so that she could feel happier most of the time instead of sad and helpless.

From the intake session with Yolanda and other discussions that followed, her licensed professional counselor was able to conceptualize her concerns as follows:

Career: Yolanda has a poor work identity and difficulty in balancing life roles. She has had difficulty in maintaining a level of work performance that was expected by several employers. Realistically, she is carrying a heavy load of responsibility, but her inconsistent performance at the workplace is an indication of personal problems. Depression and excessive anger associated with borderline personality disorder need to be addressed. Even though Yolanda wants her work to be satisfactory, her inconsistent patterns of behavior make it difficult for her to meet required work standards. Indecisive clients like Yolanda can be helped by learning step-by-step procedures in the decision-making process as well as training that addresses interpersonal relationships. In Yolanda's case, personal and career problems should be addressed simultaneously. The focus on the interrelationships of concerns will include how distorted beliefs and negative cognitions can affect all life roles.

Affective: Poor self-esteem and feelings of inferiority and helplessness are indications of emotional instability. Yolanda is subject to mood swings, from high levels of energy to the other end of the spectrum, which includes depression, lethargy, and fatigue. Her inconsistent behavior more than likely contributes to relationship problems at work and in the home. Mood swings could make her emotionally vulnerable for poor decision making that could lead to serious consequences and concerns in all life roles.

Cognitive–behavioral: Yolanda's view of herself is primarily negative; in fact, she has a very low opinion of herself. She stated that she sees herself as ugly, fat, and stupid. Negative views of self such as the ones expressed by Yolanda can lead to depression; anger; and inconsistent, erratic behavior. Obviously, this kind of behavior will not be tolerated in the workplace. When Yolanda's thinking process focuses on past mistakes it is difficult for her to think positively about the future; thus, she often becomes depressed and may be subject to even self-mutilation.

Culture: Yolanda is a second-generation Hispanic whose parents were born and reared in Mexico. She was born shortly after they arrived in Texas. Yolanda self-identifies as a Mexican American and embraces many traditional values. She has a collectivist worldview, which suggests that she is family and community oriented. The inconsistent behavior that she displays, however, confuses both her parents and her children. Yolanda's inability to foster family relationships could contribute greatly to her bouts with depression and poor self-concept. It should be very helpful to involve the family in Yolanda's quest to overcome personal and career concerns.

One of the treatments for borderline personality disorder is designed to help clients cope with stressors that trigger depressive episodes. Clients are first taught to identify emotional responses to stress and second to learn how to regulate their emotions. The rationale here is that clients who are able to identify troublesome thoughts can purposely re-experience them and in the process extinguish the fear associated with certain events and situations (Barlow & Durand, 2005; Linehan, 1993).

All helpers must be alert to cultural variables when selecting interventions. For example, some Hispanic clients may believe that mental health concerns are caused by evil spirits; thus, they may turn to their church for assistance to overcome their major concerns. Some may seek help from a folk healer or curandera or curandero. Not all Hispanics share these beliefs, but helpers should be aware of potential conflicts with Hispanic cultural factors when selecting interventions (Paniagua, 2005).

Ho (1992) suggested that Hispanics expect immediate solutions to their concerns, or at least tentative ones, at the end of the first session. Hence, the helper should be prepared to offer some straightforward and concrete recommendations that could be helpful to the client. In the case of Yolanda, for example, a homework assignment to practice relaxation techniques could be recommended. Informing Yolanda and her parents of future interventions in which they will participate could also win support from the family. The next session could include family members. Recall that in collectivist societies major decisions about a family member's future are usually decided by the family as a whole.

Throughout this book, cognitive–behavioral approaches have been highlighted regarding their effectiveness. A different twist in their use with Hispanics could make them even more effective. The use of systematic desensitization, for example, could include Hispanic scenes to represent certain environmental events. Hispanic helpers could be used to assist in the intervention process. The major point here is that Hispanic women like Yolanda hold basic beliefs about what is appropriate when interacting with family members. Yolanda, for instance, is likely to have difficulty expressing assertive behavior toward her husband or father. When there is a disagreement, Yolanda would likely first acknowledge the authority of important others (*respecto*) before expressing any assertive comments (Paniagua,

2005). On the other hand, cognitive–behavioral techniques are learning oriented, which makes them more acceptable than psychodynamic procedures
that encourage frank discussions of private family matters.

Returning to expectations of Hispanic clients and their families, one must
plan to submit highly structured interventions that are not intrusive, especially in the beginning counseling sessions. Making a list of desirable and
appropriate careers in conjunction with family members, finding information about potential jobs, and constructing a budget would more than likely
be acceptable interventions. As ones builds trust, more personal data can be
compiled in order to address both personal and career concerns.

Cultural factors can help counselors address a wide range of concerns that
are found in borderline personality disorder. Yolanda could benefit from
cognitive–behavioral interventions such as systematic desensitization, cognitive restructuring, modeling, assertive training, and culturally sensitive problem-
solving techniques. A highly structured career development plan could
include interest and personality identification, learning more about different
occupations, modeling for enhancing self-efficacy, and focusing on the interrelationships of all life roles. Some very thoughtful and helpful guidelines for
the prevention of attrition with Hispanic clients by Paniagua (2005) can be
found in Box 12.2.

Box 12.2   Guidelines for the Prevention of Attrition With Hispanic Clients

1. Use *formalismo* (formalism) during first contact with the client, but gradually move to *personalismo* (personalism) in subsequent contacts.

2. Assure the client that members of his or her church can be included in the client's assessment and treatment.

3. Conduct a brief separate interview with the father to recognize his authority in the family.

4. Talk about spiritual events that the client believes can lead to emotional problems (e.g., *mal puesto,* or hex; *mal de ojo, or* evil eye).

5. Do not suggest that the client take actions that may compete with the cultural ideals of *machismo* and *marianismo* (e.g., husband controls the family; wife is submissive and passive).

6. Ensure that when the client leaves the first session, you have provided him or her with concrete recommendations regarding how to handle the problem: avoid giving the client the impression that you need to gather more information in subsequent sessions before providing recommendations.

7. Because the client is likely to expect medication, discuss the possibility of prescribing medication during the first and subsequent sessions.

8. Be aware that time is not a fundamental variable in Hispanic cultures; do not ask the client why he or she is late for therapy.

These three case studies have provided some examples of how career, work, and mental health are interrelated. The cases presented included symptoms of disorders that were severe and very inclusive. In addressing the concerns of the clients in these case studies, I have suggested a wide range of interventions that are coordinated to address the interrelationships of concerns. In a whole-person approach to helping, counselors focus on behavior from a biopsychosocial perspective. An integrated system of helping takes into account influences on behavior from biological, psychological, and social/cultural domains. The reciprocal relationship among influences suggests that biological factors can influence psychological patterns of behavior, for example. Observation of behavior as a multidimensional, multifaceted process includes a wide range of behaviors that are interrelated and connected. The above case studies have presented only a few interrelated concerns, but they should make the point that counselors are to be alert to symptoms of psychological disorders that can disrupt and/or interfere with career choice and development.

Summary

Career counseling models developed in the latter part of the 20th century were focused on helping clients make optimal career choices. These models also addressed personal concerns that might interfere with the career development process. The changing nature of work has underscored the need for helping adults make career transitions and develop strategies to combat personal problems such as stressful work environments.

The cognitive–behavioral approaches suggested in this chapter include problem solving, assertiveness training and behavioral rehearsal, systematic desensitization, cognitive restructuring, the role of cognitive schemas, Ellis's A-B-C theory of personality, self-enhancing thoughts, homework assignments, behavioral change by Meichenbaum, and SIT. The rationale for cognitive–behavioral approaches suggests that behavior is driven by cognitions. The major focus of cognitive–behavioral approaches is on client concerns and symptoms that evolve from cognitive schemas.

The first case study portrayed how anxiety disorders can affect a person's career choice and development. Another case explores how hypochondriasis can disrupt all life roles. The final case explores the concerns of an Hispanic women with symptoms of borderline personality disorder. In all cases, personal and career concerns are addressed.

Supplementary Learning Exercises

1. Describe the rationale for using cognitive–behavioral techniques as interventions for faulty beliefs.

2. Defend the use of problem-solving techniques as a means to cope with problems on a daily basis.

3. Develop a scenario for role playing by clients that addresses stressful relationships.

4. Defend the following statement regarding the rationale for using cognitive restructuring: "Behavior is learned and thus can be unlearned and relearned."

5. How would you restructure and replace negative schemas of thinking?

Appendix A _____

Acculturation Scales

Group   Title

African Americans   Racial Identity Attitude Scale

Helms, J. E., & Parham, T. A. (1996). The Racial Identity Scale. In R. J. Jones (Ed.), *Handbook of tests and measurements for Black populations* (pp. 167–174). Hampton, VA: Cobb & Henry.

African Americans   Developmental Inventory of Black Consciousness

Milliones, J. (1980). Construction of a Black consciousness measure: Psychotherapeutic implications. *Psychotherapy: Theory, Research, and Practice, 17,* 175–182.

American Indians   Rosebud Personal Opinion Survey

Hoffman, T., Dana, R. H., & Bolton, B. (1985). Measured acculturation and MMPI–168 performance of Native American adults. *Journal of Cross-Cultural Psychology, 16,* 243–256.

Asian Americans   Asian American Multidimensional Acculturation Scale

Chung, R. H., Kim, B. S., & Abrew, J. M. (2004). Asian American Multicultural Acculturation scale: Development, factor analysis, reliability, and validity. *Cultural Diversity and Ethnic Minority Psychology, 10,* 66–80.

Central South Americans   Abbreviated Multidimensional
(Caribbean, Mexican, Spanish)   Acculturation Scale

Zea, C., Asner-Self, K. K., Birman, D., & Buke, L. P. (2003). The abbreviated Multidimensional Acculturation Scale: Empirical validations with two Latino/Latina samples. *Cultural Diversity and Ethnic Minority Psychology, 9,* 107–126.

Chinese, Japanese, Koreans   Suinn–Lew Asian Identity Scale

Suinn, R. M., Ahuna, C., & Khoo, G. (1992). The Suinn–Lew Asian Self-Identification Acculturation Scale: Concurrent and factorial validation. *Educational and Psychological Measurement, 47,* 401–407.

Cubans   Cuban Behavioral Identity Questionnaire

Garcia, M., & Lega, L. J. (1979). Development of a Cuban ethnic identity questionnaire. *Hispanic Journal of Behaviorial Sciences, 1,* 247–261.

Japanese Americans   Ethnic-Identity Questionnaire

Masuda, M., Matsumato, G. H., & Meredith, G. M. (1970). Ethnic identity in three generations of Japanese Americans. *Journal of Social Psychology, 81,* 199–207.

Mexican Americans   Acculturation Rating Scale for Mexican Americans

Cuellar, I., Arnold, B., & Maldanonado, R. (1995). Acculturation Rating Scale for Mexicans II: A revision of the original ARSMA scale. *Hispanic Journal of Behavioral Sciences, 17,* 275–304.

Mexican Americans   Acculturation Balance Scale

Pierce, R. C., Clark, M., & Kiefer, C. W. (1972). A "bootstrap" scaling technique. *Human Organization, 31,* 403–410.

Mexican Americans   Cultural Lifestyle Inventory

Mendoza, R. H. (1989). An empirical scale to measure type and degree of acculturation in Mexican-American adolescents and adults. *Journal of Cross-Cultural Psychology, 20,* 372–384.

Puerto Ricans, Mexican   Brief Acculturation Scale for Hispanics
Americans

Norris, A. E., Ford, K., & Bova, C. A. (1996). Psychometrics of a brief acculturation scale for Hispanics in a probability sample of urban Hispanic adolescents and young adults. *Hispanic Journal of Behavioral Sciences, 18,* 29–38.

South Asian, Hispanic, Anglo Americans   Multicultural Acculturation Scale

Wong-Rieger, D., & Quintana, D. (1987). Comparative acculturation of Southeastern Asians and Hispanic immigrants and sojourners. *Journal of Cross-Cultural Psychology, 18,* 145–162.

Vietnamese, Nicaraguan, Refugees   Acculturation Questionnaire

Smither, R., & Rodriquez-Giegling, M. (1982). Personality, demographics, and acculturation of Vietnamese and Nicaraguan refugees to the United States. *International Journal of Psychology, 17,* 19–25.

SOURCE: Compiled from Paniagua (2005).

Appendix B _____

The Diagnostic and
Statistical Manual of Mental
Disorders *(Fourth Edition, Text
Revision) Classification System*

Axis I

Identifies clinical disorders except for personality disorders and mental
retardation
Example: 305.00 Alcohol Abuse

Axis II

Identifies current personality disorders and mental retardation
Example: 301.83 Borderline Personality Disorder

Axis III

Identifies current relevant medical conditions

Axis IV

Identifies any psychological or environmental problems relevant to diagnosis
Example: Educational issues, occupational issues, and housing issues

Axis V

Global assessment of functioning
Examples on scale of 100 to 0

Code:

100–91 Superior functioning

81–90 Absent or minimal symptoms

71–80 Expectable reactions to stressors

61–70 Some mild symptoms

51–60 Moderate symptoms

41–50 Serious symptoms

31–40 Some impairment in reality testing or communication

21–30 Behavior influenced by delusions or hallucinations or serious impairment in communication and judgment

11–20 Some danger in hurting self and others

1–10 Persistent danger in hurting self or others

References _____

Allen, T. D., Herst, D. E. L., Bruck, C. S., & Sutton, M. (2000). Consequences associated with work-to-family conflict: A review and agenda for future research. *Journal of Occupational Health Psychology, 5,* 278–308.

American Psychiatric Association. (2000). *Diagnostic and statistical manual of mental disorders* (4th ed., text revision). Washington, DC: Author.

Amirkhan, J. H., Risinger, R. T., & Swickert, R. J. (1995). Extraversion: A "hidden" personality factor in coping? *Journal of Personality, 63,* 189–212.

Andersen, M. K., & Taylor, H. F. (2006). *Sociology: Understanding a diverse society* (4th ed.). Belmont, CA: Wadsworth Thomson.

Arthur, M., & Rousseau, D. (1996). *The boundaryless career.* New York: Oxford University Press.

Bandura, A. (1986). *Social foundations of thought and action: A social cognitive theory.* Englewood Cliffs, NJ: Prentice Hall.

Bandura, A. (1997). *Self-efficacy: The exercise of self-control.* New York: Freeman.

Bandura, A. (2001). Social cognitive theory: A genetic perspective. *Annual Review of Psychology, 52,* 1–26.

Barlow, D. H. (2002). *Anxiety and its disorder: The nature and treatment of anxiety and panic* (2nd ed.). New York: Guilford Press.

Barlow, D. H., & Durand, V. M. (2005). *Abnormal psychology: An integrative approach.* Belmont, CA: Wadsworth Thomson.

Barrett, P. M., Duffy, A. L., Dads, M. R., & Rapec, R. M. (2002). Cognitive–behavioral treatment of anxiety disorders in children: Long-term (6 year) follow-up. *Journal of Clinical Psychology, 69,* 135–141.

Bartoldus, E., Gillery, B., & Sturges, P. J. (1989). Job related stress and coping among home-care workers with elderly people. *Health and Social Work, 14,* 204–210.

Baumeister, R. F. (1989). The problem of life's meaning. In D. M. Buss & N. Cantor (Eds.), *Personality psychology: Recent trends and emerging directions* (pp. 138–148). New York: Springer-Verlag.

Beck, A. T. (1976). *Cognitive therapy and the emotional disorders.* New York: International Universities Press.

Beck, A. T., & Freeman, A. (1990). *Cognitive therapy of personality disorders.* New York: Guilford Press.

Bennett, G. K., Seashore, H. G., & Westman, A. G. (1974). *Differential Aptitude Test.* San Antonio, TX: Psychological Corporation.

Berk, L., & Landau, S. (1993). Private speech of learning disabled and normally achieving children in classroom academic and laboratory contexts. *Child Development, 64,* 556–571.

Berns, R. M. (2004). *Child, family, school, community: Socialization and support* (6th ed.). Belmont, CA: Wadsworth Thomson.

Betz, N. E., & Corning, A. F. (1993). The inseparability of career and personal counseling. *Career Development Quarterly, 42,* 137–142.

Betz, N. E., & Hackett, G. (1981). The relationship of career-related self-efficacy expectations to perceived career options in women and men. *Journal of Counseling Psychology, 28,* 399–410.

Bleuler, E. (1908). Die Prognose der Dementia praecox (Schizophreniegruppe) [The prognosis of dementia praecox (Schizophrenia, a group and/or class of disorders)]. *Allgemeine Zeitischrift fur Psychiatric, 65,* 436–464.

Bodrova, E., & Leong, D. J. (1996). *Tools of the mind: The Vygotskian approach to early childhood education.* Englewood Cliffs, NJ: Prentice Hall.

Borkovec, T. D., & Costello, E. (1993). Efficacy of applied relaxation and cognitive–behavioral therapy in the treatment of generalized anxiety disorder. *Journal of Consulting and Clinical Psychology, 61,* 611–619.

Bradley, J. C., Brief, A. P., & George, J. M. (2002). More than the Big Five: Personality and careers. In D. C. Feldman (Ed.), *Work careers: A developmental perspective* (pp. 27–63). San Francisco: Jossey-Bass.

Brawman-Mintzer, O. (2001). Pharmacologic treatment of generalized anxiety disorder. *Psychiatric Clinics of North America, 24,* 119–137.

Brems, C. (2001). *Basic skills in psychotherapy and counseling.* Belmont, CA: Wadsworth Thomson.

Brislin, R. (2000). *Understanding culture's influence on behavior* (2nd ed.). Belmont, CA: Wadsworth Thomson.

Brodie, D. (1999). *Untying the knot: Ex-husbands, ex-wives, and other experts on the passage of divorce.* New York: St. Martin's Griffin.

Bronfenbrenner, U. (1979). *The ecology of human development.* Cambridge, MA: Harvard University Press.

Brown, D., & Associates. (2002). *Career choice and development* (4th ed.). San Francisco: Jossey-Bass.

Brown, D., Brooks, L., & Associates. (1996). *Career choice and development* (3rd ed.). San Francisco: Jossey-Bass.

Brown, G. W., Harris, T. O., & Hepworth, C. (1994). Life events and endogenous depression. *Archives of General Psychiatry, 51,* 525–534.

Bruce, M. L., & Kim, K. M. (1992). Differences in the effect of divorce on major depression in men and women. *American Journal of Psychiatry, 149,* 914–917.

Buss, A. H., & Plomin, R. (1984). *Temperament: Early developing personality traits.* Hillsdale, NJ: Lawrence Erlbaum.

Cantor, N. (1990). From thought to behavior: "Having" and "doing" in the study of personality and cognition. *American Psychologist, 45,* 735–750.

Cantor, N., & Langston, C. A. (1989). "Ups and downs" of life tasks in a life transition. In L. A. Pervin (Ed.), *Goals, concepts in personality and social psychology* (pp. 127–167). Hillsdale, NJ: Lawrence Erlbaum.

Cappelli, P. (1999). *The new deal at work: Managing the market-driven workforce.* Boston: Harvard Business School Press.

Castillo, R. J. (1997). *Culture and mental illness: A client-centered approach.* Belmont, CA: Wadsworth Thomson.

Cattell, R. B. (1982). *The inheritance of personality and ability: Research methods.* New York: Academic Press.

Cattell, R. B., Cattell, A. K., & Cattell, H. E. (1993). *Sixteen Personality Questionnaire* (5th ed.). Champaign, IL: Institute of Personality and Ability Testing.

Charney, D. S., & Drevets, W. C. (2002). Neurobiological basis of anxiety disorders. In K. L. Davis, D. Charney, J. T. Coyle, & C. Nemeroff (Eds.), *Neuropsychopharmacology: The fifth generation of progress* (pp. 901–951). Philadelphia: Lippincott Williams & Wilkins.

Chiu, S., & Alexander, P. A. (2000). The motivational function of preschoolers' private speech. *Discourse Processes, 30,* 133–152.

Choi, S. C., Kim, U., & Choi, S. H. (1993). Indigenous analysis of collective representations: A Korean perspective. In U. Kim & J. W. Berry (Eds.), *Indigenous psychologies: Research and experience in cultural context* (pp. 193–210). Newbury Park, CA: Sage.

Cohen, S., & Wills, T. A. (1985). Stress, social support, and the buffering hypothesis. *Psychological Bulletin, 98,* 310–357.

Comas-Diaz, L., & Grenier, J. R. (1998). Migration and acculturation. In J. Sandoval, C. L. Frisby, K. F. Geisinger, J. D. Scheuneman, & J. R. Grenier (Eds.), *Test interpretation and diversity* (pp. 213–241). Washington, DC: American Psychological Association.

Coon, D. (2001). *Introduction to psychology: Gateway to mind and body* (9th ed.). Belmont, CA: Wadsworth Thomson.

Corazzini, J. G. (1997). Using research to determine the efficacy and modes of treatment in university counseling centers. *Journal of Counseling Psychology, 44,* 378–380.

Corey, G. (2005). *Theory and practice of counseling and psychotherapy* (7th ed.). Belmont, CA: Brooks/Cole–Thomson.

Cormier, S., & Nurius, P. S. (2003). *Interviewing and change strategies for helpers* (5th ed.). Belmont, CA: Wadsworth Thomson.

Costa, G. (1996). The impact of shift and night work on health. *Applied Ergonomics, 27,* 9–16.

Costa, P. T., & McCrae, R. R. (1984). Personality as a lifelong determinant of well-being. In C. Z. Malatesta & C. E. Izard (Eds.), *Emotion in adult development* (pp. 141–158). Beverly Hills, CA: Sage.

Costa, P. T., & McCrae, R. R. (1988). Personality in adulthood: A six-year longitudinal study of self-reports and spouse ratings on the NEO Personality Inventory. *Journal of Personality and Social Psychology, 54,* 853–863.

Costa, P. T., & McCrae, R. R. (1992). *NEO-PI-R professional manual.* Odessa, FL: Psychological Assessment Resources.

Costa, P. T., Jr., & Widiger, T. A. (Eds.). (1994). *Personality disorders and the five-factor model of personality.* Washington, DC: American Psychological Association.

Crites, J. O., & Savickas, M. I. (1996). Revision of the Career Maturity Inventory. *Journal of Career Assessment, 4,* 131–138.

Csikszentmihalyi, M., & Schnieder, B. (2000). *Becoming adult: How teenagers prepare for the world of work.* New York: Basic Books.

Danna, K., & Griffin, R. W. (1999). Health and well-being in the workplace. *Journal of Management, 25,* 357–384.

Dawis, R. V., & Lofquist, L. H. (1984). *A psychological theory of work adjustment: An individual differences model and its application.* Minneapolis: University of Minnesota Press.

Digman, J. M. (1990). Personality structure: Emergence of the five-factor model. *Annual Review of Psychology, 41*, 417–440.

Doyle, R. E. (1998). *Essential skills and strategies in the helping process* (3rd ed.). Pacific Grove, CA: Brooks/Cole.

Drucker, P. F. (2002). *Managing in the next society.* New York: Truman Tally Books/Dutton.

Duxbury, L. E., & Higgins, C. A. (1991). Gender differences in work/family conflict. *Journal of Applied Psychology, 76*, 60–74.

D'Zurilla, T. J., & Nezu, C. M. (1999). *Problem-solving therapy: A social competence approach to clinical intervention* (2nd ed.). New York: Springer Publishing.

Edwards, J. R. (1992). A cybernetic theory of stress, coping, and well-being in organizations. *Academy of Management Review, 17*, 238–274.

Ellis, A. (1994). *Reason and emotion in psychotherapy* (rev. ed.). New York: Kensington.

Ellis, A., Gordon, J., Neenan, M., & Palmer, S. (1997). *Stress counseling: A rational motive behavior approach.* New York: Springer Publishing.

Erikson, E. H. (1963). *Childhood and society* (2nd ed.). New York: Norton.

Erikson, E. H. (1968). *Identity: Youth and crisis.* New York: Norton.

Eysenck, H. J. (1967). *The biological basis of personality.* Springfield, IL: Charles C Thomas.

Eysenck, H. J. (1990). Genetic and environmental contributions to individual differences: The three major dimensions of personality. *Journal of Personality, 58*, 245–261.

Eysenck, H. J., & Eysenck, M. W. (1985). *Personality and individual differences: A natural science approach.* New York: Plenum Press.

Fava, G. A., Grandi, S., Rafinelli, C., Fabbri, S., & Cazzaro, M. (2000). Explanatory therapy in hypochondriasis. *Journal of Clinical Psychiatry, 61*, 317–322.

Feldman, D. C. (1985). The new careerism: Origin, tenets, and consequences. *Industrial Psychology, 22*, 39–44.

Feldman, D. C. (Ed.). (2002). *Managing careers in organizations.* San Francisco: Jossey-Bass.

Fink, G. (2000). *Encyclopedia of stress.* San Diego, CA: Academic Press.

Franklin, J. E., & Francis, R. J. (1999). Alcohol and other psychoactive substance use disorders. In R. E. Hales, S. C. Yudofsky, & J. A. Talbort (Eds.), *Textbook of psychiatry* (3rd ed., pp. 363–423).Washington, DC: American Psychiatric Press.

Frawley, W. (1997). *Vygotsky and cognitive science: Language and the unification of the social and computational mind.* Cambridge, MA: Harvard University Press.

French, J. R. P., Caplan, R. D., & Van Harrison, R. (1982). *The mechanism of job stress and strain.* New York: Wiley.

Freud, S. (1946). *Ego: A mechanism of defense.* New York: International Universities Press.

Galaif, E. R., Newcomb, M. D., & Carmona, J. V. (2001). Prospective relationships between drug problems and work adjustment in a community sample of adults. *Journal of Applied Psychology, 86*, 337–350.

Galliano, G. (2003). *Gender: Crossing boundaries.* Belmont, CA: Wadsworth Thomson.

Geertz, C. (1975). From the native's point of view: On the nature of anthropological understanding. *American Scientist, 63*, 47–53.

Gelso, C., & Fretz, B. (2001). *Counseling psychology* (2nd ed.). Belmont, CA: Wadsworth Thomson.

Gilbert, D. (2003). *The American class structure: In an age of growing inequality.* Belmont, CA: Wadsworth Thomson.

Glassman, M. (1994). All things being equal: The two roads of Piaget and Vygotsky. *Developmental Psychology, 14,* 186–214.

Glatt, C. E., Tampilic, M., Christie, C., Deyoung, J., & Freimer, N. B. (2004). Re-screening serotonin receptors for genetic variants identifies population and molecular genetic complexity. *American Journal of Medical Genetics, 124,* 92–100.

Goldberg, L. R. (1992). The development of markers for the Big Five factor structure. *Psychological Assessment, 4,* 26–42.

Goldenberg, H., & Goldenberg, J. (2002). *Counseling families today.* Pacific Grove, CA: Brooks/Cole.

Goldfried, M. R., & Davidson, G. C. (1994). *Clinical behavior therapy* (expanded ed.). New York: Wiley.

Goodman, J. (1993, April). *Using nontraditional appraisals, tools, and techniques.* Presentation given at the annual conference of the Michigan Career Development Association, Kalamazoo.

Gottfredson, L. S. (1981). Circumscription and compromise: A developmental theory of occupational aspirations. *Journal of Counseling Psychology, 28,* 545–579.

Gottfredson, L. S. (2002). Gottfredson's theory of circumscription and compromise. In D. Brown & Associates (Eds.), *Career choice and development* (4th ed., pp. 85–149). San Francisco: Jossey-Bass.

Gray, J. A., & McNaughton, N. (1996). The neuropsychology anxiety: Reprise. In D. A. Hope (Ed.), *Nebraska Symposium on Motivation: Vol. 43. Perspectives of anxiety, panic, and fear* (pp. 61–134). Lincoln: University of Nebraska Press.

Greenberg, M. S., & Beck, A. T. (1989). Depression versus anxiety: A test of the content-specificity hypothesis. *Journal of Abnormal Psychology, 98,* 9–13.

Gunderson, J. G. (2001). *Borderline personality disorder: A clinical guide.* Washington, DC: American Psychiatric Press.

Gunderson, J. G., & Links, P. S. (2001). Borderline personality disorder. In G. O. Gabbard (Ed.), *Treatment of psychiatric disorders* (Vol. 2, 3rd ed., pp. 2273–2291). Washington, DC: American Psychiatric Press.

Haenen, M. A., de Jong, D. J., Schmidt, A. J., Stevens, S., & Visser, L. (2000). Hypochondriacs' estimation of negative outcomes: Domain-specificity and responsiveness to reassuring and alarming information. *Behavior Research and Therapy, 38,* 819–833.

Hankin, B. L., & Abramson, I. Y. (2001). Development of gender differences in depression: An elaborated cognitive vulnerability–transactional stress theory. *Psychological Bulletin, 127,* 773–796.

Harmon, L., Hansen, J. C., Borgen, F., & Hammer, A. (1994). *Strong Interest Inventory manual.* Palo Alto, CA: Consulting Psychologists Press.

Hartung, P. J. (1999). Interest assessment using card sorts. In M. L Savickas & A. R. Spokane (Eds.), *Vocational interests: Their meaning, measurement, and counseling use* (pp. 235–252). Palo Alto, CA: Davies-Black.

Havighurst, R. J. (1972). *Developmental tasks and education* (3rd ed.). New York: David McKay.

Hays, K. E. (1995). Putting sport psychology into (your) practice. *Professional Psychology: Research and Practice, 16,* 33–40.

Healy, C. C. (1982). *Career development: Counseling through life stages*. Boston: Allyn & Bacon.

Healy, C. C. (1990). Reforming career appraisals to meet the needs of clients in the 1990s. *The Counseling Psychologist, 18*, 214–226.

Heimberg, R. G., Salzman, D. G., Holt, C. S., & Blendell, K. A. (1993). Cognitive–behavioral group treatment for social phobia: Effectiveness at five-year follow-up. *Cognitive Therapy and Research, 17*, 325–339.

Heine, S. J., & Renshaw, K. (2002). Interjudge agreement, self-enhancement, and liking: Cross-cultural divergences. *Personality and Social Psychology Bulletin, 28*, 578–587.

Heinricks, R. W. (1993). Schizophrenia and the brain: Conditions for a neuropsychology of madness. *American Psychologist, 48*, 221–233.

Herr, E. L., Cramer, S. H., & Niles, S. G. (2004). *Career guidance and counseling through the life-span: Systematic approaches* (6th ed.). Boston: Pearson Education.

Higginbotham, E., & Weber, L. (1992). Moving up with kin and community: Upward social mobility for black and white women. *Gender & Society, 6*, 416–440.

Hinton, D., Chau, H., Nguyen, I., Nguyen, M., Phant, T., & Quinn, S. (2001). Panic disorder among Vietnamese refugees attending a psychiatric clinic: Prevalence and subtypes. *General Hospital Psychiatry, 23*, 337–344.

Hirschfield, D. R., Rosenhaum, J. F., Biederman, J., Boldac, E. A., Farone, S. V., Snidman, M., et al. (1992). Stable behavior inhibition and its association with anxiety disorder. *Journal of the American Academy of Child & Adolescent Psychiatry, 31*, 103–111.

Ho, M. K. (1992). *Minority children and adolescents in therapy*. Newbury Park, CA: Sage.

Hofstede, G. (1984). *Culture's consequences: International differences in work related values* (abridged ed.). Beverly Hills, CA: Sage.

Holland, J. L. (1992). *Making vocational choices* (2nd ed.). Odessa, FL: Psychological Assessment Resources.

Holland, J. L., Powell, A. B., & Fritzsche, B. A. (1994). *The SDS professional user's guide*. Odessa, FL: Psychological Assessment Resources.

Horwath, E., & Weissman, M. (1997). Epidemiology of anxiety disorders across cultural groups. In S. Friedman (Ed.), *Cultural issues in the treatment of anxiety* (pp. 21–39). New York: Guilford Press.

Hotchkiss, L., & Borow, H. (1996). Sociological perspective on work and career development. In D. Brown, L. Brooks, & Associates (Eds.), *Career choice and development* (3rd ed., pp. 281–326). San Francisco: Jossey-Bass.

House, J. S., Landis, K. R., & Umberson, D. (1988, July 29). Social relationships and health. *Science, 241*, 540–545.

Hui, C. H. (1988). Measurement of individualism–collectivism. *Journal of Research in Personality, 22*, 17–36.

Ivey, A. E., & Ivey, M. B. (2003). *Intentional interviewing and counseling* (5th ed.). Pacific Grove, CA: Brooks/Cole–Thomson.

Jacoby, S. (1999). Are career jobs headed for extinction? *California Management Review, 42*, 123–145.

Johansson, C. B. (1975). *Self-Description Inventory*. Minneapolis, MN: National Computer Systems.

Johnson, S. L., Winett, C. A., Meyer, B., Greenhouse, W. J., & Miller, I. (1999). Social support and course of bipolar disorder. *American Psychologist, 180, 558–566.*

Kagan, J. (1997). Temperament and the reactions to unfamiliarity. *Child Development, 68,* 130–143.

Kail, R. V., & Cavanaugh, J. C. (2004). *Human development* (3rd ed.). Belmont, CA: Wadsworth Thomson.

Kalat, J. L. (2004). *Biological psychology* (8th ed.). Belmont, CA: Wadsworth Thomson.

Kelly, G. A. (1955). *The psychology of personal constructs.* New York: W. W. Norton.

Kemeny, M. E. (2003). The psychobiology of stress. *Current Directions in Psychological Science, 12,* 124–129.

Kessler, R. C., McGonagle, K. A., Zhao, S., Nelson, C. B., Hughes, M., Eshlemen, S., et al. (1994). Lifetime and 12-month prevalence of *DSM–III–R* psychiatric disorders among persons aged 15–54 in the United States: Results from the national comorbidity survey. *Archives of General Psychiatry, 51,* 8–19.

Kipper, D. A., & Ritchie, T. D. (2003). The effectiveness of psychodrama techniques: A meta-analysis. *Group Dynamics: Theory, Research, and Practice, 7,* 13–25.

Kirkcaldy, B. D., Shephard, R. J., & Furnham, A. F. (2002). The influence of Type A behavior and locus of control upon job satisfaction and occupational health. *Personality and Individual Differences, 33,* 1361–1371.

Kirkmayer, L. J. (2001). Cultural variation in the clinical presentation of depression and anxiety: Implications for diagnosis and treatment. *Journal of Clinical Psychiatry, 62,* 22–28.

Klienman, A. (1988). *Rethinking psychiatry: From cultural category to personal experience.* New York: Free Press.

Kohn, M. L. (1969). *Class and conformity: A study of values.* Homerwood, IL: Dorsey Press.

Kohn, M. L. (1976). Social class and parental values: Another conformation of the relationship. *American Sociological Review, 41,* 538–545.

Kohn, M. L. (1977). *Class and conformity* (2nd ed.). Chicago: University of Chicago Press.

Kohn, M. L., & Schooler, C. (1983). *Work and personality: An inquiry into impact of social stratification.* Norwood, NJ: Ablex.

Kokko, K., & Pulkkinen, L. (2000). Aggression in childhood and long-term unemployment in adulthood: A cycle of maladaptation and some protective factors. *Developmental Psychology, 36,* 463–472.

Kossek, E. E., & Ozeki, C. (1998). Work–family conflict, policies, and the job–life satisfaction relationship: A review and directions for organizational behavior–human resource research. *Journal of Applied Psychology, 83,* 139–149.

Kraepelin, E. (1898). *The diagnosis and prognosis of dementia praecox.* Paper presented at the 29th Congress of Southwestern German Psychiatry, Heidelberg, Germany.

Krumboltz, J. D. (1988). *Career Beliefs Inventory.* Palo Alto, CA: Consulting Psychologists Press.

Krumboltz, J. D. (1993). Integrating career and personal counseling. *Career Development Quarterly, 42,* 143–148.

Krumboltz, J. D., Mitchell, A., & Gelatt, H. G. (1975). Applications of social learning theory of career selection. *Focus on Guidance, 8,* 1–16.

Krumboltz, J. D., & Sorensen, D. L. (1974). *Career decision making.* Madison, WI: Counseling Films.

Kurman, J. (2001). Self-enhancement: Is it restricted to individualistic cultures? *Personality and Social Psychology Bulletin, 27,* 1705–1716.

Laursen, B., Pulkkinen, L., & Adams, R. (2002). The antecedents and correlates of agreeableness in adulthood. *Developmental Psychology, 38,* 591–603.

Lazarus, R. S., & Launier, R. (1978). Stress-related transactions between person and environment. In L. A. Pervin & M. Lewis (Eds.), *Perspectives in interactional psychology* (pp. 287–327). New York: Plenum Press.

Leahy, R. (1983). *The child's construction of social inequity.* New York: Academic Press.

Leana, C. R. (2002).The changing organizational context of careers. In D. C. Feldman (Ed.), *Work careers: A developmental perspective* (pp. 274–294). San Francisco: Jossey-Bass.

Lee, S. (2001). From diversity to unity: The classification of mental disorders in the 21st century China. *Cultural Psychiatry: International Perspectives, 24,* 421–431.

Lent, R. W., Brown, S. D., & Hackett, G. (2002). Social cognitive career theory. In D. Brown & Associates (Eds.), *Career choice and development* (4th ed., pp. 255–312). San Francisco: Jossey-Bass.

Lieb, R., Wittchen, H-U., Hofler, M., Fuetsch, M., Stein, M. B., & Merikangas, K. R. (2002). Parental psychopathology, parenting styles, and the risks of social phobia in offspring. *Archives of General Psychiatry, 57,* 859–866.

Liese, B. S. (1994). Brief therapy, crisis intervention and the cognitive therapy of substance abuse. *Crisis Intervention, 1,* 11–29.

Linehan, M. M. (1993). *Cognitive–behavioral treatment of borderline personality disorder.* New York: Guilford Press.

Liu, X., Kurita, H., Uchiyama, M., Okawa, M., Liu, L., & Ma, D. (2000). Life events, locus of control, and behavioral problems among Chinese adolescents. *Journal of Clinical Psychology, 56,* 1565–1577.

London, M. (2002). Organizational assistance in career development. In D. C. Feldman (Ed.), *Careers work: A developmental approach* (pp. 323–346). San Francisco: Jossey-Bass.

Marcia, J. E. (1980), Identity in adolescence. In J. Adelson (Ed.), *Handbook of adolescent psychology* (pp. 159–187). New York: Wiley.

Marsella, A. J., Sartorius, N., Jablensky, A., & Fenton, F. R. (1985). Cross-cultural studies of depressive disorders: An overview. In A. Klienman & B. Good (Eds.), *Culture and depression: Studies in the anthropology and cross-cultural psychiatry of affect and disorder* (pp. 299–324). Berkeley: University of California Press.

Massey, D. (1996). The age of extremes: Concentrated affluence and poverty in the twenty-first century. *Demography, 33,* 395–412.

Matsumoto, D. (1991). Cultural influences on facial expressions of emotion. *Southern Communication Journal, 56,* 128–137.

Matsumoto, D., & Juang, L. (2004). *Culture and psychology* (3rd ed.). Belmont, CA: Wadsworth Thomson.

Matsumoto, D., Weissman, M., Preston, K., Brown, B., & Kupperbusch, C. (1997). Context specific measurement of individualism–collectivism on the individual level: The IC Interpersonal Assessment Inventory (ICIAI). *Journal of Cross-Cultural Psychology, 28,* 743–767.

McCrae, R. R., & Costa, P. T., Jr. (1985). Openness to experience. In R. Hogan & W. H. James (Eds.), *Perspectives in personality* (Vol. 1, pp. 145–172). Greenwich, CT: JAI Press.

McCrae, R. R., & Costa, P. T., Jr. (1991). Adding Liebe and Arbeit: The full five-factor model and well-being. *Personality and Social Psychology Bulletin, 17,* 227–232.

McCrae, R. R., & Costa, P. T., Jr. (1997). Personality trait structure as a human universal. *American Psychologist, 52,* 509–516.

McCrae, R. R., Costa, P. T., Jr., Terracciano, A., Parker, W. D., Mills, C. J., De Fruyt, F., & Mervielde, I. (2002). Personality trait development from age 12 to age 18: Longitudinal, cross-sectional, and cross-cultural analysis. *Journal of Personality and Social Psychology, 83,* 1456–1468.

McCrae, R. R., & John, O. P. (1992). An introduction to the five-factor model and its applications. *Journal of Personality, 60,* 175–215.

McGuffin, P., Rijsdjk, F., Andrew, M., Sham, P., Katz, R., & Cardno, A. (2003). The heritability of bipolar affective disorder and the genetic relationship to unipolar depression. *Archives of General Psychiatry, 60,* 497–502.

Meichenbaum, D. (1977). *Cognitive behavior modification: An integrative approach.* New York: Plenum Press.

Meichenbaum, D. (1985). *Stress inoculation training.* New York: Pergamon Press.

Meichenbaum, D. (1993). Stress inoculation training: A 20-year update. In P. M. Lehrer & R. L. Woolfolk (Eds.), *Principles and practice of stress management* (2nd ed., pp. 373–406). New York: Guilford Press.

Mishel, L., Berstein, J., & Schmitt, J. (2001). *The state of working America: 2000–2001.* Ithaca, NY: Cornell University Press.

Mitchell, L. K., & Krumboltz, J. D. (1996). Krumboltz's learning theory of career choice and counseling. In D. Brown, L. Brook, & Associates (Eds.), *Career choice and development* (3rd ed., pp. 233–276). San Francisco: Jossey-Bass.

Mitchell, L. K., Levin, A. S., & Krumboltz, J. D. (1999). Planned happenstance: Constructing unexpected career opportunities. *Journal of Counseling and Development, 77,* 115–124.

Morey, L. C. (1988). Personality disorders in *DSM–III* and *DSM–III–R*: Convergence, coverage, and internal consistency. *American Journal of Psychiatry, 145,* 573–577.

Morrow, S., Gore, P., & Campbell, B. (1996). The application of a socio-cognitive framework to the career development of lesbian women and gay men. *Journal of Vocational Behavior, 48,* 136–148.

Mortenson, T. G. (2001, October). Family income and higher education opportunity, 1970–2000. *Postsecondary Education Opportunity,* 1–9.

Muchinsky, P. M. (2003). *Psychology applied to work* (7th ed.). Belmont, CA: Wadsworth Thomson.

Mueser, K. T., Torrey, W. C., Lynde, D., Singer, P., & Drake, R. E. (2003). Implementing evidence-based practices for people with severe mental illness. *Behavior Modification, 27,* 387–411.

Muris, P. (2002). Relationships between self-efficacy and symptoms of anxiety disorders and depression in a normal adolescent sample. *Personality and Individual Differences, 32,* 337–348.

Musto, D. E. (1992). America's first cocaine epidemic: What did we learn? In T. R. Kosten & H. S. Kleber (Eds.), *Clinician's guide to cocaine addiction: Theory, research, and treatment* (pp. 3–15). New York: Guilford Press.

Nairne, J. S. (2003). *Psychology the adaptive mind* (3rd ed.). Belmont, CA: Wadsworth Thompson.

National Center for Health Statistics. (2003). *Health United States.* Rockville, MD: U.S. Department of Health and Human Services.

National Institute of Mental Health. (2003). *Breaking ground, breaking through: The strategic plan for mood disorders research* (NIH Publication No. 03–5121). Bethesda, MD: National Institutes of Health.

National Opinion Research Center. (1953). Jobs and opportunities: A popular evaluation. In R. Bendix & S. M. Lipset (Eds.), *Class, status, and power* (pp. 9–13). Glencoe, IL: Free Press.

Neimeyer, G. J. (1989). Application of repertory grid technique to vocational assessment. *Journal of Counseling and Development, 67,* 585–589.

Nevill, D. D., & Super, D. E. (1986). *The Salience Inventory Manual: Theory, application, and research.* Palo Alto, CA: Consulting Psychologists Press.

Newman, B. M., & Newman, P. R. (2003). *Development through life: A psychological approach* (8th ed.). Belmont, CA: Wadsworth.

Okun, B. (2002). *Effective helping* (6th ed.). Pacific Grove, CA: Brooks/Cole–Thomson.

Okun, B. F., Fried, J., & Okun, M. L. (1999). *Understanding diversity: A learning-as-practice primer.* Pacific Grove, CA: Brooks/Cole.

Osborn, D., & Zunker, V. G. (2006). *Using assessment for career development* (7th ed.). Belmont, CA: Brooks/Cole–Thomson.

Osipow, S. H. (1979). Occupational mental health: Another role for counseling psychologists. *The Counseling Psychologist, 8,* 65–70.

Osipow, S. H. (1990). Convergence in theories of career choice and development: Review and prospect. *Journal of Vocational Behavior, 36,* 122–131.

Paniagua, F. A. (2005). *Assessing and treating culturally diverse clients: A practical guide* (3rd ed.). Thousand Oaks, CA: Sage.

Parsons, F. (1909). *Choosing a vocation.* Boston: Houghton Mifflin.

Patel, V., & Andrade, C. (2003). Pharmacological treatment of severe psychiatric disorders in the developing world: Lessons from India. *CNS Drugs, 17,* 1071–1080.

Paunonen, S. V., & Ashton, M. C. (2001). Big Five factors and facets and the prediction of behavior. *Journal of Personality and Social Psychology, 74,* 538–556.

Peterson, G. W., Sampson, J. P., & Reardon, R. C. (1991). *Career development and services: A cognitive approach.* Pacific Grove, CA: Brooks/Cole.

Plomin, R., & Petrill, S. A. (1997). Genetics and intelligence: What's new? *Intelligence, 24,* 53–77.

Rice, P. L. (1998). *Health psychology.* Pacific Grove, CA: Brooks/Cole.

Rice, P. L. (1999). *Stress and health* (3rd ed.). Pacific Grove, CA: Brooks/Cole–Thomson.

Roberts, B. W., Caspi, A., & Moffit, T. (2003). Work experiences and personality development in young adulthood. *Journal of Personality and Social Psychology, 84,* 582–593.

Roberts, D. F. (2000). Media and youth: Access, exposure, and privatization. *Journal of Adolescent Health, 27*(Suppl.), 8–14.

Robinson, S. L. (1996). Trust and breach of the psychological contract. *Administrative Science Quarterly, 41,* 574–599.

Roe, A. (1956). *The psychology of occupations.* New York: Wiley.

Roemer, L., Orsillo, S. M., & Barlow, D. H. (2002). Generalized anxiety disorder. In D. H. Barlow (Ed.), *Anxiety and its disorder: The nature and treatment of anxiety and panic* (2nd ed., pp. 477–515). New York: Guilford Press.

Rotter, J. B. (1982). Social learning theory. In N. T. Heather (Ed.), *Expectations and actions: Expectancy-value models in psychology* (pp. 241–260). Hillsdale, NJ: Lawrence Erlbaum.

Rounds, J. B., Henly, G. A., Dawis, R. V., Lofquist, L. H., & Weiss, D. J. (1981). *Manual for the Minnesota Importance Questionnaire.* Minneapolis: University of Minnesota, Psychology Department Work Adjustment Project.

Rounds, J. B., & Tracey, T. J. (1990). From trait-and-factor to person–environment-fit counseling: Theory and process. In W. B. Walsh & S. J. Osipow (Eds.), *Career counseling: Contemporary topics in vocational psychology* (pp. 1–44). Hillsdale, NJ: Lawrence Erlbaum.

Ryckman, R. M. (2004). *Theories of personality* (8th ed.). Belmont, CA: Wadsworth Thomson.

Sampson, J. P., Peterson, G. W., Lenz, J. G., Reardon, R. C., & Saunders, D. E. (1996). *Career Thoughts Inventory: Professional manual.* Odessa, FL: Psychological Assessment Resources.

Sapolsky, R. M., & Ray, J. C. (1989). Styles of dominance and their endocrine correlates among wild, live baboons. *American Journal of Primatology, 18,* 1–13.

Savickas, M. I., & Hartung, P. J. (1996).The Career Development Inventory in review: Psychometric and research findings. *Journal of Career Assessment, 4,* 247–259.

Savickas, M. L. (2002). Career construction: A developmental theory. In D. Brown & Associates (Eds.), *Career choice and development* (4th ed., pp. 149–206). San Francisco: Jossey-Bass.

Schuckit, M. A., & Smith, T. L. (1996). An 8-year follow-up of 450 sons of alcoholic and control subjects. *Archives of General Psychiatry, 53,* 202–210.

Schultz, D. P., & Schultz, S. E. (2005). *Theories of personality* (8th ed.). Belmont, CA: Wadsworth Thomson.

Schwenk, C. (1999). Marijuana and the workplace. Westport, CT: Quorum Books.

Segerstrom, S. C., Taylor, S. E., Kemeny, M. E., & Fahey, J. L. (1998). Optimism is associated with mood, coping, and immune change in response to stress. *Journal of Personality and Social Psychology, 74,* 1646–1655.

Seligman, M. E. (1975). *Helplessness: On depression, development and death.* San Francisco: W. H. Freeman.

Sewell, W. H., & Shah, V. P. (1977). Socioeconomic status, intelligence, and attainment of higher education. In J. Karabel & A. H. Halsey (Eds.), *Power and ideology in education* (pp. 32–41). New York: Oxford University Press.

Shaffer, D. R. (2002). *Developmental psychology: Childhood and adolescence* (6th ed.). Belmont, CA: Brooks/Cole–Thomson.

Sharf, R. S. (2002). *Applying career development theory to counseling* (3rd ed.). Pacific Grove, CA: Brooks/Cole–Thomson.

Sharf, R. S. (2004). *Theories of psychotherapy and counseling* (3rd ed.). Pacific Grove, CA: Brooks/Cole–Thomson.

Sharpe, M. (1997). Chronic fatigue. In D. M. Clark & C. G. Fairburn (Eds.), *Science and practice of cognitive behavior therapy* (pp. 381–414). Oxford, UK: Oxford University Press.

Sigelman, C. K., & Rider, E. A. (2003). *Life-span human development* (4th ed.). Belmont, CA: Wadsworth Thomson.

Simmons, R. G., & Rosenberg, M. (1971). Functions of children's perception of the stratification system. *American Sociological Review, 36,* 235–249.

Slavin, L. A., Rainer, K. L., McGeary, M. L., & Gowda, K. K. (1991). Toward a multicultural model of the stress process. *Journal of Counseling and Development, 70,* 156–163.

Spokane, A. R. (1991). *Career intervention.* Englewood Cliffs, NJ: Prentice Hall.

Sprock, J. (2000). Gender-typed behavioral examples of histrionic personality disorder. *Journal of Psychopathology and Behavioral Assessment, 22,* 107–122.

Stone, M. H. (2001). Schizoid and schizotypal personality disorders. In G. O. Gabbard (Ed.), *Treatment of psychiatric disorders* (Vol. 2, 3rd ed., pp. 2237–2250). Washington, DC: American Psychiatric Press.

Subich, L. M. (1996). Addressing diversity in the process of career assessment. In M. L. Savickas & W. B. Walsh (Eds.), *Handbook of career counseling theory and practice* (pp. 277–291). Palo Alto, CA: Davies-Black.

Sullivan, S. (1999). The changing nature of careers: A review and research agenda. *Journal of Management, 25,* 457–484.

Suls, J., Green, P., & Hillis, S. (1998). Emotional reactivity to everyday problems, affective inertia, and neuroticism. *Personality and Social Psychology Bulletin, 24,* 127–136.

Sulsky, L., & Smith, C. (2005). *Work stress.* Belmont, CA: Wadsworth Thomson.

Super, D. E. (1955). The dimensions and measurement of vocational maturity. *Teachers College Record, 57,* 151–163.

Super, D. E. (1963). Self-concepts in vocational development. In D. E. Super, R. Starishevsky, N. Marlin, & J. P. Jordaan (Eds.), *Career development: Self-concept theory* (pp. 17–32). New York: College Entrance Examination Board.

Super, D. E. (1970). *Work Values Inventory.* Boston: Houghton Mifflin.

Super, D. E. (1974). *Measuring vocational maturity for counseling and evaluation.* Washington, DC: National Vocational Guidance Association.

Super, D. E. (1980). A life-span, life-space approach to career development. *Journal of Vocational Behavior, 16,* 282–298.

Super, D. E. (1984). Career and life development. In D. Brown, L. Brooks, & Associates (Eds.), *Career choice and development* (pp. 197–261). San Francisco: Jossey-Bass.

Super, D. E., (1990). A life-span, life-space approach to career development. In D. Brown, L. Brooks, & Associates (Eds.), *Career choice and development: Applying contemporary theories to practice* (2nd ed., pp. 197–261). San Francisco: Jossey-Bass.

Super, D. E., & Overstreet, P. L. (1960). *The vocational maturity of ninth-grade boys.* New York: Teachers College Columbia University.

Super, D. E., Thompson, A. S., & Lindeman, J. P. (1988). *Adult Career Concerns Inventory: Manual for research and exploratory use in counseling.* Palo Alto, CA: Consulting Psychologists Press.

Swanson, J. L., & Fouad, N. A. (1999). *Career theory and practice: Learning through case studies.* Thousand Oaks, CA: Sage.

Tokar, D. M., Fisher, A. R., & Subich, L. M. (1998). Personality and vocational behavior: A selective review of the literature, 1993–1997. *Journal of Vocational Behavior, 53,* 115–153.

Triandis, H. C. (Ed.). (1995). *New directions in social psychology: Individualism and collectivism.* Boulder, CO: Westview Press.

Triandis, H. C., Bontempo, R., Villareal, M. J., Asai, M., & Lucca, N. (1988). Individualism and collectivism: Cross-cultural perspectives on self ingroup relationships. *Journal of Personality and Social Psychology, 4,* 323–338.

Triandis, H. C., Marin, G., Lisansky, J., & Betancourt, H. (1984). Simpatica as a cultural script of Hispanics. *Journal of Personality and Social Psychology, 47,* 1363–1375.

Triandis, H. C., McCusker, C., & Hui, C. H. (1990). Multi-methods probes of individualism and collectivism. *Journal of Personality and Social Psychology, 59,* 1006–1020.

Trull, T. J. (2005). *Clinical psychology* (7th ed.). Belmont, CA: Wadsworth Thomson.

Turk, C. L., Heimberg, R. G., & Hope, D. A. (2001). Social phobia and social anxiety. In D. H. Barlow (Ed.), *Clinical handbook of psychological disorders: A step-by-step treatment manual* (3rd ed., pp. 99–136). New York: Guilford Press.

Tutor, J. (1991). The development of class awareness in children. *Social Forces, 49,* 470–476.

Tyson, P. R., & Vaughn, R. A. (1987, April). Drug testing in the work place: Legal responsibilities. *Occupational Health and Safety,* 24–36.

Uchitelle, L., & Kleinfeld, N. R. (1996). The price of jobs lost. In New York Times, *The downsizing of America* (pp. 3–36). New York: Times Books.

Viken, R. J. H., Rose, R. J., Kaprio, J., & Koskenvuo, M. (1994). A developmental genetic analysis of adult personality: Extraversion and neuroticism from 18 to 59 years of age. *Journal of Personality and Social Psychology, 66,* 722–730.

Violato, C., & Holden, W. B. (1988). A confirmatory factor analysis of a four-factor model of adolescent concerns. *Journal of Youth and Adolescence, 17,* 101–113.

Walter, V. (2000). *Personal Career Development Profile.* Champaign, IL: Institute for Personality and Ability Testing.

Walther, A. N. (1991). *Divorce hangover.* New York: Pocket Books.

Warner, R. I., & Steel, B. S. (1999). Child rearing as a mechanism for social change: The relationship of child gender to parent's commitment to gender equity. *Gender & Society, 13,* 503–517.

Warr, P. B. (1987). *Work, unemployment, and mental health.* Oxford, UK: Clarendon Press.

Warwick, H. M. C., Clark, D. M., Cobb, A. M., & Sailovskis, P. M. (1996). A controlled trail of cognitive–behavioral treatment of hypochondriasis. *British Journal of Psychiatry, 169,* 189–195.

Watson, D. L., & Tharp, R. G. (2002). *Self-directed behavior: Self-modification for personal adjustment* (8th ed.). Pacific Grove, CA: Brooks/Cole–Thomson.

Watts, A. G., Super, D. E., & Kidd, J. M. (1981). *Career development in Britain.* Cambridge, UK: Hobson's Press.

Watts, T. (1995). Towards a policy strategy for lifelong career development: A transatlantic perspective. *Career Development Quarterly, 45,* 41–53.

Werner, J. M. (2002). Public policy and the changing legal contract of career development. In D. C. Feldman (Ed.), *Work careers: A developmental approach* (pp. 245–274). San Francisco: Jossey-Bass.

Wetherell, J. L., Gatz, L., & Craske, M. G. (2003). Treatment of generalized anxiety disorder in older adults. *Journal of Consulting and Clinical Psychology, 71,* 31–40.

Whiston, S. C. (2000). *Principles and application of assessment in counseling.* Belmont, CA: Brooks/Cole–Thomson.

Widiger, T. A. (1992). Review of the NEO Personality Inventory. In J. S. Conoley & J. J. Kramer (Eds.), *Eleventh mental measurements yearbook* (pp. 605–606). Lincoln: University of Nebraska Press.

Wiedenfeld, S. A., O'Leary, A., Bandura, A., Brown, S., Levine, S., & Raske, K. (1990). Impact of perceived self-efficacy in coping with stressors on components of the immune system. *Journal of Personality and Social Psychology, 59,* 1082–1094.

Williams, K. J., & Alliger, G. M. (1994). Role stressors, mood spillover, and perceptions of work–family conflict in employed parents. *Academy of Management Journal, 37,* 873–868.

Wilson, J. F. (2003). *Biological foundations of human behavior.* Belmont, CA: Wadsworth Thomson.

Wolpe, J. (1958). *Psychotherapy by reciprocal inhibition.* Stanford, CA: Stanford University Press.

World Health Organization. (1981). *Current state of diagnosis and classification in the mental health field.* Geneva, Switzerland: Author.

World Health Organization. (1983). *Depression disorders in different cultures: Report of the WHO Collaborative Study of Standardized Assessment of Depressive Disorders.* Geneva, Switzerland: Author.

Yik, M. S., Bond, M. H., & Paulhus, D. H. (1998). Do Chinese self-enhance or self-efface? *Personality and Social Psychology Bulletin, 24,* 399–406.

Zedeck, S. (1992). Introduction: Exploring the domain of work and family careers. In S. Zedeck (Ed.), *Work, families, and organizations* (pp. 1–32). San Francisco: Jossey-Bass.

Zunker, V. G. (2006). *Career counseling: A holistic approach* (7th ed.). Belmont, CA: Brooks/Cole–Thomson.

Name Index _____

Subject Index _____

About the Author _____

Vernon G. Zunker, EdD (University of Houston, with postdoctoral training at the University of Texas Medical School at Galveston, where he completed a residency in clinical psychology) is Professor Emeritus, Texas State University. Dr. Zunker had a joint appointment during most of his tenure at Texas State University, where he was Director of the Counseling Center for 18 years and taught graduate courses in counseling psychology for 24 years. In addition, he established a student learning resource center, a career development resource center, and was instrumental in the development of a testing center and the university's credit-by-examination program. A licensed psychologist, Dr. Zunker was also a consultant to the Texas Rehabilitation Commission for more than two decades. He was a member of a statewide committee for several years that was charged with the responsibility of selecting psychological assessment instruments for the state vocational rehabilitation testing program that established eligibility of its clients. He has written seven editions of *Career Counseling: A Holistic Approach* (the fifth edition was translated into Chinese, and the sixth edition was translated into Korean), four editions of *Using Assessment for Career Development*, and been coauthor on three editions. He has also authored two editions of *A Dream Come True: Robert Hugman* and *San Antonio's Riverwalk* (translated into Japanese). He considers his almost 3 years of sailing in the Merchant Marine as one of his greatest learning experiences. He often told his students that as a teenager on his own in a number of foreign countries, he learned to appreciate the significance of cultural differences. He and his wife Rosalie and canine companion, Toddi, reside in San Antonio.